Journalist and author Michael O'Toole was born in Hospital, Co. Limerick and educated at the Polytechnic of Central London and Trinity College, Dublin.

He worked as aviation correspondent for the *Irish Press* group of newspapers in the 1960s and 1970s, during which time he learned to fly. He wrote and broadcast widely on aviation matters up to his death in April 2000.

He was a news editor and long time 'Dubliner's Diary' columnist with the *Evening Press*. He also worked for the *Evening Herald*, *Daily Telegraph*, RTÉ and the BBC and was Ireland correspondent for *The Tablet* for a number of years. He won a national analysis and comment media award in the 1990s.

He is the author of the best-selling *More Kicks Than Pence* and a number of short stories.

I knew Michael O'Toole as a brilliant post-graduate student of literature in Trinity College. I got to know him also as a gifted journalist. In this fascinating book, the scrupulous scholar and the lucid, concise journalist combine to produce a well researched, gripping work which will surprise and educate all its readers. This is a shocking, enlightening creation and something of a masterpiece.

– Brendan Kennelly

Aviation safety is a serious subject, but Michael O'Toole has made it entertaining and educational as well, unfolding a history of aviation in Ireland – the aircraft, the airlines and the people – in his painstakingly researched and engagingly written stories of some of the country's most notorious air crashes

– Graham Warwick
US editor, *Flight International*

Cleared for
DISASTER

Ireland's Most Horrific Air Crashes

MICHAEL O'TOOLE

Edited by Maureen O'Toole

MERCIER PRESS
WHAT YOU NEED TO READ

MERCIER PRESS
Douglas Village, Cork
www.mercierpress.ie

Trade enquiries to Columba Mercier Distribution,
55a Spruce Avenue, Stillorgan Industrial Park, Blackrock, Dublin

Mercier Press receives financial assistance from
the Arts Council/An Chomhairle Ealaíon

The publishers would like to thank Anthony Dinan of the *Irish Examiner* for permission to reproduce photographs for the text and cover.

Printed and Bound by J. H. Haynes & Co. Ltd, Sparkford

Contents

Acknowledgements

I would like to thank the many people from all over the world who contributed to Michael's research for this book.

I know he would wish to acknowledge particularly the help and support of our children, Orla, Feargal and Justin, their spouses and partners, Michael, Melissa and Ciara, my sister, Bette Browne, my niece, Fidelma Browne, and his friends, Arthur and Deirdre Flynn, David Davin-Power, Donal Goggin and Captain Felim Cronin of the well-known Cronin flying family.

A very special thanks must go to Captain Cronin. Michael had almost completed *Cleared for Disaster* at the time of his death. The chapter on the Tuskar Rock crash remained to be finished and I completed this, something which I could not have done without Felim's expertise, wisdom and patience.

Maureen O'Toole
June 2006

For Orla, Feargal and Justin

'Plane down at Shannon! Will I rise the monsters?'

Paddy Clare, the 'nightown man' of the *Irish Press,* was addressing the last weary editorial executive left on duty at Burgh Quay that All-Ireland Sunday morning of 5 September 1954. He had just received a tip off from the paper's Shannon correspondent that a potential aviation disaster had occurred near Shannon Airport.

But the time was between 5 and 6 a.m. and the parsimonious nature of the *Irish Press* management was such that Paddy knew that in the normal course of events all he should do was leave a memo detailing whatever information he had gleaned during his shift. This would be picked up by the news editor who would be coming on duty for the next day's *Irish Press* later in the day, possibly as late as midday.

What he should NOT, repeat not, do was take any step which might incur expense, such as deploying more reporters or photographers than those already allotted 'markings' for the day in the newsroom bible: the diary of events to be covered.

However these were not normal times. A few days earlier, the *Irish Press* group had launched a new evening paper, the *Evening Press,* and the youthful, but sturdy, infant publication was already showing sings of requiring fresh approaches and fresh expenditures. Hence, Paddy's query. Should he take the fateful step of arousing people who could sanction expenses, such as editors, managing editors and group art editors from their beds?

After much heart searching, and only because of Paddy's mention of the new evening paper factor, the acting chief sub-editor gave permission to 'rise the monsters'.

Meanwhile, because of a larger, and more tragic, replication of the antediluvian procedures of the *Irish Press*, passengers from the KLM Constellation *Triton*, were smothering in aviation fuel, choking to death in mud, or drowning in the chilly waters of the Shannon estuary.

Their story has been told, poignantly and posthumously, in this enthralling book by Michael O'Toole who was destined to become one of the most distinguished alumni of the *Evening Press*.

Michael, whom I came to know well – and to admire – during my own sojourn with the *Evening Press*, had three passions in life: his wife, Maureen, his journalism and a love of everything to do with flying which led not merely to reading and writing about the subject, but to his becoming a pilot. All three passions have come together in this work.

Maureen has completed the one chapter outstanding at the time of his death, that on the mysterious crash of the Aer Lingus Viscount, *St Phelim*, off the Tuskar Rock, which some thought was caused by an off course British missile. Michael's mastery of the craft of wordsmith, coupled with his knowledge of his subject, leap from the page.

At any time, air crashes exercise a literally fatal attraction. But they do so especially in today's world when so many of us, so often, are involved in air travel. Unfortunately, it is also the world of the Iraq war and the suicide bomber. We know it could happen in Ireland.

One of the most gripping chapters in this book, 'The Cruellest Sea', details an occasion on which 'something' happened, approximately 500 miles off the Irish coast during March 1951: a giant American Globemaster vanished from the skies. There were no survivors. It was widely rumoured that this plane was carrying an atomic bomb, as Globemasters frequently did.

What we know for certain, in Michael O'Toole's words, is that:

The Globemaster was carrying top brass of the US services and strategic air command [the command which kept nuclear bombers in the air, twenty-four hours a day during the Cold War, TPC] including a brigadier general, three colonels, two majors, twenty captains and four lieutenants. It was also believed to be carrying highly confidential documents.

Whatever it was carrying the search for that plane's wreckage was one of the largest in aviation history. An armada of ships took part, a flotilla of aircraft. Long after the slightest hope of finding anyone alive had vanished, a most intensive sea and air search was maintained from Shannon. What were they looking for? We don't know.

We do know that Shannon Airport was taken over to such an extent that when a bewildered Seán McBride returned there one morning from a visit to Washington, where he had been telling President Truman that Ireland could not join the Atlantic Pact until partition was ended, he had to walk through 'a tangle of "foreign war planes" parked all over the ramp'.

One of these planes was a British Lincoln bomber, the first time that a British armed plane had landed in the Republic.

In view of the current debate about Shannon's being used by the Americans because of the Iraq war, this chapter alone would make the book well worth reading. But I can confidently assure the reader that the book contains more, much more, all of it richly rewarding.

Tim Pat Coogan

CHAPTER 1

Catastrophe at Rineanna: the Early Shannon Crashes

ALTHOUGH the first air crossings of both the Irish Sea and the Atlantic (1910 and 1919 respectively) ended in crash landings, the first really serious accident to a commercial airliner in Ireland was at Shannon Airport, then better known as Rineanna, on Friday, 16 July 1943. Earlier, in March 1941, a four-engined de Havilland 86A of Aer Lingus (EI-ABK – fleet name *Éire*) had been forced down on a beach at Malahide, Co. Dublin, some seven kilometres northeast of Dublin Airport. While its nose was badly damaged, it was possible to fly it off again after some temporary repairs.

The first of the many crashes that Shannon would experience during the coming half century occurred at 1.40 p.m. on a pleasant mid-summer afternoon and in full view of the welcoming party waiting on the ramp to greet the VIPs it was carrying. With civil aviation still in its infancy, crashes were still terrifyingly frequent and already that year there had been seven fatal accidents, two of them highly sensational. The American novelist and journalist, Ben Robertson, was one of twenty-four fatalities when a Pan American Airways Boeing 314 flying boat crashed on landing on the river Tagus in Lisbon on 22 February. And on 1 June, in a crash which remains controversial to this day, the actor Leslie Howard, along with sixteen others, died when a DC-3 operated by KLM on behalf of BOAC (British Overseas Airways Corporation) was shot down by the Luftwaffe over the bay of Biscay en route from neutral Lisbon to Whitchurch Aerodrome, near Bristol.

In the Shannon incident, a DH91 Frobisher of BOAC – registered G-AFDK and with the fleet name *Fortuna* – started to yaw (twist in one direction) violently while on final approach to runway 14 and, having rolled over a low wall and lost its tailplane from hitting a row of bushes, it smashed into a small field short of the runway threshold. Fortunately – and probably owing to the fact that the fuselage was of plywood rather than metal – there was no fire.

The new Shannon land base had been operational for just over two years.

Unlike most of those that were to follow, the Frobisher crash was non-fatal. Indeed, it was to an extent something of a light-hearted affair as the only casualty was a large and ancient goat, the decaying carcass of which was trapped beneath the fuselage and provided the air accident investigators, working in the heat of mid July, with a huge incentive to get the job finished quickly.

Although the transformation from air force base to civilian airport was fairly evident in 1943, Shannon was still under military control. Rineanna was the headquarters of No. 1 Coastal Patrol Squadron which comprised mainly two Supermarine Walrus amphibians and four Ansons. Wartime censorship was in full force in Ireland that summer and the first reports of this historic accident didn't reach the Irish newspapers until 10 August when the three Dublin dailies carried almost identical accounts of a 'crash landing' at Rineanna. The stories were based on a press association dispatch from London. The date of the accident was not disclosed, nor was the airport at which the flight originated.

But the newspapers did manage to get an almost complete passenger list past the official censors. It revealed that the Frobisher was carrying four members of the BOAC board and four members of the airline's senior management. In fact, there were five members of the senior management team. It was not revealed that two of the passengers – Gerard d'Erlanger and Pauline Gowers – were major figures in the British war effort. D'Erlanger was head of the air transport auxiliary (ATA) which then comprised some 700 pilots operating from fifteen bases who performed the vital role of ferrying new aircraft from the factories to the RAF bases. (Four years after the crash, d'Erlanger would be appointed a director of Aer Lingus, as the BOAC representative. In those days BEA and BOAC between them owned forty per cent of Aer Lingus.)

There were a sizeable number of women pilots in the ATA and this section of the organisation was headed by the 'Miss Pauline Gower' of the press reports who in military life was Commandant Pauline Gower, OBE, director of the Women's ATA. (An interesting feature of the women pilots of the ATA is that a computerised analysis of the hours flown in delivering 310,000 aircraft, done many years after the war had ended, showed that the women pilots had a better safety record than the men.)

The overlap between civil and military aviation was by then well established. Even before the outbreak of hostilities, Britain's major airline (then known as Imperial Airways) had been placed on a semi-military footing and operated as an adjunct to the RAF. For several months before the declaration of war, RAF pilots flew on German and other European routes with their civilian counterparts so as to familiarise themselves with the locations of cities they would subsequently bomb.

Two of BOAC's flying boats, *Cabot* and *Caribou*, were requisitioned as long-range reconnaissance aircraft and one of the airline's most famous captains was among several BOAC staff killed on active service. The ATA, which was run largely by d'Erlanger and Gower, was responsible for ferrying aircraft from the factories to the RAF bases in Britain and overseas. At the time of the Shannon crash, it had almost reached its full complement of 700 pilots – many of them women – who operated between 15 bases in the UK. Between them, they delivered 310,000 aircraft during the hostilities.

Had the Frobisher's pilot, Captain Geoffrey Palliser Moss, not been able to partially control the aircraft by sheer force of muscle power, thus preventing it from spinning, the consequences for Britain's war effort in the air could have been substantial.

Officially, the purpose of the journey by these aviation VIPs was to enable them to inspect BOAC's facilities at the new Shannon land base from which passengers arriving by flying boat across the estuary at Foynes could be ferried to England. But it is likely there was another reason for the flight: the prospect of a brief but welcome respite from war-torn England for a group of overworked and war weary people. Although by 1943 – the year in which, in the view of the historian A. J. P. Taylor, world leadership moved from Great Britain to the United States – the heavy air raids were over, during the week of the crash there had been bombing raids by the Luftwaffe over the northeast coast, Hull, East Anglia and the southeast, including London.

The plan for the BOAC party was, most likely, that a none too onerous inspection of the Rineanna land base would conveniently combine with a pleasant weekend enjoying the good food and priceless tranquility of the Clare/Limerick region before being dropped off at Hendon Aerodrome in North London after which *Fortuna* would continue on to Whitchurch Aerodrome near Bristol, the wartime base of BOAC.

The aircraft in which they were making the trip began life as the D.H.91 Albatross: a beautifully streamlined and superbly aerodynamic four-engined low wing monoplane of wooden construction, which first flew on 20 May 1937. It was powered by four de Havilland Gipsy Twelve engines driving constant-speed propellers, and had electrically retractable main landing gear units. It was designed to air ministry specifications and conceived as a transatlantic mail plane. The range for transatlantic operations was never achieved. It was, however, eminently suitable for a shuttle service between the UK and Iceland and several were used by the RAF for this purpose.

Five Albatrosses were adapted for use by Imperial Airways (forerunner of BOAC) who styled it the Frobisher. The refinements included a more sophisticated slotted flaps system to replace the original split, trailing-edge flaps. They normally carried twenty-two passengers and a crew of four and were used extensively by BOAC on the Whitchurch–Lisbon service as well as Whitchurch–Shannon. This flight had a crew of five which included two stewardesses to look after nine passengers – a clear indication of the VIP status of the passengers.

Even by the standards of the time, the Frobisher, though aesthetically and technically eminent, was a rather unfortunate aircraft. Of the seven in the BOAC fleet, two crashed while landing at Reykjavik (G-AEVV in August 1941; G-AEVW in April 1942); another (G-AFDL) was lost at Pucklechurch, near Bristol, in October 1940, and a fourth (G-AFDI) was destroyed by enemy action during an air raid on Whitchurch.

The Rineanna crash occurred a mere three-quarters of a mile from the end of the runway and in sight of the welcoming party gathered to receive the VIP passengers. Hilary Watson, chief of BOAC's Irish operations, headed immediately to the wreck and was among the first to arrive. With an axe from a rescue vehicle he hacked through the wooden fuselage – its passenger windows blacked out in keeping with wartime regulations – and found one of the directors, Simon Marks (son of the founder of Marks and Spencer and then the M&S chairman), terrified and still strapped to his seat. According to Marks' biographer, Paul Bookbinder, in *Simon Marks: Retail Revolutionary*, Marks attempted to introduce himself to Watson who responded by saying: 'Mr Marks, this is not the time for formalities. This plane is about to explode like a bomb.' He then proceeded to drag him unceremoniously from the wreck. Marks gave a different slant in his written statement to the inspector of accidents. His brief account of the crash ended by saying that he got out 'without any difficulty'.

Miss Gower's statement about her terrifying experience in the cabin of the Frobisher with its blacked-out windows, is another example of true British grit: 'It occurred to me that some part of the aircraft had become detached,' she said, 'and a few moments afterwards we crashed.'

But the most dramatic of these statements is that of the thirty-five-year-old pilot, Captain Geoffrey Palliser Moss, which contains a graphic description of the terrifying few minutes leading up to the crash. By the standards of the day, Moss was very experienced. He had 4,000 flying hours, even though only eighteen were on this particular aircraft type. In adversity he performed brilliantly and the inquiry cleared him of all blame.

He told the inspector of accidents how he had applied full opposite rudder immediately the yaw started, but this failed to control the swing. He then opened the throttles and the swing corrected. The nose then immediately started to dip and he went perilously low. He applied all his strength in trying to pull the control column back but failed to move it more than an inch. A 'nose-in' was, he felt, imminent:

'I asked the flight engineer to close the throttles and help me pull back on the control column. I then took my foot off the rudder pedal and the yawing returned. I put my foot on the dashboard and, with the help of the flight engineer, succeeded in getting the column back about halfway between neutral and full.'

Catastrophe was avoided. The aircraft traversed a field of haycocks for sixty yards before crashing sideways over a loose stone wall. The tail and rear end had already smashed off after coming into contact with a row of bushes.

The Frobisher crash resulted in the almost instantaneous appointment of the first inspector of accidents of the new Irish state. R. W. O'Sullivan, who was chief aeronautical engineer to the Irish air corps, was given the title of inspector of accidents and dispatched to Rineanna. He went on to investigate practically all of the major air accidents within the state, culminating in the difficult and painstaking investigation of the Aer Lingus Viscount *St Phelim* (EI-AOM) at Tuskar Rock in March 1968.

In his memoirs, *An Irish Airman's Sketchbook* (1988), O'Sullivan recalled how the distinguished survivors of the Frobisher were anxious to get away as soon as possible and were fretful of being delayed through over-zealous officialdom. He met them outside their Limerick hotel in the coach that was taking them to the airport and was warmly applauded when he told them there would be no interrogation and it would suffice for each of them to send him a short statement through the BOAC station manager.

Finding the cause of the crash wasn't difficult. Two eyewitnesses told how they had seen what they believed to be leaflets falling from the aircraft as it approached. When they went to pick them up they found they were pieces of plywood. One woman collected six pieces measuring around two by one feet square. Mr O'Sullivan soon found that the skin of the starboard wing simply tore off when the flaps were activated. This caused the starboard flap to come up again, leaving the port wing flap fully extended. The aircraft then started to yaw through an angle of almost ninety degrees.

A check of the aircraft's maintenance records showed that the skin of the starboard wing had been partially replaced during a recent overhaul. Unfortunately, the engineers neglected to glue down the new surface and it was held in place only by being attached to the brass brads (nails) of the rear spar (the main longitudinal beam of the wing).

With *Fortuna* written off, only two Frobishers remained in the BOAC fleet. These had entered service in 1938 and 1939 and their five year periods of obsolescence were due in December 1943 and June 1944. Not surprisingly, the board decided to bring the date of their retirement forward and they were scrapped at the end of September 1943.

The good luck that BOAC enjoyed at Rineanna on 16 July wasn't to last long. Twelve days later, one of its Short Sunderland flying boats, flying in poor weather and desperately trying to locate Foynes, crashed into Mount Brandon, Co. Kerry. This time there were ten fatalities and fifteen survivors.

Captain Michael Cusack looked down from the left hand cockpit window of the gleaming silver and green DC-3, registration EI-ACA, flagship of the Aer Lingus fleet, just after 9 p.m. on Tuesday, 18 June 1946. The twenty-six-year-old and newly-married commander of the daily scheduled Shannon to Dublin service could see the small knot of passengers make their way in the gathering dusk from the wooden terminal to the aircraft.

At the rear passenger door, the sole air hostess, Anna Greevy (elder sister of the internationally famous mezzo soprano, Bernadette Greevy), stood waiting to welcome them. Just past twenty, she was one of the eight original air hostesses hired by the airline earlier that year. On this very day, her sister, Marie Greevy, started work with Air France. She would later become general manager of Sabena's Irish operation.

In the cockpit with Michael Cusack was co-pilot Brendan Murray, a twenty-three-year-old Limerick man recently demobbed from the RAF; he had served during the worst years of the war flying Handley Page Halifax bombers. The third member of the crew, radio officer James Ring, a native of Kildorrey, Mallow, Co. Cork, sat behind Cusack beside the radio racks and facing towards the starboard side.

The fifteen passengers included two priests, a US based monsignor and a local curate. Little did the young air hostess realise as she greeted the two clergymen that within fifteen minutes she would have to restrain one of them from standing up in his seat at the head of the aeroplane to pronounce a general absolution as they turned back towards the airport with flames spouting along the starboard side of the aircraft.

Co-pilot Murray wasn't the only former RAF pilot on board *Charlie Alpha* on what was to be its final flight. Travelling as a passenger was another former RAF man, Air Commodore John Oliver, a veteran of both world wars who, back in 1918, was decorated by King George V with the air force cross. Now aged forty-eight, he had retired from the RAF two months prior to the accident and was working as an executive with the Goodyear tyre company. As the emergency developed, the air commodore – to the consternation of the young air hostess – decided that he should play an active role in evacuating the aircraft.

Charlie Alpha was the pride of the Aer Lingus fleet. Registered on 1 April 1940, it was the first of the 19 DC-3s which were the backbone of the Aer Lingus fleet during the 1940s and 1950s. They enabled the infant airline to make the transition from small regional carrier to medium sized European airline. Throughout the difficult later war years *Charlie Alpha* had plied the dangerous airways between Dublin and Liverpool in camouflage and often with its windows blacked out.

It was the only Aer Lingus DC-3 to be bought directly from the manufacturers. Another (EI-ACB) was actually registered but, because the outbreak of war played havoc with the development of new Aer Lingus routes, it was sold to Pan American prior to delivery. Most of the other aircraft were converted military versions of the DC-3, war surplus machines known as the C47, and bought more or less as a job lot for a few thousand pounds each.

Having come off the production line, *Charlie Alpha* was flown across the US to New York where it was dismantled, crated and shipped to Antwerp to be reassembled for Aer Lingus by Fokker at its Schipol headquarters. This was not the only occasion that this lovely aeroplane had to endure the ignominy of being shipped over the seas in crates. On 19 April 1941, it was severely damaged when it collided with a post on landing at Barton Airport, Manchester. A recovery team sent over from Dublin took it apart and on 1 June it arrived back in Dublin on board the *Lady Kilkenny*. *Charlie Alpha* did not fly again until August 1942. Later it became commonplace to fit temporary additional fuel tanks in DC-3s and ferry them across the Atlantic. One such delivery flight, that of a Sabena DC-3 (OO-CBH) came to grief in a boreen in Kinvara, Co. Galway, a month after the destruction of *Charlie Alpha* when the pilot crash-landed after mistakenly reckoning he had run out of fuel.

Charlie Alpha's last take-off was to be from the old 05/23 main runway at Shannon. Shortly after 9.30 p.m. Cusack turned the DC-3's nose into the gentle summer breeze and ran each engine at 1,500 rpm, checking the generators for the dreaded 'mag drop' (an electrical fault which can cause a reduction in the power of the engine). The weather conditions were favourable. General visibility was given at twenty-five miles, with a shower in sight to the southwest. The surface wind was measured at 8 knots. By 9.35 p.m., Murray had requested and received take-off clearance. Cusack then swung the DC-3 on to the runway and, after activating the booster pumps, opened the throttles. Within seconds of rolling into the airflow the airspeed indicator was reading 35 knots and Cusack lifted the tail by easing the control column forward. Now, for the first time since boarding, the fifteen passengers found themselves sitting at an even keel. Less than a minute later, the co-pilot called out the combined VI-rotation speed of 86 knots. Cusack eased back the control column and sent *Charlie Alpha* lumbering into the sky.

From her crew seat in the rear, air hostess Anna Greevy could not see the ground fall away. She had never had any fear of flying, and even after a couple of months experience as air crew, every take-off was still something of a wonder as, in the words of John Gillespie Magee's famous poem, one 'slips the surly bonds of earth'.

That year there were only fifteen hostesses in the entire airline. In the drab Ireland of the mid 1940s, the job was seen as immensely glamorous. At the turn of the century, as Mrs Anna France, and for many years living in London, she looked back with great pride and affection on her years with Aer Lingus:

'Explaining the excitement and the sense of what amounted to missionary zeal that practically everyone in Aer Lingus felt in those days isn't easy,' she said. 'The airline was still very young and on the brink of what we believed to be major development.

'We had a marvellously charismatic general manager in Gerry Dempsey. He inspired everyone. Every single one of us really believed that we had a vital role to play, not only for Aer Lingus but for the whole country. And we felt so lucky and so privileged in not just having a job but to have such an exciting and worthwhile one.'

Soon after the take-off, Anna Greevy unfastened her seat belt in order to mingle with her passengers and, as was common in those more leisurely days, to point out features along the route. Although the DC-3 had a small galley there was no catering on this short sixty-minute flight. The normal routing would have them soaring at around 5,000 feet over the northern tip of Lough Derg, the first of the great Shannon lakes, and then in a northeasterly curve over the Great Central Plain of Ireland and the lush pastures of Meath or Kildare before sighting Collinstown with the Irish Sea and Lambay Island as its backdrop.

Anna's first duty was to walk through the narrow cabin, carefully observing her passengers and attempting to calm any apprehension or unease with a confident smile or a reassuring word. About halfway towards the cockpit, she became aware that a passenger seated on the right hand side was anxiously tugging at her jacket and pointing at the window. 'Excuse me,' he inquired anxiously, 'but is this normal?'

Small gouts of yellowish flames and black smoke were coming from the top of the engine. Inexperienced as she was, Anna Greevy knew that they were far from normal. Substantial tongues of flame, smokeless and purplish in colour, from the underside of the DC-3's Pratt and Whitney R-1820 (1,200hp) piston engines, though perfectly normal, often caused inexperienced passengers much alarm. But what the hostess saw on this occasion was entirely different. She realised immediately that everyone on board was at peril.

In the cockpit, the captain and first officer were already aware of a problem. The first indications were a coughing sound from the starboard engine followed by a loss of power and a swing to starboard. Cusack corrected the swing by applying opposite rudder and, having found there was no fuel pressure showing for the starboard engine, opened the cross-feed valve. When this failed to revive the engine, Cusack ordered Murray to get up the fuel pressure by means of the Wobble pump – an emergency, hand-operated device.

This was the correct emergency procedure for engine failure without fire. Neither pilot suspected at this stage that an engine was on fire and neither knew that their remedy was exacerbating the problem by feeding more fuel to an engine that was already ablaze.

Anna Greevy remembered the moment well: 'In those first couple of seconds many things flashed through my mind,' she recalls. 'I remember saying to myself, "I'm going to die, we are all going to die. It isn't fair, because I have so much to do. I'm not ready for this. I'm not prepared". Then, I think, I said a short, silent prayer – probably an act of contrition.

'Suddenly, everything changed, just as if a shutter had come down. I found I was able to put everything out of my mind except the need to go through the emergency drill and do everything in my power to help the passsengers.'

When Anna Greevy opened the cockpit door, neither Captain Cusack nor his co-pilot was aware of the engine fire. Neither was the third member of the operational crew, Radio Officer Jim Ring.

Ring was sitting directly behind the captain's left hand seat but at right angles to it. As Anna Greevy opened the cockpit door he had a clear view of the rapidly advancing fire.

Over fifty-five years later and living in retirement in Kilbarrack, Dublin, Jim Ring still had a vivid recollection of the flight: 'I had noticed the swing when the engine lost power, but it wasn't very pronounced. I remember seeing Michael Cusack's hand reaching for the cross-feed valve.

'Then Anna opened the door and because I was facing directly towards the starboard side, I could see that the fire was well advanced, spreading right down the length of the fuselage and burning through the fabric-covered starboard aileron. I'll never forget my sense of horror, and I immediately tapped out an SOS in Morse to Shannon. As I was tapping out the message I could see that Michael Cusack's neck was getting redder and redder.

'He was already turning back towards the airport and he said to Anna: "Go back and get everyone strapped in". After she had gone, Brendan Murray said very quietly: "Michael, I think you had better put her down".'

In his seat towards the rear of the starboard side, Air Commodore Oliver was aware of his peril. In his statement to the inspector of accidents, he said: 'About three minutes after take-off I smelt burning. Very shortly after that I saw a light flashing outside the starboard windows and knew that there was a fire inside the engine nacelle.

'The air hostess noticed this at about the same time and went forward and told the captain. She returned and in the calmest possible manner said: "Will you all please do up your belts. The pilot is returning to the aerodrome". The flames started to spread and were roaring down the side of the cabin.'

The plight of EI-ACA had not gone unnoticed on the ground. At least two people, an Aer Lingus traffic clerk and a Pan American Airways engineer, both working on the tarmac, noticed that an engine was on fire. The traffic clerk took immediate action and phoned the control tower. The officer who spoke to him told him not to worry – the take-off had been normal.

This exchange of words was referred to in a memo dated 29 June 1946, from the general manager of Aer Lingus, J. F. Dempsey, to the chairman, the all-powerful and much feared secretary of the department of industry and commerce, John Leydon. In his memo, Dempsey wrote: 'I am informed that following the take-off, the aircraft passed back over the airport and that one of our traffic staff observed what he thought to be fire and immediately reported to "Control". It is alleged that "Control" replied that the aircraft was alright and was proceeding normally. It now appears that only about another minute elapsed before our aircraft called "Control" informing "Control" that he was in trouble and was returning.

'Had the pilot realised in the first instance that the trouble in his starboard engine was fire, he would not, of course, have turned on the cross-feed valve. I am not suggesting that there is anything material in what appears to be the failure of "Control" to take more positive action following the receipt of the report from our Traffic Clerk but, knowing your anxiety to fully investigate not only the cause of the fire but the subsequent actions of all concerned, I am passing this information to you.'

As she returned to the cabin, Anna Greevy found one of the clergymen preparing to stand up to impart a general absolution. The young air hostess suggested it would be every bit as effective if he gave it while seated. Reluctantly, the cleric obeyed.

'By this time all the other passengers knew that we were on fire. Even though you could sense the fear, there was no panic. I assured them that the captain was dealing with the situation, that we would return to Shannon, and I urged everyone to stay in their seats with their seat belts tightly fastened.'

The Aer Lingus operations manual for the DC-3 contained a seventeen-point emergency drill for coping with engine fires. The first eight items were considered vital and were underlined. They read:

1. Mixture – idle and off.
2. Feather button – press.
3. Throttle on dead engine – closed.
4. R.P.M. on Dead Engine – fully coarse.
5. Fire extinguisher (when engine stopped) – select and operate.
6. Fuel isolation cock – closed.
7. Power setting (live engine) as required.
8. Fuel valve – off.

The other items included adjusting the trim tabs, checking generators, pressure and suction.

Cusack and Murray would not have enough time to go through all these procedures. The DC-3, although mainly of metal construction, had fabric-covered control surfaces and *Charlie Alpha*'s starboard aileron (a hinged surface in the wing) was already burning fiercely and making control over banking (tilting sideways to make a return) extremely difficult. Cusack knew that it was probably a matter of minutes before he could lose his rudder to the flames.

Wisely, he agreed with the judgement of his co-pilot and decided to put the DC-3 down, its landing gear retracted, on a marshy patch where the Shannon industrial estate now stands. As former air force pilots, Cusack and Murray were no novices at coaxing crippled aircraft out of the skies. On this occasion they performed brilliantly, even though they made one rudimentary error – an error which turned out to be most fortunate for all on board. In the short time available to them, the two pilots neglected to cut off the cross-feed to the burning engine. With high octane petrol feeding it, the fire burned fiercely – so fiercely, in fact, that it burned through the engine mounting and the blazing engine broke off and fell into a field. A minute or two longer and a fuel tank might have exploded.

As the blazing DC-3 headed back towards Shannon, Anna Greevy noticed to her dismay that several passengers had unfastened their seat belts and one had actually left his seat and was making towards the back of the aircraft. When she remonstrated with him, he replied, firmly but courteously 'I am an air commodore of the RAF, and I know what I'm doing. Now you and I are going to get that door open before we hit the ground and end up trapped in here.'

The air commodore, who had been impressed by the coolness of the hostess, sounded convincing. 'Whatever the regulations or the training manuals said, he was a lot bigger than me and anyhow his demeanor and manner of speech inspired real confidence. I decided that the proper thing to do was to let him get on with it.

'The door of the DC-3 opened directly outwards and getting it open against the slipstream took our combined strength. For the last hundred feet or so of the descent we were both lying on the floor, still pushing at the door and clinging on for dear life to the nearest seat struts.'

In his statement after the crash, the air commodore said that at first the hostess made 'strenuous efforts' to stop him opening the door. 'Then the aircraft made several lurches which gave me the feeling that it was out of control from that moment.'

The moment of impact is still stamped on Anna Greevy's memory: 'There were a couple of hideous shudders as the belly of the aircraft made contact with the marshy ground. My foot was bleeding profusely from a bad gash and a few of the passengers who had undone their seat belts were also thrown about and picked up some injuries.

'But I knew the second we hit that we were OK. It was a brilliant piece of flying by Michael Cusack. He had so little time.' The chief inspector of accidents, R. W. O'Sullivan, agreed. The pilot, he noted, acted 'with admirable calmness and great skill'.

Jim Ring believes that if the air commodore had not insisted on opening the door prior to the touch-down, it would almost certainly have jammed upon impact. 'He certainly had the right idea, even if it was contrary to what was laid down in the emergency procedures. His action may have saved several lives.'

No great degree of detective work was required in finding the cause of the accident. The vibrations during the take-off caused a fuel pipe coupling to come loose, thus spraying petrol all over the back of the engine. The coupling design was in fact faulty and was later superseded.

Having helped evacuate her passengers, Anna Greevy was taken to the County Hospital in Ennis. 'I wanted to get back home to Clontarf and hated the idea of going to hospital but the company insisted. The only accommodation available was in the maternity department and I was put into this large ward with several expectant mothers.

'We didn't have a phone at home in those days and my parents were informed of the crash by a woman down the avenue who ran a nursing home and whose number I had given for use in an emergency. At first they thought I had lost my leg and they were in a terrible state. Then the Radio Éireann news gave a fuller picture and they calmed down.

'In those innocent days of very primitive communications they decided that they should send me a telegram to the airport which was given to me at the hospital. It took them ages to make up their minds what to say. In the end they settled for: "Congratulations on your escape – Mammy & Daddy". 'I was so thrilled to hear from them. And I still have the telegram.'

Anna Greevy was back in the air within a couple of weeks. She later became chief hostess of Aer Lingus, leaving in 1954 to marry and settle in London.

Michael Cusack went on to fly the new state-of-the-art L-749 Constellations, bought for the opening of an Atlantic service in 1948 but subsequently sold to BOAC after a bitterly controversial political decision to abandon the proposed North Atlantic service. He left the airline soon afterwards to fly freighters in India and to take part in the Berlin airlift. Later, he resumed his studies in dentistry which he had started before he joined the Irish air corps in the early years of the war and, during the long vacations, flew DC-3s with Skyways of Liverpool. Once he had qualified as a dentist, he built up a successful practice in London before returning to Dublin where he practised for many years in Westland Row. He died in 1996 while playing golf at Portmarnock Golf Links.

Brendan Murray continued his career with Aer Lingus and became a much respected captain on Boeing 737 jets. He had to leave flying early owing to ill health and served for a time as the airline's chief safety officer. He died before reaching retirement age. His daughter, Tina, followed him into the industry as an Aer

Lingus pilot, rising to become a captain with the airline.

Jim Ring was one of several radio officers whose flying careers ended when Aer Lingus stopped using radio officers in 1948. He qualified as a navigator and as an aircraft dispatcher, married an Aer Lingus hostess, Claire Cooney, and worked for many years in flight operations, retiring in 1983 as operations service superintendent.

The year 1946 wasn't a good one for the DC-3, in particular, or for air safety in general. Many other DC-3 passengers and crews weren't as lucky as those who walked away from the wreckage of *Charlie Alpha* in the Rineanna marshland. During 1946, a total of forty DC-3s crashed with the loss of 246 lives. Considering that, at maximum, the DC-3 then carried only twenty-eight passengers (EI-ACA was a twenty-one seater) it is a disturbing record and one that shows how much safer flying has become.

The passengers aboard *Charlie Alpha* owed their lives to the unlikely combination of brilliant flying coupled with pilot error. If Cusack and Murray had followed the book and turned off the cross feed to the blazing engine, it is highly likely that, instead of falling off, it would have caused a fuel tank to explode.

CHAPTER 2

The Not Too Cruel Sea ... North Atlantic Ditchings

THE conquest of the North Atlantic started in earnest on 18 May 1919, when Harry Hawker, one of the great test-pilots of the day, took off from Newfoundland in his Sopworth biplane powered by a single 320hp Rolls Royce Eagle engine. This was the first attempt to fly the Atlantic non stop. Hawker and his navigator, Lieutenant Commodore L. K. Mackenzie-Grieve, had almost reached the halfway mark when an engine problem forced them to ditch alongside a small Dutch cargo ship called the *Mary*.

They were lucky. The ship launched a lifeboat and both airmen were rescued. As the *Mary* had no wireless, they were presumed lost. Finally, on 25 May, a visual signal was sent to a shore station in the outer Hebrides. This wasn't Hawker's first forced landing on water. Six years earlier, while in a gliding turn for an emergency landing in the Irish Sea off Loughshinny in north Co. Dublin, his oil-soaked boot slipped off the rudder bar causing him to lose control and plunge into the water. He was lucky on that occasion too as he succeeded in swimming away from the wreckage with no injuries.

Almost a month to the day after Hawker and Mackenzie-Grieve had been picked up, Captain John Alcock and Lieutenant Arthur Whitten Brown accomplished the first non stop crossing of the Atlantic. Their plane was a twin-engined Vickers Vimy bomber powered by two Rolls-Royce Eagle engines. They covered the route from St John's, Newfoundland, to Clifton, Co. Galway, in sixteen hours and twelve minutes. The first airship crossing of the Atlantic was accomplished the following month when the airship R-34 made the crossing from Scotland to New York taking four days to make the journey.

By the time Charles Lindbergh made his historic crossing from Roosevelt Field, New York, to Le Bourget, Paris, on 20–21 May 1927, more than seventy others had crossed the Atlantic by air. Lindbergh, however, was the first to go it alone – that was what made his flight the most famous of all Atlantic crossings. He, too, was lucky. Several others who tried to emulate him weren't and the US coastguard became so weary of trying to rescue ill-prepared Atlantic flyers that the US government banned all solo crossings. It was because of this ban that Douglas ('Wrong-Way') Corrigan invented his famous 'compass error' excuse which he continued to claim until his death took him eastwards to Ireland and not westwards to California as he had intended.

Ditching in the 2,000-mile stretch of ocean that lies between Newfoundland and Ireland has always been a terrifying prospect for even the most intrepid aviator. At their worst, the Atlantic waves can reach fifty feet. Putting a crippled airplane on to an Atlantic swell without having it break up and sink on impact calls for luck as well as great piloting skills. It is an exercise which, even today, cannot be fully practised in the most sophisticated flight simulators.

The Boeing 314 Crash, 14 October 1947

Of all the ditchings in the North Atlantic, that of the Boeing 314 flying boat *Bermuda Sky Queen* on 14 October 1947 remains the most noteworthy. Purists will insist that 'ditching' is the wrong word as only land planes can be ditched. But the cumbersome B314 which was designed for tranquil waters was at little more advantage than a land plane. The fact that its sixty-two passengers and seven crew members survived their nightmarish ordeal without physical injury was largely due to the skill and professionalism of two captains: the commander of the flying boat who made a magnificent landing amid thirty-foot waves, and the commander of the US coastguard cutter, *George M. Bibb*, whose conduct of the rescue operation was a model of intelligent and creative seamanship, and courage.

Captain Paul B. Cronk, the forty-seven-year-old captain of the *Bibb*, along with several members of his crew, were subsequently decorated by the US government for their efforts. Captain Charles Martin, the thirty-three-year-old commander of the *Bermuda Sky Queen* was subjected to a civil fine of $200 'for his alleged violations of the Civil Air Regulations in the conduct of the flight'.

Prior to that magnificent piece of airmanship Captain Martin had presided over a piece of flight planning which must rate as one of the most bizarre in the history of commercial aviation. When the *Bermuda Sky Queen* lifted off at Foynes on the afternoon of Monday, 13 October 1947, it was overloaded by 5,000 lb in excess of its certified gross weight and the estimates of fuel consumption and ground-speeds given to the captain were mathematical impossibilities.

The operator of the B314, American International Airlines, was one of several charter airlines that had mushroomed in the US at the end of the war. Traffic over the North Atlantic was booming and the shipping companies, still trying to reorganise themselves after the restrictions of the war years, were unable to cope. There were rich pickings for charter airlines able to provide seats at rates lower than the premium first-class fares still being charged by the scheduled carriers in their DC-6s and Lockheed Constellations.

The *Bermuda Sky Queen* was no stranger in Foynes. In her present incarnation, she had already made a trip through the base on 30 September that year when she arrived from Poole, Dorset, and continued across the Atlantic with fifty-two passengers and a crew of seven. As she arrived from Poole on 13 October with sixty-one passengers and eight crew members she was making aviation history. Never before had so many people set out on an Atlantic crossing by air.

The Boeing 314 was the biggest airliner on the post-war Atlantic routes. As with so many other aircraft, the concept for the design came from Pan American. On 31 July 1936, Boeing contracted with Pan American to build six 314 flying boats powered by four 1,500hp Wright GR-2600 Double Cyclone engines, giving a maximum speed of 193mph and a range of 3,500 miles from a maximum fuel capacity of 4,200 US gallons. The first B314 made its maiden voyage on 7 June 1939 and passenger service started three weeks later.

BOAC also operated the B314 on the Atlantic but they and Pan American withdrew it from this route in 1946. Although the original specifications were for up to seventy-four passengers in four cabins, Pan American normally carried only thirty-five passengers – but in extreme luxury. Their 314s each had a dining-room seating seventeen passengers, a promenade deck where people could walk and watch the Atlantic breakers, and a honeymoon suite at the rear.

The charter company for which Captain Martin worked had no interest in pampering its customers. The four cabins of the *Bermuda Sky Queen* had been stripped of all luxury furnishings. Gone were the dining-room, the promenade deck and the rear stateroom. In their place were sixty passenger seats, all upright and with no reclining facility. Only one cabin attendant – a steward – was carried, and none of the crew wore a uniform. Such meagre facilities for a crossing estimated to take seventeen hours would test the endurance of the most robust passenger. More than half a century before the term was invented, this was 'no frills' service with a vengeance.

Although the crew lacked experience in Atlantic navigation, it comprised some excellent men. Captain Martin had been a wartime pilot with the US navy and, as his handling of the emergency landing was to show, he was capable of brilliant airmanship. After this unhappy incident, he went on to have a successful career as a pilot with Delta, one of the most respected airlines in the US. Martin's co-pilot, Addison Thompson, had 4,000 flying hours to his credit and, like the captain, was on his second Atlantic round trip. Second Officer John H. Shafer, Flight Engineer Walter Yaramishyn, Assistant Flight Engineer Robert Hamilton and Radio Officer Keith Woodmansee were all properly licensed and qualified.

Their landing at Foynes after flying from Poole in Dorset on the afternoon of 12 October caused quite a stir. Since the arrival of the first Atlantic landplane at the new land base in Rineanna across the estuary, the Foynes operation had been steadily winding down. Although the last movement from Foynes wasn't until October 1948, the two big operators – Pan American and BOAC – had already pulled out. The arrival of any flying boat to Foynes in 1947 would be a great novelty, but the arrival of the *Bermuda Sky Queen* was much more. Because it had sixty-nine souls on board, the *Bermuda Sky Queen* was set to make aviation history. Never before had so many people been carried on a commercial airplane across the Atlantic.

From the start, the omens were bad. A weather forecast promising gale force headwinds caused an overnight delay and the passengers – most of them oil company executives and their families – were put up in the local passenger hostels. Among the passengers was a US sea captain and his crew of nine who had delivered a tanker to the UK. Twelve children – two of them babes in arms – were listed on the manifest.

The following morning Captain Martin, along with First Officer Thompson and Second Officer Shaefer, went to the Shannon meteorological station and studied the latest data. Subsequently they worked out their flight plan. Using figures given to him by the crew, Captain Martin estimated that his 4,000 gallons of fuel would keep him in the air for twenty-two hours and that the 1,730-mile hop from Foynes to Gander would be accomplished in seventeen hours. Even if the predicted headwinds increased substantially, his five hour safety margin would still, he reasoned, be more than adequate.

Unfortunately, the figures given to the captain were way out of line. The throttle and boost settings recommended to him would provide not twenty-two hours of flying time but seventeen and a half, cutting the safety margin to a mere thirty minutes. Another fatal flaw in the calculations was the failure to take into account the effect the gross overloading would have on the B314's ground-speed and that, even if these was no increase in the speed of the headwinds, the estimated speed of 130 knots would not be reached until well into the flight when much of the fuel had been burned off.

In the event, the headwinds increased dramatically and icing conditions at 6,000 feet further hampered their progress. At 1.55 a.m. the B314 made contact with the US coastguard cutter *George M. Bibb*, one of the thirteen weather ships which at that time were anchored throughout the Atlantic to provide meteorological, communications and rescue services to aviation. The *Bermuda Sky Queen* had now flown 892 miles since leaving Foynes and had consumed ten hours and twenty-five minutes of the twenty-two hour estimated fuel range. The *Bibb*'s radio operator reported winds of 40 to 45 knots at 6,000 feet. Captain Martin obtained permission to descend to 4,000 feet in search of better conditions. At 5 a.m. the second officer, who had been resting in a crew bunk, was awakened to compute an accurate location based on the weather data just received. The results were chilling.

According to these new calculations, the B314 had been battered by gale force headwinds of over 60mph which had reduced its groundspeed to a derisory 59 knots. Even before the flight engineer started to work out the fuel situation in regard to the remaining 550 miles to Gander, everyone on the flight deck knew they weren't going to make it. The calculations revealed there was only enough fuel left for two hrs and forty-five minutes of flight.

The only option now was to put the flying boat down close to the weather ship. It was a horrific prospect. The hull of the B314 was designed for contact with tranquil sheltered waters. On this October morning in the mid Atlantic a fierce gale was whipping the ocean's surface into thirty-foot waves, any of which might rip the hull of the flying boat apart and send everyone on board to an ocean grave. Only a combination of outstanding airmanship and incredible luck could ensure that the *Bermuda Sky Queen* survived such a landing. And even if Martin was to succeed in keeping it afloat, how would the passengers be rescued in such horrific conditions?

At 7.58 a.m., with Gander 460 miles to the west and the *Bibb* about 300 miles to the east, Captain Martin turned the B314 around and sent out a distress call. It was picked up by a Trans Canada Airlines freighter and a Pan American Airways DC-4 heading for Shannon. Within minutes, all air and sea traffic in the region as well as coastal stations had been notified. The radio officer on a BOAC Constellation notified the *Bibb* that Captain Martin would attempt an emergency landing close to the ship at around 8 a.m.

The commander of the *Bibb*, Paul B. Cronk, was asleep in his bunk when word of the emergency came. He and most of his hundred-man crew had come through a difficult seventy-two hours, assisting numerous aircraft through the bad weather by means of radar checks and meteorological reports. When his quartermaster called him to appraise him of the *Bermuda Sky Queen*'s plight he could scarcely comprehend that there were sixty-nine souls on board the stricken flying boat. The notion of a passenger load greater than the forty-three passengers carried by the DC-4 Skymasters that then dominated the North Atlantic route was almost beyond his grasp.

Grumpy because of the lack of sleep, Cronk dressed and came out on deck. When the B314 eventually appeared on the horizon and made a low pass over the *Bibb* he and his fellow officers could scarcely believe their eyes. Compared with the TCA and Pan American DC-4s that were already circling the area, the *Bermuda Sky Queen* looked like a monster. With a sinking heart, Cronk surveyed the thirty-foot waves and went into the chart room to make contact with Captain Martin. He suggested to the flying boat captain that the *Bibb* might calm the sea down by circling and that Martin might be able to settle in the circled area. Martin replied that he would have to find his own niche among the waves.

Aboard the *Bermuda Sky Queen* the passengers remained calm. Most were unaware of their peril. One woman who asked the steward what was going on was told that they were touching down to refuel. One passenger reported that the steward asked her to break up her card game as 'we are going down to get a weather report'. 'We thought it odd,' she said, 'but everyone reacted calmly.'

Captain Martin made four low passes over the gigantic swell before giving the order: 'Open the emergency escape hatches.' He then levelled off, closed the throttles and, raising the nose to shed the remaining airspeed, allowed his giant aircraft to sink into the stall that brings every flight to its natural end.

But in this case it was neither a smooth runway nor a stretch of calm water that lay ahead. From the left hand window of the Trans Canada DC-4 Captain Steve Albulet watched in horror as the B314 struck the water and appeared to vanish behind a huge wave. Albulet knew that several ditchings of this kind had ended in disaster as the hulls of the flying boats disintegrated under the enormous pressure of the waves. As he held his breath, Captain Albulet saw the sea settle over the B314. Then, a few seconds later, his heart rose as he saw the *Bermuda Sky Queen* rise out of the sea as if it were a submarine coming to the surface.

In the four cabins, the light that came through the portholes was extinguished as the sea closed in. In the darkness the passengers found themselves thrown violently forward only to be checked by their seat belts. Items of loose luggage flew about the cabins, ending up in a heap against the forward bulkheads. The impact was so violent and the strain of the seat belts so severe that many passengers were winded.

In the chart room of the *Bibb* Captain Cronk was reluctant to call the flying boat as he feared the carnage that might be occurring in it. Then came the clear, calm voice of Captain Martin: 'We are O.K. We will taxi up to you.'

Martin had made one of the finest and most famous landings in aviation history. He had judged the moment perfectly, waiting until the falling wave was no longer capable of destroying the flying boat's hull. His skill had saved both the lives of his passengers and his aircraft.

But any euphoria that the unfortunate passengers may have felt after the successful landing evaporated as soon as Martin applied power to the engines and started to taxi towards the weather ship. The B314 bounced about like a cork, sending practically every passenger on board into paroxysms of seasickness.

During the eleven hours in which it would take to complete the rescue, many of these passengers would reach such a stage of sickness that they no longer cared whether they lived or died.

As the flying boat came close to the ship it was suddenly seized by the backwash of a giant wave. Martin immediately cut the power but he was unable to prevent his craft from crashing against the *Bibb* with such force that the nose of the flying boat and the no. 3 engine were severely battered. As the ship and flying boat separated, the B314's starboard wing tip struck the *Bibb*'s catwalk causing damage to both.

As Captain Cronk surveyed the scene he knew that the saga of the *Bermuda Sky Queen* had only begun and that its passengers were still at great peril. Even though Martin continued to avoid the worst of the sea's broadsides, the hull was no longer watertight. But with the gale showing no sign of abating, Cronk could not think of a way of getting the passengers off. He consoled himself in the knowledge that as long as she remained afloat there was hope.

But in the passenger cabins of the B314 hope was dwindling

fast. Since the moment of touch-down, practically all of the passengers and most of the crew had been violently seasick. They were strapped into cramped seats in what had now become highly unsanitary conditions. The children cried piteously and demanded to know why their parents were subjecting them to this misery. As darkness approached, Captain Martin – himself in the throes of seasickness – feared that the hull was about to break up and that his passengers would soon be so debilitated from seasickness that they would be unable to help themselves. He called the *Bibb* and pleaded with Cronk to try and get them off before dark.

Even though the sea was still far too rough for lifeboats to survive, Cronk decided that unless some action was taken the unfortunate passengers would lose all hope. He ordered that three of the merchant seamen on board the flying boat should volunteer for a trial run by having themselves launched in a dinghy. Three seamen, led by Captain Quinn, immediately volunteered. The first dinghy burst. After successfully launching a second, they jumped into it and cut themselves free. Cronk edged his ship towards them.

It took almost an hour to get the seamen on board the cutter and Cronk knew that their survival was entirely due to the fact that they were experienced in rescue procedures. Trying this method with ordinary passengers would be fatal.

Cronk devised another plan. He would launch one of the big twenty-man rafts and tow it across to the flying boat using one of the buoyant surf boats. The raft would then serve as a loading platform with passengers transferring to the surf boat to be ferried to the ship. Dusk was already falling as the rescue began.

A merchant seaman waited in the raft to grab passengers as they jumped. First out was a man bearing a tiny bundle. Passenger Bill Bostock jumped with his eighteen-month-old daughter, Sandra. His wife followed, guiding their five-year-old son. Another son jumped but missed the raft and went into the sea. He was soon hauled on board. A sixth passenger, Mrs Gwendolyn Ritchie, made up the load and the surfboat set off into the gale for the cutter.

After three further trips, all made in darkness and with the aid of the ship's searchlights, thirty-one passengers had been released from the hell of the *Bermuda Sky Queen*. But the weather was worsening and the surfboat was becoming seriously waterlogged. For what was clearly going to be the last attempt of the night, sixteen passengers were taken off and put on the raft. Near disaster followed. The excess weight caused the raft to break away from the flying boat. The surfboat crew pursued it and succeeded in getting the passengers on to their craft which now almost sank. Three seamen had to jump back on to the raft and take three passengers with them. The tangled lines of the raft fouled the surf boat's propeller making steering impossible. A huge wave carried the boat and the raft towards the cutter and rammed them under its stern. The surfboat capsized and the people on the raft were also thrown into the raging sea. Cronk and his men refused to acknowledge defeat and one by one all the passengers were hauled out of the water. But the surfboat was lost.

An attempt was now made to row across to the flying boat. Cronk selected his six most experienced men and they set off towing another raft. The heavy seas defeated them and they had to return. Cronk called Captain Martin. 'How do you feel about spending another night on the plane?' he asked. Martin replied in one word: 'Affirmative.'

At dawn, the wind had gone down and the seas had calmed considerably. Within two hours the last remaining passengers and the crew of the *Bermuda Sky Queen* were taken off. The nightmare was over.

The sturdy B314 remained bobbing in the water and Cronk received orders to sink it lest it prove a hazard to shipping. Before setting course for Boston with his load of grateful passengers, Captain Cronk ordered that the ship's cannon be turned on the *Bermuda Sky Queen*. Within minutes it was at the bottom of the ocean.

Ireland's chief inspector of air accidents, Mr R. W. O'Sullivan, was sent to New York for the official inquiry. His trip, as a file in the national archives shows, was not without its own drama. In a memo dated 7 January 1948, Mr O'Sullivan complained that 'on the day before departure and therefore leaving no time to protest', he was informed that his subsistence allowance would be reduced from $15 to $10 a day.

'I consider it most unjustified,' he wrote, 'to cut the subsistence rate by thirty-three and a third per cent at a time when the cost of living in the United States, and particularly in New York, has increased by leaps and bounds to an unprecedented high figure.'

Hotel accommodation, he pointed out, was a matter of great difficulty in New York and Washington and there was practically no choice in the matter. Breakfast worked out at $1.75, lunch was $3.75 and dinner $5.75. Coffee in mid-morning and afternoon tea would add a further fifty to seventy-five cents. 'To this,' he wrote, 'must be added a sum to cover tips and gratuities to porters, maids and waiters. Here again the customary 10 per cent has been found unacceptable. The minimum tip which can be offered in safety in New York is 25 cents and a figure of 15 per cent of one's bill evinces the merest courtesy ...'

The problems created by Captain Martin and the *Bermuda Sky Queen* were far ranging.

The Douglas C-54A Crash, 15 August 1949

Sunday, 15 August 1949, was not Captain Edward 'Ed' Bessey's day. After a four-day rest stop in Rome, the company station wagon bringing him and his crew of seven men and two women to Ciampino Airport was over half an hour late. His forty-nine passengers, most of them emigrants and displaced persons bound for Venezuela via Shannon and New York, sweltered in the departure hall awaiting permission to board the Transocean DC-4 Skymaster that stood waiting on the tarmac.

The passengers were unlikely to complain, but Orvis M. Nelson, the square-jawed, hard-driving founder and president of one of the world's most remarkable and unusual airlines, was. Nelson, a veteran DC-4 pilot and 'Mr Transocean' himself was at Shannon that very day as part of a worldwide tour of his airlines' facilities.

Nelson drove his pilots hard. The son of a Norwegian emigrant whose family knew another family of Norwegian emigrants called Lindbergh, he had spent his early youth wielding an axe in his father's pine and hardwood tracts along the Prairie River and at the mill in Tamarack, Minnesota. He learned to fly in the US army and held a degree in mathematics. He flew the mails for six months during the disastrous experiment in which the US army took over from civilian pilots and lost seven of his classmates. Having left the forces, he landed a job as a pilot with United Airlines.

Nelson was an entrepreneur at heart and a job for life in one of the country's leading airlines wasn't what he really wanted. Like many a like-minded pilot of his generation, he longed for the opportunity to start his own airline. His chance came in May 1946 when he bought two government surplus Douglas C-54A four-engined transports at $90,000 each. Before it finally went bankrupt in 1960, Nelson had built Transocean into a huge supplemental carrier with a fleet of 114 aircraft. A wheeler-dealer whose catch-cry was 'anything, anywhere, anytime' and whose proudest boast was that he once bought a surplus DC-4 for $30,000, worked the hell out of it for two years and then sold it for $500,000, he expected his captains to be not only skilful pilots but resourceful businessmen as well. A captain who brought a planeful of immigrants to, say, Venezuela, would be expected to look around for a suitable load of cargo to pay for the fuel on the way back to the home base in Oakland, California.

Nelson also liked to boast that he once nearly lost his life because of the Irish sweepstake. After stopping in Puerto Rico on a northbound flight from Venezuela, where he had completed a flight from Rome similar to the one which Captain Bessey was now taking out of Rome, he decided to take a load of passengers to New York from San Juan.

During the engine run-up before taking off he discovered a cracked cylinder in one engine. He off-loaded his passengers, dumped some of his fuel and, with his crew of five – including his wife who was acting as stewardess – took off on three engines for the 1,700 mile trip to his home base. 'I was surprised to find that the airplane was very slow getting off the ground, but we finally staggered off the end of the runway,' he told the Transocean historian, Richard Thruelsen. 'Then I had difficulty in gaining altitude – in fact, we were a couple of hours out before I got her up past 5,000 feet.'

After landing, 3000 lbs of illegal Irish Hospitals Trust Sweepstake tickets were found in the belly compartment of the aircraft, which contained the hydraulic system. Almost simultaneously, another load of tickets was found in another Transocean DC-4 at Gander. In both cases, the tickets had been loaded at Shannon on the eastbound sector of the flights. The FBI was called and eventually five Transocean employees were convicted and jailed for smuggling the tickets.

Ed Bessey, a thirty-five-year-old veteran of forty Atlantic and sixty Pacific crossings had been with Nelson almost from the start of the airline. He had a total of 8,600 flying hours, of which 2,500 were in DC-4s. Like most of the early Transocean pilots, he had taken part in a massive ferrying operation in which 150 Curtiss C-46 Commandos were flown from California to China. Industry sceptics expected the fledgling airline to lose at least a dozen aircraft on these demanding flights. Not a single aircraft was lost and the operation gave Nelson a well-earned reputation as an organisational genius and an airline chief who knew how to pick good pilots.

A large, bulky man, well over six-feet tall, Bessey was well known and liked in Shannon. His reply to a devout staff member who questioned him as to his religious beliefs was often quoted at the airport. Asked what he really believed in, Bessey replied: 'Four good engines and tanks full of gas.'

Gerry Deeney, a former RAF pilot and for many years station manager for Seaboard and Western Airlines (later Seaboard World Airlines) at Shannon, remembers Bessey as a very affable man. 'He was very highly regarded and commanded respect easily,' Deeney says. As well as transiting through Shannon on numerous occasions, Bessey once took a DC-4 on a special demonstration flight around the Clare and Galway coasts organised by Orvis Nelson for local hoteliers and VIPs.

The aircraft which Bessey and his crew took over in Rome that Sunday afternoon was a converted Douglas C-54A with the registration number N-79998, manufacturer's serial number 3076. The C-54As started life as fully militarised versions of the DC-4 transport, capable of lifting fifty troops or 32,500 lbs of cargo. A total of 220 C-54As were built – 100 at Douglas' Santa Monica plant, and 155 in Chicago. Bessey's aircraft was powered by four Pratt and Whitney R-2000 engines and had a fuel capacity of 3,326 gallons.

In addition to his normal crew of a co-pilot, second officer, navigator, flight engineer, radio officer and two cabin attendants, Captain Bessey also had on board, listed as a crew member, the famous US aviatrix Ruth Rowland Nichols. Miss Nichols, who was then forty-six, was returning to the US from a world tour. Although she had a commercial pilot's licence and a string of records and achievements, including the women's world speed record and the women's world altitude record, she was not a Transocean employee and the fact that she had been flying the aircraft prior to the accident caused some controversy. Questioned about her role in the flight, Nelson made no apologies for the fact that she had been flying the Skymaster under supervision and the subsequent inquiry found no connection between her role in piloting the aircraft and the subsequent ditching.

Nelson later described the crew as 'veterans' which, in a sense, they were. The captain's 2,500 hours on this type of craft wouldn't have been considered 'heavy' by the standards of the time. His co-pilot, Richard Hall, though only twenty-nine, also had 2,500 hours on DC-4 aircraft. The second officer, John Moore, was forty-one, and while he had a total of 10,500 hours flying time, 1,200 had been in DC-4 equipment. The navigator, James A. Baumann, was thirty, and had been with the company for just a year. He had trained as a navigator with the US navy and had 3,000 hours of navigational flight experience – 1,500 hours being in DC-4s.

As they arrived in Ciampino, Bessey wasted no time in getting the Skymaster off the ground. To conserve time, he divided the pre-flight duties among the crew. Along with Moore, the second officer and Baumann, the navigator, he went to the meteorological centre to collect the weather data. Moore then prepared the flight clearance, which he filed with Rome air traffic control, while navigator Baumann computed the flight plan based on a routing to Shannon via airways over Paris.

Baumann had no discussions with either the first or second officers, nor did the navigator or second officer have knowledge of the correct aircraft weight and fuel load until after the flight documents were completed and they had reported to the aircraft. In his haste to get away, the captain did not examine any of the flight documents before departure.

The flaws which would result in the loss of eight lives and the destruction of the aircraft were already present. The second officer had indicated on the flight clearance that they had fuel for sixteen hours of flight. The navigator had done his calculations on the basis that there was fuel for twelve hours. But after they had boarded the aircraft they found that in fact there was only 2,200 gallons of fuel on board – sufficient for eleven hours.

As the company's standard consumption rate for the DC-4 was 200 gallons per hour, this was not sufficient for the required fuel reserve – two hours at normal cruise – after flight to Shannon and then the alternate, Paris Orly.

Captain Bessey was told of this but, because weather conditions were predicted to be relatively clear, he decided that there was sufficient fuel and that Dublin should be the alternative airport. He also decided to make a shortcut by flying direct to Shannon from Marseille rather than over airways and via Paris as planned by navigator Baumann. Rome ATC were not informed of the change in alternate airports.

At 4.08 p.m. on Sunday, the Transocean Skymaster lifted off from Ciampino and headed west. The take-off was done by First Officer Hall, with Bessey serving as co-pilot. They levelled off at 8,500 feet and Bessey retired to a crew bunk leaving Hall in command and Second Officer Moore as co-pilot. Except for the fact that the no. 3 engine operated roughly when the mixture was in auto lean, the flight was without incident.

The flight reported over Marseille at 6.20 p.m. and over Rennes at 8.50 p.m. While the navigator was shooting the stars (taking a position from the stars), Captain Bessey returned from his bunk to resume command of the flight. The navigator now fixed the time of arrival for Shannon at 11.45 p.m. The flight transmitted to Shannon radio that it was over Land's End at 10.27 p.m. The navigator then gave the captain a new ETA for Shannon – 12.10 a.m.

They had been flying for nearly seven hours at 8,500 feet when, at 11 p.m., they descended to 3,500 feet which was above a layer of stratus cloud. As they came over the French coast, the navigator obtained a three-star fix which, he testified, told him they were fifty-three miles northwest of Brest and fifteen miles west of the flight's intended track. He estimated that their speed over the ground was 138 knots.

The flight now continued on reduced power on a heading of 310 degrees. The captain started to become concerned about his position and asked the navigator to obtain a Loran fix (in which position is determined from the intervals between signal pulses received from widely spaced radio transmitters). Baumann tried but failed. Then, between 12.30 and 12.40 a.m. he obtained a three star celestial fix which, when plotted, showed that they had missed Shannon and were 175 miles out over the North Atlantic. Ten minutes later Bessey turned the Skymaster around and headed back to Shannon. They had been in the air for a total of nine hours and six minutes and now had fuel for only one hour and thirty minutes.

Bessey's distress signal was picked up by three other aircraft in the vicinity. The Skymaster was spotted by the crew of a TWA Constellation which had just taken off from Shannon en route to New York. Captain Charles Adams made contact with Bessey and offered to guide him back to Shannon. Later, when ditching became inevitable, Captain Adams followed the Skymaster down to 300 feet and dropped flares over the ocean.

By 2.40 a.m. Captain Bessey's belief in 'four good engines and tanks full of gas' had taken on a very hollow ring. Via an escorting plane, he reported dramatically to Shannon: 'I am running very low on fuel.' Then: 'I have lost no. 4 engine.' This was followed a few minutes later by: 'I have now lost no. 3 engine.' Two engines had now failed because of fuel starvation. He still had two good engines but the tanks were empty. He was still over the Atlantic, seven miles northwest of Lurga Point and the seaside resort of Kilkee when he decided that the time had come for him to put down in the ocean.

In the cabin, the stewardess and purser had helped the Italian emigrants into their life-jackets. Although the stewardess, Luigina Cerabona, spoke Italian, there were communications difficulties. Mercifully, there was no panic. But when the moment for evacuation came, seven passengers panicked and plunged into the sea without having properly inflated their life-jackets. They were immediately drowned.

Captain Bessey's landing, like that of Captain Martin of the *Bermuda Sky Queen* two years earlier, was textbook stuff. The sea was fairly calm and, even more fortunately, there was an English trawler and the Limerick steamship freighter, *Lanahrone,* in the vicinity. Bessey judged the moment perfectly and, even though the tail broke off on the shock of impact, the Skymaster remained afloat for about fifteen minutes. The crew launched the life rafts and, after the initial debacle in which eight passengers were lost, succeeded in controlling the evacuation in an orderly and efficient manner. By daybreak, all of the survivors and the bodies of the victims had been picked up.

The flight deck crew were the last to leave the sinking airliner. As he climbed through the hatch in advance of the captain, Radio Officer Herbert Asbel was struck by part of a disintegrating wing and knocked unconscious. He slid into the water and was drowned.

As the accident had occurred on the high seas, the US civil aeronautics board assumed control of the inquiry. On 14 September 1950, it released its report which put the blame squarely on the commander. 'There can be little doubt,' it said, 'that the flight met with disaster because of inadequate flight planning and haphazard performance of flight duties.

'During the planning stage of the flight, the crew did not confer with one another and they had no agreement nor accurate knowledge of route, fuel hours on board, fuel requirements, or duration of flight.

'The board determines,' it concluded, 'that the probable cause of this accident was the failure of the captain to exercise the proper supervision over his crew during flight planning and while en route.'

CHAPTER 3

Rivals even in Death: The TWA and PAA L-49 Constellation Crashes at Rineanna, 1946–48

THE new year of 1946 was a momentous time in the history of civil aviation. Only in the Americas had commercial air transport been uninterrupted by the world war which had ended a few months previously. Even there, development had been retarded by both the wholesale requisitioning of civilian aircraft for military transports, and the drafting of pilots into the services. With the surrender of Germany and Japan though, new airlines had started to spring up all over Europe and the US as machines and men made surplus by the peace started to come on the open market in great numbers. The established airlines were feverishly re-equipping and rejuvenating themselves for what was obviously going to be a golden age in civil air transport. Nowhere was this surge of activity more frenetic than in the effort to gain supremacy of the coveted North Atlantic routes.

The Atlantic was seen as the great prize – the pilots and engineers of Juan Trippe's Pan American Airways had already conquered the Pacific. Trippe had always seen himself as aviation overlord of the oceans. He had fought long and deviously to stave off what he regarded as a ploy by the British to dominate the flying boat routes through establishing the main Americas base in Canada and having passengers ferried to US centres by airlines such as his. The outbreak of war not only put an end to these plans but resulted in the USA becoming the dominant aircraft manufacturing nation of the world – a dominance which the British aircraft industry would never succeed in breaking.

The era of the flying boats on the North Atlantic had been – as Charles Lindbergh had always predicted – short-lived. It started in June 1937, suffered an initial lull – mainly because the British were ill prepared – and endured severe restrictions because of the hostilities.

By the time the war ended, the US manufacturers Douglas had on the market a civilian version of its C-54 transport known as the DC-4 or Skymaster. Although unpressurised and therefore unable to climb above the vicious North Atlantic storms, it had four good Pratt and Whitney R-2000 Twin Wasp engines and, with stops in Gander, Shannon, or both, was well capable of crossing the Atlantic at a cruise speed which, according to the manufacturer, could reach 227 miles an hour.

Atlantic operations started at the new land base in Rineanna eight miles across the estuary from Foynes on 24 October 1945. On that date the first scheduled commercial landplane to cross the Atlantic arrived in Rineanna, en route to London. This was the DC-4 Flagship of the short-lived American Export Airlines. Among its fourteen passengers, all but one of them invited guests, was J. F. Dempsey, general manager of Aer Lingus.

American Export Airlines was an offshoot of the American Export Lines shipping company, and it soon merged with American Airlines Transatlantic Division and became American Overseas Airlines (AOA). To the consternation of Juan Trippe, who passionately believed in a government-sponsored monopoly in favour of Pan American (the famous 'chosen instrument' concept) the Civil Aeronautics board (CAB) had licensed three carriers to operate on the Atlantic: Pan American, American Export and TWA. American Export were authorised to serve the whole of northern Europe north of the fiftieth parallel, with the rest of the continent divided up between Pan American and TWA. American Export and Pan American were given rights to London while TWA had exclusive rights to Paris. Eventually, in 1950, Pan American took over AOA.

If 1946 was a good one for aviation in general, it was a miserable one for TWA. Transcontinental and Western Airlines the airline originated in 1930 with the merger of Transcontinental Air Transport (TAT) and two smaller carriers. TWA had built up a formidable domestic network when, in 1939, Howard Hughes, heir to the Hughes Tool Company fortunes and later the world's most famous recluse, took control. Trippe's Pan American was already a titan among world airlines and now Hughes held similar ambitions for TWA. The fearsome rivals had much in common. Both were pilots – Hughes a particularly distinguished one – and clever businessmen. Each was ruthless, secretive and devious. Hughes, a drawling Texan, was said to have all the attributes of a brilliant aeronautical engineer without any kind of formal training or education in the field. Trippe, a wily Yale-educated WASP, believed in going to the top and disliked having to make a case to anyone less that the president of the USA. Each had a passionate desire to have his airline dominate the North Atlantic and each went to great lengths to outfox the other. A US senator who had dealings with Trippe at around this time said: 'Mr Trippe made the impression upon me of a man living under the conviction that he had a divine call to operate and control American aviation in the transoceanic field.' But in the end, it was Hughes who outfoxed Trippe and in June 1969 Pan American lost its position as leading carrier on the Atlantic to TWA.

In 1946, it didn't look as if it was going to work out like that. Trippe's Pan American already had a foothold on the route and TWA was on the verge of bankruptcy. But Hughes had one powerful advantage over Trippe – one that would ultimately be a large factor in the demise of the free world's most powerful airline. Unlike Pan American, TWA had a well-developed domestic network from which to 'feed' passengers onward to Europe. Both had the L-49 Constellation.

Hughes had scored a brilliant coup on 1 March 1946 by putting the L-49 on TWA's transcontinental route from New York to Los Angeles. United Airlines started a New York–San Franscisco route the same day using DC-4s. But the pressurised L-49 did the coast to coast run in eleven hours as against thirteen or fourteen in the unpressurised and far less comfortable DC-4. From the start, the passenger appeal of the Constellation was huge. Pan American introduced its first L-49 service on the New York–Bermuda run and went on to introduce it on the North Atlantic on 14 January, three weeks before TWA.

While it is true that the L-49 Constellation was very much the brainchild of Howard Hughes, the commonly held notion that he actually designed the aircraft is a fallacy. Hughes had first approached Lockheed in 1939 with his idea for a super luxury, pressurised transport capable of flying coast to coast from New York to Los Angeles. When quoted a price of $425,000 each, Hughes said: 'Go ahead and build fifty. TWA can't pay, so I'll pay for them myself.'

But the events of 7 December 1941 at Pearl harbour – 'the date which will live in infamy' as President Roosevelt put it – changed much in US civil aviation and all production of the Constellation was immediately reserved for the military. Hughes had to wait until November 1945 to get the first L-49 TWA branded: the TWA colours – twin red stripe along a silver fuselage; TWA in large lettering towards the rear of the fuselage where it narrows to meet the tailplane with its triple fins; the letters TWA – within a circle this time – beneath the cockpit windows; and a final and larger TWA lettering emblazoned on the upper side of the port wing. Because TWA had been a strictly domestic airline during the time of the L-49s development, Hughes, with uncharacteristic generosity, had allowed Juan Trippe to come in on the project and order a fleet of the wonder aircraft for Pan American. Both airlines now prepared to use it to the fullest in battling each other on the North Atlantic.

But from the start there had been trouble with the L-49s' engines. Several engine fires and prop failures had been reported and, since the aircraft was the state-of-the art airliner of the day, these were subject to massive media attention. Steadily, the L-49 was building up a bad press, even though by July 1946 some 200 million passenger miles had been flown safely by the many L-49s in airline service.

Then, on 11 July 1946 came disaster. A TWA L-49 (NC86513) on a routine training flight crashed in Reading, Pennsylvania, after the crew became blinded by smoke in the cockpit. After Captain Dick Brown sensed a smell of burning he asked the flight engineer to go back to investigate. He returned and declared that the whole cabin was on fire. With his head through the cockpit window, Captain Brown made a desperate attempt to land. He failed. The aircraft struck power cables and crashed. Captain Brown, badly injured, was the sole survivor. TWA had already suffered a crash of another L-49 (NC86510) on a training flight in Washington DC., but there had been no casualties. Now three of its pilots and an engineer were dead and grotesque photographs of the big Constellation, overturned and with most of its centre section burnt away, were being splashed on the front pages of newspapers all over the world. Almost immediately, the CAB ordered the grounding of all the L-49s.

The investigators quickly discovered that the cause of these electrical fires was a faulty 'through stud' – a small electrical conductor that allowed power to flow through the pressurised fuselage while preserving the pressure seal. Because of their proximity to the fuselage, arching (jumping across to the fuselage) was a hazard. The fact that they were adjacent to high-pressure hydraulic lines greatly increased the fire hazard. In language that would hardly be used in such a report today, the CAB roundly denounced the 'through studs' as being of 'a crudely deficient design'.

Before the year was out, TWA would have to endure a much greater tragedy with the fiery crash of another of its L-49s, the *Star of Cairo*, on a small boggy island close to the new Shannon Airport at Rineanna. Ironically, just as they followed each other in commerce, these two great airlines would also follow each other in tragedy. The TWA disaster of 28 December 1946 at Shannon – the first crash of a civil airliner involving fatalities in Ireland – would be followed by another and even worse one sixteen months later with the crash of Pan American's L-49 *Empress of the Skies* on 15 April 1948.

The Star of Cairo Crash, 27 December 1946

The *Star of Cairo* was the first 'overwater' type Constellation delivered to TWA and had earlier carried the fleet names *Paris Sky Chief* and *Najavo Sky Chief* before being designated *Star of Cairo* in February 1946. It was delivered to TWA on 21 November 1945, and registered N90773, fleet number 550. It was powered by four Wright 745C18BA engines with Hamilton propellers.

After the July 1946 groundings it was converted to an L-49-46-26 standard with an improved electrical system, new engine exhaust systems and additional fire extinguisher systems. It was the first Constellation, and the first TWA aircraft, to land at Shannon. On that occasion it established a new Atlantic speed record by crossing from Gander in six hours and fifty-five minutes. On 10 February 1946 it made a transit stop at Shannon with two US cardinals travelling to Rome for the first post-war papal consistory. It was also used on 3 November 1946 for TWA's special preview flight for invited guests from New York La Guardia to Paris Orly.

TWA flight 6863 began boarding at Orly Airport Paris shortly before 11 p.m. on 27 December 1946. For many of the fourteen passengers the prospect of the long Atlantic crossing to New York in a state-of-the-art Constellation must have been high adventure. It was, after all, a mere forty-seven years since the Wright brothers had made the celebrated first sustained and controlled flight at Kitty Hawk, North Carolina, in a frail timber and canvas biplane with a forty-foot wingspan and a 16hp engine.

For the twenty-five-year-old hostess who greeted them at the head of the boarding steps, this was to have been her eighth Atlantic crossing. Vena Ferguson was born in Deii Rapids, South Dakota, and had worked as a secretary in a New York bank before joining TWA in May 1944. She would soon be faced with the greatest test that can come the way of any aircrew member: the challenge of rescuing and caring for severely injured passengers in a major crash involving fire and explosion. Miss Ferguson, though in deep shock and suffering minor physical injuries, would discharge these responsibilities with great courage and professionalism and thereby earn a special commendation from the civil aeronautics bureau.

One passenger to whom the prospect of an ocean crossing would be more or less routine was fifty-four-year-old Captain Pierre Dreyfus. Dreyfus was the son of Colonel Alfred Dreyfus, whose rigged conviction – and subsequent vindication – for military treason based on the rampant anti-Semitism of the French army officer corps caused an international sensation in the 1890s and later led to a reorganisation of the French army.

Pierre Dreyfus had followed his famous father into the military and served with great distinction, gaining the Croix de Guerre and the Légion d'honneur award. Having served with the Gaullist forces, he gained admission to the USA in 1942 where he flourished as an industrialist and was active in Jewish charities. He had an apartment in fashionable Fifth Avenue in New York's Manhattan. His brother-in-law told the *New York Times* that he was returning there after travelling to France to see his wife and attend the wedding of their daughter. Captain Dreyfus' nineteen-year-old college student son was waiting for him at La Guardia Airport, unaware that he was already dead in a boggy, uninhabited island in the Shannon estuary.

For another Jew, fifty-seven-year-old Polish-born Herman Koegal, the flight was to be the transition from an eight year long nightmare to a family reunion and a new beginning in the land of the free.

Mr Koegal had been a well to do clothing manufacturer in Berlin when, in 1938, the Nazis forced him to return to Poland. A year later the tide of persecution sent him to Russia. The Russians sent him to Siberia and, when the Germans invaded, he was sent to Turkestan in Soviet central Asia. After the war he made his way back to Poland and, through the efforts of his daughter, an American citizen, he got permission to enter the USA. When the airline representatives called to her Manhattan apartment at 260 West 72nd Street, they found it festooned with streamers and 'Welcome Home' signs. Mr Koegal, too, was to perish on Inishmacnaughtan.

One passenger for whom the flight must have been the adventure of a lifetime was Mrs Edith Delaby-Waterbury, not yet twenty and the mother of a four-and-a-half-month-old baby, Charles Bruce Delaby. She had married a twenty-eight-year-old US soldier, Charles Delaby, in France. Her husband had been demobbed before the baby was born and now she was bringing him to the home her husband had made for them in Newark, New Jersey.

She and the baby would suffer burns and fractures in the crash and for a critical twenty-four hours Mrs Waterbury would hover between life and death in St John's Hospital, Limerick. But she and her baby were to be among the lucky ones. At home in Belmont Avenue, Newark, Charles Waterbury was told initially that his wife and child were safe. He rushed out to the nearest church to offer prayers in thanksgiving. Then in the confusion that frequently prevails in the early stages of air disasters, he was contacted again and told that both were dead.

The *New York Times* of 30 December reported that Mr Waterbury, 'bleary eyed from lack of sleep', was more cheerful yesterday as he nervously fingered a cablegram from St John's Hospital

Limerick, which read: 'Condition your wife slightly improved.'

Dr Alexander Haim Pekelis, age forty-four, of Larchmount, New York, was returning from Basle where he had been a delegate of American labour zionists to the annual World Zionist Conference. A brilliant international lawyer, he had held university teaching posts in Florence, Leipzig, Vienna and Paris before entering the USA in 1940. He was editor-in-chief of the *Columbia University Law Review* – the first non-American to hold the post. He too was to die on the island of Inishmacnaughtan that December night.

The *Star of Cairo* lifted off for the last time from the Orly runway at 11.16 p.m. and climbed on to a westerly course which would bring it, via Cherbourg and St Mawgan, to Shannon. It was, hostess Vena Ferguson recalled, a particularly smooth flight. 'Practically all the passengers went to sleep soon after the take-off,' she told the CAB inquiry. During the 113-minute flight to Shannon, she and the twenty-one-year-old purser, John Logan, went through the cabin handing out blankets and pillows and serving coffee to the few passengers who remained awake.

At 1.35 a.m. the *Star of Cairo* reported that they were over the Waterford coast at 7,000 feet and descending. They were then cleared to cross the Limerick Junction fan marker at 5,000 feet and warned of other traffic on the west leg. At 1.53 a.m. the radio officer, Herbert Burmeister, reported that they were over the radio range station at 5,000 feet. Shannon ATC asked him to report when they had started their procedure turn. At precisely 2 a.m., Burmeister reported that it was on procedure turn. The controller then cleared it for final approach to runway 14 and read out the weather conditions: 'Rain and drizzle; visibility two miles; cloud, ten-tenths at 900 feet; six-tenths at 400 feet; three-tenths broken at 300 feet; wind 120 degrees, 4 knots; altimeter setting 30-04.'

Burmeister acknowledged receipt of this message and at 2.05 a.m. reported at 1,200 feet. At this stage he was given an amendment to landing conditions: 'Cloud now ten-tenths at 400 feet;

four-tenths at 250 feet; visibility one mile; wind 120 degrees, 5 knots; altimeter setting 30.04.' The controller then asked that they give him a ceiling check.

At approximately 2.08 a.m., the aircraft was seen in the neighbourhood of the airport, approaching from the east. A number of the observers – including crash crews and airline personnel – thought it was unusually low while passing over the field. They saw it turn to the north through approximately forty degrees and then make a left turn to line up with runway 14 for landing.

When it was approximately halfway through this turn, disaster came. The port wing tip and outboard propeller struck the ground.

Patrick O'Sullivan, a crash crew driver, was one of those who observed the final moments of the flight. He told the investigators that he watched the aircraft come over the runway with its landing lights on and then pull up. He remarked to a colleague that the pilot must have been lower than he intended and was going round for another attempt.

He then lost track of the aircraft in the cloud. But, as he told the inquiry: 'a few minutes later we saw a terrific red glow blazing up in the direction of Carrigarry. We also heard some loud explosions.'

During those final minutes of the flight, Vena Ferguson had observed the 'landing light coming on and had gone through the cabin to awake those passengers who were sleeping and to ensure that their seat belts were fastened. She then went to the rear of the aircraft and strapped herself into seat no. 38. John Logan, the purser, strapped himself into seat no. 39 beside her. Across the aisle sat passenger David Tannenbaum who, like Logan and Ferguson, would prove to be heroic in the face of the catastrophe that was about to happen.

There was no warning. Vena Ferguson told the inquiry that she remembered only feeling a bump and the strain of the seat belt. 'After that I have no conception of how long we remained in the tail of the aircraft until we got out,' she said.

The *Star of Cairo* hit the ground at a point about ninety feet beyond a six-foot high embankment. Its speed, the investigators reckoned, was 149mph. The port wing-tip and outboard propeller hit the soggy ground almost simultaneously and dug in. The aircraft swung to the left as the port wing started to break up. This caused the fuel tanks to rupture and there was an immediate explosion followed by a raging inferno. As the aircraft careered through the boggy terrain and started to break up, several members of the cockpit crew were thrown clear. Seconds before the explosion the entire rear section broke away and continued to slide rearwards in a relatively intact condition to a distance of 360 feet.

Having unfastened their seat belts, hostess Ferguson, purser Logan and passenger Tannenbaum found themselves standing at the edge of a gaping and jagged wound in the fuselage where the tail section had broken away. Instinctively, they jumped on to the marshy ground and immediately found themselves ankle deep in mud.

The pilot, thirty-three-year-old Captain Herbert Tansey, was knocked unconscious upon impact and thrown clear – still strapped to his seat. As he came to, he found his leg, which later had to be amputated, pinioned beneath a pile of debris. The sky was lit up by the flames, and the moans and screams of the injured and the dying were all around him.

Another TWA captain, who was one of the first to reach the crash site, gave a moving description of finding his stricken colleague still trapped in the wreckage. Captain Dean Miller told the inquiry: 'I said: "Hello Herb". He recognised me and said: "Where is this place?" I said it was an island northwest of the field. Tansey said: "I can't understand it. I am positive I was flying at 500 feet on the altimeter. The altimeter was reading 500 feet …"'

They had come down on Inishmacnaughton, a 260 acre island situated on the eastern shore of the river Fergus, near its junction with the Shannon. Four miles west of Bunratty, the island is so low-lying that much of it is subjected to seasonal flooding.

The rescue operation, considering the difficulties of the terrain and the limited resources of the time, was swift and efficient. No word of criticism in regard to it was contained in the reports of either the Irish or the US investigations. On the contrary, there was acknowledgement and appreciation of the risks many of the rescue workers took in wading through the mudflats while carrying stretchers and blankets for the victims. Estimates of the time it took to reach the crash site vary. The hostess, Vena Ferguson, reckoned that it took almost two hours, while the garda sergeant based at Shannon, Mr J. J. Hickey, told the inquest on the victims that he and other rescue workers had reached the scene at 2.45 a.m.

When the first rescuers arrived, knee deep in mud having waded through the mudflats, a dismal and terrifying scene awaited them. What was left of the *Star of Cairo* was spread over a distance of some 300 yards, most of it still burning. In the light of the flames they saw several bodies on the marshy ground and heard the moans and cries of those still alive.

The rescue equipment available in Shannon in 1946 was primitive. There were no helicopters in Ireland at that time, nor were there any amphibian crafts capable of transporting rescue workers and casualties over the treacherous mudflats for which the Shannon estuary is notorious. The torturous business of dragging stretchers across the mud and then repeating the journey with the wounded and dead continued for several hours. At a point where the stretchers could be transferred to rowing boats, the airport medical officer, Dr James O'Boyle, and Red Cross workers from Limerick, had set up a medical centre where the injured were given pain-killing injections and basic first aid.

G. P. Gallivan, then a TWA flight dispatcher and later to make his name as a playwright, recalls the night of the crash: 'I was on late duty and was boarding the bus for Limerick as the *Star of Cairo* came in,' he recalls. 'By the time the bus had made its first stop on the Ennis Road, the TWA station wagon was there to take us back to the airport. There was a great deal of confusion. Three or four of us were taken in a small boat to the island to see what we could do. There were fires, mud and pieces of wreckage scattered all over the place. We started to pull some people free but in our enthusiasm to help – to be set against ignorance – we might well have done more harm than good.' Gallivan was one of those who donated blood to help save Captain Tansey's life.

Gerry Gallivan has another memory of the crash that still haunts him: 'TWA flew the relatives of the dead to Shannon and I remember meeting the father of one dead crew member. The poor man – I have long forgotten his name – was completely broken. The victim had been the last of his five sons. The four others had been killed in the war.'

Charles Hennigan, one of the first crash crew workers to arrive, said in a statement to the inquiry: 'I heard the screams of a baby in the rushes. As I reached it someone else picked it up. He gave the baby to the hostess. The baby was drenched wet so the hostess asked for a fire to be lit. We built the fire with wood and bits of the wreckage that would burn. Soon we had six or seven of the casualties grouped around it. One of them died. A case of liquor was found and some was given to those casualties who were able for it.'

The baby was Charles Bruce Waterbury, the four-and-a-half-month-old son of French GI bride, Edith Augustine Waterbury. He had suffered slight burns in the crash and a fractured thigh in the fall from the wreck.

The young mother was far more seriously injured and for the next couple of days hovered between life and death in St John's Hospital, Limerick. The *New York Times* of 30 December reported: 'Mrs Edith Delaby Waterbury, French war bride who was flying to join her American husband in Newark, N.J. rallied further during the day when she came out of delirium and found her son, Charles Bruce, four-and-a-half-months-old, in a crib beside her bed. Earlier she was quoted in the same paper as saying she didn't expect to see her husband again but that she hoped her son would.

In another room at St John's, the thirty-four-year-old second radio officer, Dudley Hill of Alexandria, Virginia, who had suffered massive chest injuries, was also fighting for his life. He was not to be as lucky. He died the following day.

Thirty miles away in the County Hospital, Ennis, the commander of the *Star of Cairo*, Captain Herbert Tansey, was also fighting for his life. At thirty-three, he was one of TWA's most senior pilots. Now his career as a professional pilot was at an end as surgeons decided that to save his life they must amputate the leg that had been crushed beneath the debris. Even before Tansey had been taken to hospital, Captain Larry Trimble, chief flight supervisor of TWA's international division, who was in Carmody's Hotel, Ennis, on the night of the crash and immediately went to the crash site, interviewed him on his stretcher at 3.30 a.m.

'Are you strong enough to talk, Herb,' Trimble asked. Tansey repeated what he had told his other colleague earlier on: 'I was at 500 feet, coming in on the approach, and then I went on instruments and we hit. I can't understand it – the altimeter was showing 500 feet.' From his hospital bed, Tansey told the Irish chief inspector of accidents, Mr R. W. O'Sullivan, that as he went into the final turn he was faced with total darkness and thought that all the airport lights had gone out. This, Mr O'Sullivan reasoned, was because the aircraft, on a steep approach path, had passed behind a low hill on the island outside the airport and on this very dark night had passed out of sight of the airport lights just before hitting the ground.

Both inquiries exonerated Captain Tansey and the co-pilot, Clifford Sparrow. The cause of the crash lay in the wreckage and was soon established. Detailed examination of the wreckage by a high-powered team from Lockheed established that a mechanic had wrongly assembled the pipe lines from the static pressure heads to the altimeter. One of these pressure heads was located outside the fuselage while the second, designed for use in icing conditions at altitude was located in the nose wheel well. This last one, the alternate static source, had never been intended for use while near the ground but, because of the error, it was the one which Captain Tansey had been depending on and which led him to believe he was at a much higher altitude than he actually was. Lockheed immediately specified different screw threads for the couplings so that it would be impossible for them to be wrongly connected ever again.

The official CAB inquiry opened before Colonel Robert Crisp and a team of assessors in the East Room of the Hotel New Yorker on 30 January 1947. The colonel opened the proceedings by explaining the ground rules. This, he said, was purely 'an administrative inquiry of a fact-finding nature, in which there were no adverse parties and no adverse interests.' 'No one has been made a defendant or a respondent,' he said, 'and no legal liability attaches to anyone.'

One of the early witnesses was Vena Ferguson, whose behaviour on the night of the disaster earned her the commendation from the CAB. Crisp's first question to her was a leading one: 'Miss Ferguson, you are a TWA stewardess?' To which she replied 'I am a TWA air hostess.'

The CAB report was adopted on 27 February and released the following month.

For Lockheed, still staggering from the effects of the earlier debacle, the result was a huge relief. The L-49, already highly suspect, had been vindicated. Although the Irish report contained no words of censure against TWA, the CAB report was damning. As with the Irish report, it found the primary reason for the crash was 'the reversal of primary and alternate static source lines which led the pilot to conduct his approach to the airport at a dangerously low altitude.'

But the CAB went further. It said: 'A contributing factor was the negligence of maintenance personnel in certifying to the satisfactory functioning of the static system although the test required to determine such a condition was not accomplished. A further contributory factor was the restriction of vision from the cockpit resulting from fogging of the unheated windshield.'

The CAB report also contained some mild criticisms of the Shannon meteorological services and the airport's telecommunications system which caused consternation in the department of industry and commerce at their Kildare Street headquarters. 'It is obvious that neither the company nor the Shannon Meteorological service accurately anticipated the extent to which the ceilings and visibility in the Shannon area would lower during the period of the flight,' the report stated.

A formal letter of complaint was issued and R. W. O'Sullivan was dispatched to the USA to negotiate 'agreed reports' with the CAB. There was a tussle between the civil aviation division and the establishment branch in regard to the payment of his expenses. Papers released under the thirty-year rule reveal that some civil servants believed the US government should pay for his trip. After it was pointed out that the Americans could then insist on recouping the cost of sending their inspectors to Shannon, it was agreed to bear the cost of his air travel to New York with a subsistence allowance of $15 dollars a day for a maximum of six days and a single sum of £15 sterling to cover entertainment. A minute of the establishment branch dated 13 April 1947 states that Mr O'Sullivan 'was instructed to proceed to Washington and to arrange with the US authorities for the deletion of the undesirable references.' In the event, his mission was largely successful. He was in New York when it became obvious that he would have to travel to Washington and, after cabling for permission, he was cabled back: 'Visit Washington approved. Advise urgently duration. No sanction entertainment.'

The L-49 Constellation became a safer aeroplane as a consequence of the TWA crash. In its many variations, it continued to serve TWA until, more than a decade later, the first generation jets rendered the magnificent final version, the 1649 Starliner, of which forty-four were built, obsolete. For TWA, desperately trying to stave off bankruptcy, floundering in the deep economic depression, and still recovering from the joint traumas of the earlier L-49 crash and a bitter strike by its 800 pilots which had shut down the airline between 21 October and 15 November 1946, it was truly the winter of discontent. By early 1947, TWA stock had plummeted from $71 to $9, and saving the airline would tax the talents of Howard Hughes, the enigmatic and already deeply eccentric genius.

Juan Trippe, Hughes' great rival, was involved in an effort to get the Equitable Life Insurance – one of TWA's major creditors – to force the airline into bankruptcy. He was rebuffed. Soon it would be Trippe's turn to face an even worse L-49 disaster at the same remote outpost of the North Atlantic. Before his career ended he would be facing far worse economic problems than Hughes', which in the end would destroy the most powerful and the most glamorous airline the free world had ever known.

Captain Tansey's career as an airline pilot ended on Inishmacnaughtan. He had to suffer a further amputation after returning to the USA and he later received substantial damages when he sued TWA for negligence, causing the loss of his leg. But an even greater tragedy awaited him. While working as a flying instructor in California, he suffered a heart attack when instructing a novice student pilot. The student was unable to control the aircraft and he and his student were killed.

The *Star of Cairo*'s co-pilot, Clifford Sparrow, who suffered a serious fracture of the femur and bad facial wounds, was again hospitalised after his return to the USA. For him there was a happy ending. He married his physiotherapist and, after a brief period as an office worker, successfully resumed his flying career. 'On my first trip back to Shannon,' he recalls, 'I looked out of the window and saw the wreckage of the *Star of Cairo* still there on the island.'

He made many friendships in Ireland as a result of the crash, especially with the doctors and nurses who treated him. He went on to become a senior Boeing 747 captain with TWA, retiring as a pilot on 18 March 1980, two days before his sixtieth birthday – the mandatory retirement date for airline captains. He then trained as a flight engineer and continued flying with TWA until December 1985 – forty-nine years, almost to the day, after the Shannon crash. At the time of writing, he and his wife were living in retirement in Monument, Colorado.

Vena Ferguson left TWA soon after the crash and never flew as a hostess again. She became Mrs Vena Heckman, and went to live in Rolling Hills, California – a long, long way from Inishmacnaughtan.

The Empress of the Skies Crash, 15 April 1948

A few miles northwest of Ennis, not far from the point at which westbound flights leaving Shannon normally exit the Irish coast to begin the ocean crossing, lies Drumcliffe Cemetery. It should not be confused with the Drumcliffe cemetery 'beneath Ben Bulben's head' in Co. Sligo where the poet W. B. Yeats lies under the limestone slab with its famous epitaph:

> Cast a cold eye
> On life, on death.
> Horseman, pass by!

The cemetery near Ennis contains the graves of generations of Co. Clare farmers, labourers and fishermen who, with their wives beside them, lie alongside the bourgeoisie traders, professionals and artisans from the prosperous market town up the road – all now, as the bard said: 'locked in death's dateless night.'

Inside the gate of what is otherwise a typically unkempt rural Irish cemetery, stands the strange memorial to the thirty people whose lives ended tragically and violently less than eighteen miles from this spot in the early hours of 15 April 1948. On that day, the Pan American Airways L-49 Constellation *Empress of the*

Skies crashed and burned 2,380 feet short of the approach end of Shannon's east–west runway, runway 23.

The casual traveller calling at the isolated graveyard off the Ennis–Lahinch road will find a large and rather ugly headstone over a large mass grave now covered with concrete and, considering the religious sensitivities involved, garnished with an incongruous cross of white pebbles. Although the names of all thirty victims – twenty-nine of whom were originally buried here – are inscribed, several of the bodies have over the years been exhumed and taken home for re-interment.

During 1948, at least 700 people died in civil air disasters[*] – a dismal record considering the numbers then flying. Several of the most reputable airlines – among them Pan American, Air France, Sabena, KLM, Eastern Airlines and United Airlines – suffered major crashes that year. It was the first year in which the figures for the fatalities in landplane crashes began to exceed the fifty mark. It was also the year of the first recorded hi-jacking of an airliner when, on 16 July, a Consolidated OA-10 Catalina of Cathay Pacific was taken over in mid-air between Hong Kong and Macao. Twenty-six people died as a consequence.

Pan American's Flight 1/10 was one of the most prestigious services of the world's most prestigious airline. Originating in San Franscisco, the round the world service proceeded eastwards to Calcutta, where there was a change of aircraft, before returning to the USA with stops at Damascus, Istanbul, Brussels, London and Shannon. Tourist class had not yet been invented on the Atlantic. Every passenger was automatically a VIP.

On 13 April, as the passengers joining at Calcutta boarded the L-49 Constellation, none of them could have known that the airliner they were boarding had already achieved a footnote in aviation history. It was the first and only true three-engined Constellation to undertake a transcontinental flight back to the Lockheed base in California.

[*] Figure based on *World Directory of Airliner Crashes*: a comprehensive record of more than 10,000 passenger aircraft accidents, by Terry Denham (PSL, 1996).

Because of numerous engine failures, the early Constellations were known in the industry as 'the world's best trimotors'. And while numerous 'Connies' had flown on three, two and even one engine, in every case there were four engines in the nacelles (the outer casing of the engine), even if one, two or even three of them had been feathered. *Empress of the Skies* was unique in that after an emergency landing in June 1946, in which an engine had burned out and fallen off shortly after departing New York for Shannon, it took off again on three engines with the nacelle of the lost engine removed and the gap in the wing faired over (i.e. with an external metal or plastic structure added).

When it finally came to grief near the threshold of runway 23 at Shannon on 15 April 1948, it had a total of 3,861 flying hours, 2,407 of which had been accumulated since its major overhaul. It was powered by four Wright 745C18BA3 engines with Hamilton Standard 33E-60-79 propellers.

Its flight from Calcutta to Brussels had been routine and uneventful. But on finals to Brussels for a night landing the fluorescent lighting on the captain's (left) side of the cockpit failed. The only other form of cockpit lighting available on the L-49s was a chart light which in this case was focused on the automatic direction finder indicator. The captain was unable to read the flight instruments but he continued with the landing which was successfully accomplished without reference to instruments.

When the fault was investigated after landing, the lights worked perfectly and the flight departed for London. But, on approach to London, as soon as the engine power was reduced for landing, the lights on the left hand side failed again. This time the chart light was focused on the airspeed indicator. The approach was continued and the landing was accomplished without incident.

On the ground, company mechanics soon found the cause of the failure: a faulty rheostat switch. A search for a new one proved fruitless but, as in Brussels, the lights were again working perfectly. Pan American's maintenance supervisor informed Captain Frank

C. Jakel of the situation. After a brief discussion, Captain Jakel decided to continue the flight with the faulty switch. He noted the defect in the aircraft's technical log and took off from London with thirty-one souls on board at 12.35 a.m.

At thirty-five, Frank Jakel was one of Pan American's most trusted captains. Born in Los Angeles, he now lived with his wife, Elanore, and two daughters, aged two and three, in Long Island, close to Pan American's North Atlantic base. After joining the airline in May 1941, he initially flew out of the Pan American base at Brownsville, Texas. During the war he served as a ferry pilot in air transport command and, having rejoined Pan American in 1946, achieved the distinguished ranking, peculiar to Pan American, of 'master pilot'. At the time of his death he had logged 6,230 hours of which 1,564 were in Constellations.

His co-pilot on that fateful flight was Carl. M. Henson of Forest Hills, Queens, New York. He was twenty-seven and had been employed by Pan American since December 1942. He had a total of 3,310 hours (956 in Constellations) and had successfully passed an instrument check four months previously. However, just previous to this flight he had failed an instrument approach check for a landing at Shannon.

The investigators were never able to discover which of the two pilots had been flying the aircraft at the time of the crash. Because of the condition of the bodies after the intense fire, they never established whether it was Captain Jakel or First Officer Henson who was occupying the left hand seat.

The twenty-one passengers on board the *Empress of the Skies* were being attended by purser John Hoffmeier, aged forty-one, and stewardess Bernice Feller, aged twenty-four. All ten crew members and nine of the passengers were US citizens. There were also five Italians, a Frenchman and an eighteen-year-old British woman who was travelling to New York for a holiday before taking up a scholarship at Oxford. Sir Homi Metha, aged seventy-one, who had joined the flight in Calcutta, was a wealthy Indian banker.

Miss Mumiaz Shah Nawaz, aged thirty-four, was described as a journalist and poet. Her mother, a prominent member of the Moslem League, was to take grave exception to the plan to have her buried in a Christian grave but relented when convinced that there was no earthly hope of identification.

A family of three, US diplomat George Henderson, aged thirty-four, his twenty-four-year-old wife, Agnes, and thirteen-month-old son, Bruce, joined in Damascus. Mr Henderson had been serving in the US legation in Damascus and was returning to the USA on leave prior to taking up a new posting in Dhahran, Saudi Arabia. Rescue workers found the charred body of baby Bruce cradled in his mother's arms.

The initial Shannon weather forecast made available to Captain Jakel indicated that at the time of landing the ceiling (cloud base) would be 700 feet with a higher layer of cloud at 1,000 feet and visibility of four miles. At 1.59 a.m. the flight reported to Shannon that it was over the Limerick Junction fan marker at 4,500 feet. They were now twenty-five statute miles southeast of the airport and they requested permission to make a practice approach to the field using the instrument landing system (ILS).

The Shannon controller advised that three hours previously the ILS equipment had been reported faulty but had since been serviced and, although not flight-checked, was, according to its monitoring board, operating normally. At 2.10 a.m., the flight reported that it was proceeding to the outer marker, 5.2 statute miles northeast of the field. It also made what was a standard report for Pan American flights: 'mechanical condition ok.' Shannon responded with the latest weather: the cloud base was now down to 400 feet with fog patches and three miles visibility. The wind was from 325 degrees at 4mph. The pilot was told to land on runway 23 – the runway to which the ILS was projected – and to report when making the 180 degree procedural turn for the inbound instrument approach to the field. They were also requested to report when reaching the outer marker.

These requested position reports were not complied with. At 2.20 a.m., the *Empress of the Skies* reported a 'missed approach' and advised that it was going around again for a fresh approach. Simultaneously with this message, air traffic controllers got a first sighting of the aircraft through a break in the clouds. It was reported to be at 500 feet, over and in line with runway 23. The engine noise was heard to increase and the controllers saw the L-49 starting a left turn. The second approach started at 2.27 a.m. when the flight reported it was making its 180 degree procedural turn. One minute later it received an update on the weather: fog patches, visibility 2-2/12 miles, cloud base 400 feet. At 2.31 a.m. the flight reported it was approaching the outer marker. The controller then advised that another aircraft which had just taken off had reported a ceiling of 500 feet when northwest of the field.

The *Empress of the Skies* responded with the usual acknowledgement. It was its last message.

Sitting midway down the cabin, in an aisle seat looking out on the trailing edge of the wing, was the man who was to be the sole survivor of the inferno that was now only seconds away. Marc Worst, a thirty-eight-year-old Californian, was the manager of the Lockheed Aircraft Corporation's maintenance base at Shannon. An amateur pilot and veteran air traveller, he had already survived a light aircraft crash in the USA. He knew the L-49 thoroughly and was fully acquainted with its faults and its virtues. In the next couple of days, he would be able to give invaluable evidence to the investigators. His expert testimony convinced them that, the cockpit lighting apart, there was no technical malfunction during the final stages of the flight.

Worst had joined the flight in London and was returning to his Shannon base. His wife, a nurse, was waiting for him at the airport to drive him to their home in Limerick sixteen miles away. As the aircraft descended through the fog patches, Worst had been looking out for the airport lights. He told the investigators that he did not see the lights until the aircraft was directly over the field.

He felt that the aircraft was too high and it did not surprise him to hear power being applied for the pull-up. The missed approach caused him little concern. He understood what was happening, and settled back in his seat to await the second approach.

The engines appeared to be operating normally. The seat belt and 'no smoking' signs were on. He heard the flaps being extended. The attitude of the aircraft appeared to be normal.

Then followed what Marc Worst took to be a heavy landing. There was a severe bump. Then a second severe bump. A severe jolting followed and, to his horror, he saw flames sweep through the cabin from the forward part of the fuselage. He was thrown forward in his seat but was saved injury by his seat belt. As the aircraft came to a halt he noticed that though filled with flames the cabin remained substantially undamaged. All the passengers were in their seats. None cried out and none tried to move. For that terrifying moment, all were paralysed by shock. Worst undid his seat belt and started to crawl to the rear of the cabin.

Within seconds he felt himself fall through a gaping hole in the floor. 'Hell,' he thought, 'I've fallen into the cargo hold.' He hadn't. He had fallen onto wet earth and weeds in a little hole in the ground under the fuselage. He wriggled free and ran as fast as he could, escaping with only slight burns and scratches. Within seconds everyone else on board the *Empress of the Skies* had been burned to death.

At the airport Mrs Worst had heard the crash siren go off and knew that the plane carrying her husband was on fire. Courageously, she volunteered her services as a nurse and set off for the crash site with a Pan American official, missing her husband who had raced across the field to the airport to reassure her of his safety. On arrival she was told that there were no survivors. 'You cannot know how I felt, but I decided to go on,' she told the *New York Times*. Then they came and told me that Marc was the sole survivor and again you cannot believe how I felt.'

The first bump Marc Worst had felt was the landing gear hitting a stone wall. This collapsed the nose gear and main left gear and tore the main right landing gear from its mounting. All four engines were wrenched off. The empennage (an arrangement of stabilising surfaces at the tail of an aircraft) was broken into three parts which were scattered around the fuselage and wings. The fire started almost immediately and lit up the surrounding countryside.

The rescue services operated efficiently. There was nothing for them to do. The heat was so intense that it was hours before the charred remains could be removed. In several cases, it wasn't possible for the pathologists to tell which were male and which were female.

When the inspector of accidents, R. W. O'Sullivan, arrived from Dublin several hours later, one of the first things he noticed was a Pan American DC-3 aircraft flying over the crash scene. This special flight from London had brought high-powered technical teams from Pan American and the (US) civil aeronautics bureau (CAB). O'Sullivan knew instinctively that in the minds of the diverse powerful interests eager to find a quick solution to the cause of the tragedy, the reliability of Shannon's recently installed ILS – one of the first to be installed outside of the US – would be called into question. He ordered that every available test be carried out and the ILS was found to be in perfect order.

A preliminary examination of the engines, together with Marc Worst's evidence, convinced the investigators that there was no malfunction. Then came the evidence of the faulty switch and the tendency of part of the cockpit lighting to fail when engine power was reduced.

In his report on the accident, R. W. O'Sullivan dealt with the possibility of this minor deficiency being responsible for the catastrophe. 'If the fluorescent lighting failed,' he wrote, 'the instrument panel might have been left in darkness except for the red overhead light which, during the ILS approach, would normally be focused on the ILS indicator.

'The pilot's action might be to reach up behind him to re-focus this red light on the whole instrument panel, thus diverting his attention momentarily from holding the aircraft at a steady rate of descent. The sudden blackout of the instruments would prevent the loss of altitude being noticed, the radio altimeter being set in the 0–4,000 feet range would not be sensitive enough to give reliable terrain clearance during an approach below 400 feet ...'

This hypothesis, reasonable as it appears, did not particularly appeal to the CAB inspectors who in their report wrote: 'If the pilot had unobstructed visual reference to the runway, failure of the fluorescent light on his side of the cockpit would not in itself account for any particular difficulty in his completion of the landing approach.

'Airspeeds and altitudes could have been called out by the co-pilot. If there had been failure of the pilot's fluorescent light before Captain Jakel established visual reference to the runway ... there should have been sufficient time and altitude to place a flashlight into use or to focus the overhead chart light on the pilot's instrument panel ...' They concluded that: 'a failure of the fluorescent light might have contributed to this accident, but could not be, in itself, the cause.'

And so, the crash of the *Empress of the Skies*, like so many others before and since, will forever remain in that category of air accident which defied solution and was eventually labelled with a bland, catch-all explanation under the heading 'Probable Cause'. In the case of the *Empress of the Skies*, the CAB inquiry board wrote: 'The board determines that the probable cause of this accident was the continuation of an instrument approach to an altitude insufficient to clear the terrain. A contributing factor may have been the failure of the pilot's instrument fluorescent light.'

On the afternoon of Saturday, 17 April 1948, the melancholy service for the mass burial took place at Drumcliffe. Borne on CIE (the nationalised Irish transport company) trucks, the coffins were brought from Shannon and laid beside the large pit that had been excavated. Twenty-four of the victims went into the communal grave. The bodies of the other five, who had been identified, were placed in side graves. Agnes Henderson and her thirteen-month-old son were buried together.

Unusually for the Ireland of those days, it was an ecumenical occasion. The roman catholic coadjutor bishop of Killaloe, Dr Rogers, led the christian service. Anglican, methodist, presbyterian and baptist clergy followed. On the previous day, Rabbi Bernard Kerch from the Cork jewish community and an Immam from the UK conducted their own respective services. It was a low key affair. No government minister attended – the minister for industry and commerce was represented by the Shannon airport manager, Colonel Patrick Maher.

Marc Worst, the sole survivor, returned to California the day before the funeral and lived there until his death in 1983.

Thirty years later, the most senior Pan American executive at Shannon at the time of the crash, Captain Horace Brock, gave an astonishing account of the funeral in his memoirs, *Flying the Oceans: A Pilot's Story of Pan Am 1935–55*. Brock, Yale-educated and schooled in law before taking up flying, was one of the most aristocratic of Pan American flying boat captains. He had given up flying for management and was chief of Pan American's North Atlantic division at the time of the crash.

In his book, Brock gave a thoroughly fantastic account of how he had to arrange for the mass burial by calling on 'the bishop of Limerick'. The bishop, he reported, was 'a jolly, red-faced Irishman, dressed in a cassock with both feet clad in purple socks. He sat in front of a fire with his feet propped on a pillow. He extended his hand to me to kiss his ring, which I did, respectfully …

"'Your Worship," I said, not knowing the correct address "I would like to arrange a funeral for the persons killed in the crash of our airplane at Shannon yesterday."

"'Well, well," said the bishop, his face lighting up. "A funeral did you say?" and sent an acolyte out of the room who returned soon with an enormous flask of wine, sacramental, no doubt. After we all had full tumblers of the wine, it dawned on me that I had made a terrible mistake in saying "funeral". I was to learn that a funeral in Ireland involved a parade through town followed by several hundred mourners and a wake when all the mourners and everyone else would be plied with spirits by the bereaved, in this case Pan American World Airways ...

'The burial took place on a grey and drizzly day; and I gazed at the cavernous grave at the side of which the bishop said mass, followed by six holy men in their varying robes intoning their indifferent tongues. That afternoon I flew back to New York.'

Brock managed to get even the number of the victims wrong – he wrote that there had been sixty-two when, in fact, there were thirty. How sad that the tragedy of the *Empress of the Skies* should be recorded for posterity as a crude piece of paddywhackery.

CHAPTER 4

The Cruellest Sea

SECURITY was tight at Walker air force base in New Mexico, at Barksdale in Louisana and at Limestone air force base in Maine – now Loring – in the USA on 20 and 21 March 1951 as preparations were made for the take-off for Europe of the giant Globemaster Airforce Carrier.

The four-engined, eighty-ton craft, capable of carrying 222 men and transporting light tanks and cannon, was en route to Lakenheath strategic air command base in the United Kingdom.

While at the air force bases, all aircraft were under twenty-four hour guard and a register of all personnel entering or approaching the planes was maintained. The Globemaster was loaded by the crew under the supervision of the load master and the aircraft commander.

When the Second World War ended in 1945 the large number of US military aircraft stationed at UK air bases had returned home and by the following year all wartime bases had been handed back to the RAF.

However, by 1948, the British government was inviting the government of President Truman to redeploy air force units to the UK to counter increasing tension between east and west. Matters had come to a head with the Berlin blockade in April 1948 and there had been a progressive build up of US warplanes in Britain over the next few years.

The Globemaster, which in time would become quite a common visitor to Ireland on United Nations airlifts, was at that stage still a rare sight in the Irish skies. It had been found useful for conversion into a flying hospital and was capable of accommodating 111 stretcher cases. On this occasion it was equipped with the latest survival equipment and the pilot, Captain Emmitt E. Collins, was highly experienced in this type of craft.

As preparations were made for its take-off in Holy Week of 1951, the ostensible reason for the trip was a routine inspection of UK bases. However, it later emerged that it was one of two aircraft scheduled to participate in a special mission to the United Kingdom. The mission, which involved two Globemasters, had been authorised some days earlier. Both had flown from Walker air force base to Limestone and the first was already safely in the UK.

The Globemaster was carrying top brass of the US services and strategic air command, including a brigadier general, three colonels, two majors, twenty captains and four lieutenants. It was also believed to be carrying highly confidential documents.

Globemasters were used to transport nuclear weapons, and suspicions were subsequently to arise that an atomic bomb might have been among the highly secret cargo loaded on board the fateful flight. It was less than six years after Hiroshima and Nagasaki and the west was obsessed with the fear that it would be overtaken in the atomic race. President Truman was warning that the threat of another world war was just as real as it had ever been and he was seeking $18.3 million from congress for atomic research.

Spymania was rife. The previous year Klaus Fuchs had been sentenced to fourteen years imprisonment and was deprived of his British citizenship for passing secrets to the USSR. In the USA, Judge Irvin Kaufman sentenced Julius Rosenberg, a thirty-two-year-old electrical engineer and his wife, Ethel – the parents of two young children – to death in the electric chair for stealing American atom secrets and passing them on to Russia.

On board the Globemaster was fifty-year-old Brigadier General Paul Cullen, deputy commander of the second air force at

Barksdale Field. He was of Irish-American parentage and had been commanding officer of the air photographic unit at Operation 'Crossroads', the Bikini atom bomb tests, in August 1946. Before that he had served in both Europe and the Pacific in the Second World War. Born in Ica, Peru, he saw his first service in the Second World War as a military observer with the British air force in the middle east in 1941. With him on board were Colonel Kenneth Gray, Colonel E. A. McKoy, Lieutenant Colonel J. L. Hopkins and Major G. H. Stoddard.

The flight proceeded routinely from Walker to Barksdale air force base, Louisana and then on to Limestone air force base. It was scheduled to go on to Gander, Newfoundland, and from there to Mildenhall in the UK.

The Globemaster, serial number 49-244, had gone into service with the United States air force on 28 September 1950. It had flown 324 hours 45 minutes. It had undergone a second intermediate inspection on 16 March 1951 and since then had flown just 7 hours 40 minutes from Tinker air force base to Walker, prior to departing on the UK trip. At the time it left for the UK it had sixteen hours to fly before its third intermediate inspection. The engines had never had a major overhaul.

As the giant plane lumbered into the skies from Barksdale Field, Louisana at 10 p.m. on Wednesday, 21 March, it had a total of fifty-three persons on board. Thirteen were crew members and forty passengers. Thirty-five of the passengers were from Walker air force base, four were from the headquarters of the strategic air command and one from the headquarters of the second air force.

Officers of the strategic air command included Colonel Kenneth Gray, budget officer, Colonel E. A. McKoy, assigned to the directorate of material, Lieutenant Colonel J. L. Hopkins, chief of the personal division and Major G. H. Stoddard, of the directorate of plans. According to the US army, they were to make a routine inspection of US strategic air command units in Britain.

The C-124 was the largest transport in regular use by the air force. It had a top speed of 250 miles per hour, a wing span of 173 feet and its fuselage was 127 feet long. It was powered by four 3,500hp Pratt and Whitney engines.

The weather was good and the forecast on the intended flight path to the UK 'reasonable'.

The aircraft had a cargo of two KB-29 bomb bay tanks weighing 6,830 lbs and was also carrying 10,395 lbs of medical supplies, prop equipment, spare parts, and tools. The total weight of the aircraft and fuels was 146,436 lbs.

In addition to Captain Collins and his crew of ten, the aircraft was carrying two instructors who were assigned to accompany the flight to check and evaluate the commander and his crew. Major Robert S. Bell, squadron operations officer, was assigned as instructor pilot and in command of overall operations. Captain Francis N. Davies, squadron navigator, was assigned to check the navigational capability of the crew.

Major Bell conducted a general crew briefing for the flight and Captain Davies a navigational briefing. A passenger briefing covering bail-out, ditching and crash landing was carried out under the observation of the 47th air division commander, Brigadier General Harris, Lieutenant Colonel Von Arb and Lieutenant Colonel Ladd, commanding officer 2nd strategic support squadron. The plane carried its own life rafts with food, water and coloured rockets.

The flight proceeded routinely to Gander where it landed for refuelling and crew and passengers took the opportunity to stretch their legs. It took to the air again at 4.20 p.m. on Thursday afternoon.

At 1.06 a.m on the morning of Good Friday, 23 March, oceanic control at Prestwick in Scotland received a routine message from the Globemaster changing its estimated time of arrival at Lakenheath, the US air force base at Mildenhall in England, from 6.30 a.m. to 6 a.m that morning. The plane did not report any trouble.

Shannon–Prestwick oceanic control – known as Shanwick

– was a joint control operated by Shannon and Prestwick which took over from Gander when aircraft were at thirty degrees west or approximately halfway over the Atlantic.

When the Globemaster reported into Shanwick at 1.06 a.m. it was some 800 miles southwest of Ireland, in the centre of a triangle between the Azores, Iceland and Ireland and it had plenty of fuel to enable it to reach any of the three countries. In fact, at the time its message was received it had fuel reserves which would have enabled it to remain airborne for about eight and a half further hours – until 9.35 a.m.

The area in which it was flying was what meteorologists call 'cold front', a junction between a cold air mass which was undercutting a warmer air mass. The weather associated with 'fronts' is heavy thunder showers with considerable turbulence.

The Globemaster was probably flying in fog and rain but this in itself would not have been a cause for concern.

The first indication that something was wrong came when over an hour later no report of its next routine position was received from the aircraft. Shannon Aeradio, Ballygirreen, tried to raise the plane but without success.

On hearing that radio contact had been lost, British air traffic control alerted the Azores, Iceland and Gander in the hope that they had heard from the missing plane and that it was headed for the safety of one of their airports. However, nothing had been heard from Captain Collins or his crew.

Fears were now growing that the flight had run into difficulties and there was real concern for its fate if it crashed into the turbulent seas of the Atlantic.

An emergency was immediately declared and Irish, RAF and US rescue planes were scrambled. Two United States air force Superfortresses as well as RAF Lancasters, carrying dinghies and parachute lifeboats, began a widespread search along the aircraft's planned route.

Even at this early stage there was some surprise that the pilot did not manage to get a message of some kind to one of the Atlantic weather ships. This, it was speculated, would indicate that disaster might have overtaken him without warning.

Search planes flew nearly 1,000 miles into the Atlantic on a track ten miles north of the Globemaster's known route and ten miles south of that line on the run home.

Commercial airlines were alerted and all merchant shipping in the North Atlantic sea lanes were asked to keep a look out. Two liners, the luxurious *Queen Mary* and the *Empress of Canada* joined in the search while four US navy tankers were diverted to the area.

An Irish air corps Anson plane from Baldonnell made an intensive search along the north coasts of Kerry and Clare in case the C-124 had made it to land. (The Americans did not know what to make of the Anson with which they were unfamiliar. Later, as it sat among the Albatrosses, Lancasters and Lincolns parked at Shannon, the US military attaché was moved to comment: 'That Irish Anson is a mighty fine gesture. I know it takes a powerful nerve to fly a plane like that on such a mission. The United States air force and the American people will be grateful.')

Fears grew as the day advanced and no sign was found of the missing plane. Thunderous seas lashed the area most of the day and low visibility hampered the search. British and American search planes from Britain and Aldergrove in Northern Ireland braved the buffeting winds and poor visibility, staying out as long as nine hours.

History was made when an RAF Lincoln bomber flew into Shannon from southern England – the first British armed plane to land in the Republic.

Master Pilot Ronald Kelly of London said: 'We did not think when we joined the search that we would also make history.'

Shortly before nightfall, the weather cleared, visibility improved and fresh British and American crews were brought in to continue the search.

It was decided that search planes would maintain a shuttle service all night over the Atlantic area from where the plane had last reported.

At 2.15 on Saturday morning – over twenty-four hours after the giant plane had last been heard of – the crew of one of the searching B-29 Superforts sighted debris flares and what appeared to be Mae Wests (inflatable life-jackets), 450 miles west of the Irish coast. Their radio message was picked up at several points. An RAF control officer at Uxbridge, England, said the pilot had also reported sighting what he believed to be a life raft.

The RAF officer said that seas were running high and there were strong winds in the area. Gale warnings had been posted along the British coast.

Two ships were immediately diverted to the scene and the vast armada of search planes that had been sweeping the 800 mile stretch of ocean sped to the area where the flares had been reported.

Two weather ships – the *Jig* and the *Charlie* – also headed for the scene and the *Queen Mary* reported that she was in the vicinity.

In Shannon, Major Horace A. Stephenson, commanding officer of the 7th air rescue squadron from the Azores, who was commanding the US air rescue mission, told reporters that he could not say when the rescue planes would reach the area: 'I am afraid it will take some time – possibly hours – for the weather ships to get there.' He also cautioned that in the darkness the pilot might have been mistaken.

Major Stephenson then revealed that further wreckage had been sighted – sixty miles closer to the Irish coast.

US navy HQ in London reported that a navy ship had sighted an uninflated liferaft about 400 miles west of Ireland but had seen no sign of life in the area.

The plan was to bring any survivors to Shannon so Dr William Flynn, the airport medical officer, hurriedly began arranging for additional medical staff and prepared to expand the airport's medical centre facilities.

An advance sub-base for the rescue operation was set up at Shannon. Major Stephenson, who had arrived on Saturday morning in Shannon in a Skymaster aircraft of the US military air transport service, brought with him a crew of fourteen, including three majors, to take part in the search.

A number of special search planes arrived from Tripoli and Newfoundland to join the operation.

Captain Stanley Lankiewicz said that the operation would be controlled from Manston, England, while the Shannon base would deal with co-ordinating and briefing crews.

He told waiting reporters that the greatest air-sea rescue operation in the history of aviation was underway. For twelve hours fifty planes and five ships criss-crossed the area where the flares and wreckage had reportedly been sighted. As dawn crept in from the east, the first of the specially equipped rescue Skymasters took off for the same area. A second followed shortly afterwards.

The US Flying Fortress was fitted with a special self-righting lifeboat which had recently been tried out in Korea. The boat accommodated twenty persons and was fitted with a radio. It also carried blood plasma in addition to the usual emergency equipment. Piloted by Captain W. Littlejohn it flew at about 800 feet over the area where the flares had earlier been reported. Littlejohn reported back that conditions were excellent for search work. He could see no sign of wreckage.

There were now about 200 US servicemen in Shannon. Colonel Lunde, US air attaché in Dublin, acted as banker for the US airmen, exchanging their special scrip money, which was negotiable only at military establishments, for Irish currency.

Aircraft were departing hourly from Shannon for the search area, returning only to refuel.

There were a number of theories as to what had befallen the plane. A group of US air force pilots suggested that the antennae of the Globemaster became iced and this prevented signals being sent out. They surmised that the plane could have been blown up as a result of its being struck by lightning. Another theory was that the plane ran into heavy icing conditions and lost altitude. The question of sabotage was also raised and at this stage vigorously denied by the US authorities.

Meanwhile the drama continued at the search site where the engine of one of the Superfortresses caught fire. Later an engine of another search plane went on fire, forcing it to jettison the lifeboat which it was carrying under its fuselage. Both limped back to Shannon while a third SB-29 barely made it back to the airport, with fuel reserves near zero.

At 6.30 p.m. the weather chip *Charlie,* which had arrived earlier in the area, reported that it had picked up an air force valise.

Charlie – the name then used for the United States coastguard cutter *Casco* on international weather duty – sent word to the coastguard in Boston that the piece of luggage was identified as belonging to Captain Lawrence E. Rafferty of Illinois, one of the air force personnel known to have been on the missing plane.

The high hopes that had been expressed earlier in the day when the wreckage was reportedly sighted were fading rapidly.

Pilots returning to Shannon reported: 'The sea was calm. There were no whitecaps. There was very good visibility, but we saw nothing.' Officers began to openly voice their concern that all fifty-three people on the Globemaster were lost.

But the US authorities said they were determined to continue the search twenty-four hours a day until such time as no survivors could remain alive.

A spokesperson for the third air force HQ in London said: 'We definitely have not given up hope and we will continue to make a maximum effort. We are encouraged by the fact that we can concentrate on one relatively small area after finding the bag.'

Shannon airport, open for just five and a half years and then still known as Rineanna, was having difficulty coping with the influx of aircraft and men. At dusk on Saturday when many of the search aircraft arrived together they had to be stacked over the airport awaiting landing clearance. The atmosphere was that of a fly-in from a wartime bombing mission and there was much praise for the overworked air traffic controllers.

When he returned from the USA on Sunday morning, where he had had a twenty-minute meeting with President Truman in the White House and where he had told the president that Ireland would never join the Atlantic Pact unless partition was ended, Sean McBride, the minister for external affairs, had to walk through 'a tangle of foreign war planes' parked all over the ramp.

On Sunday, the US navy directed three warships, *General Muir*, *General Rose* and *General Taylor* to join the search. The aircraft carrier *Coral Sea* and two destroyers, *Fox* and *Brenner*, en route from Norfolk, Virginia, to join the United States sixth fleet in the Mediterranean, were diverted to the Atlantic area where the search was underway.

Aboard the 45,000 ton *Coral Sea*, planes were ready to take off as soon as they came within effective range of the area. The British submarine, *Thule*, the American merchant vessel, *Golden Eagle*, and an icebreaker were also making their way to the region.

Intense action continued throughout Sunday with seventy aircraft, six ships and the British submarine combing the Atlantic.

A duffle bag which was identified as belonging to one of the Globemaster's passengers was picked up by a cutter, floating in the sea some 100 miles from where the first wreckage had initially been sighted.

The search continued. Nothing was found on Monday. A box twenty-miles square where wreckage had first been sighted on Friday was searched but there was no longer any trace of it.

Hope was now fading for any survivors. Even if they had survived the impact it was unlikely they would still be alive after several days in the ocean. American authorities were clinging to admittedly 'faint hopes' that some of the men might have drifted to safety in liferafts.

On 26 March it was announced that the head office for the

release of news about the Globemaster was being transferred from Shannon to the HQ of the US air division at Ruislip

At this stage it seemed inevitable that the search would be wound up. However, to the mystification of many, the search rather than being scaled down was intensified.

US officials said they were hoping to find some clue which might explain why the giant four-engined transport plane had crashed without sending out any distress signals.

On Tuesday, the *Coral Sea* arrived in the area. Sixty-five aircraft were launched from the carrier, including three helicopters, to join the thirty-seven aircraft already engaged in the search.

The following day there were thirty-six aircraft launched from the carrier and twenty-seven flying from the UK and Shannon. Spares had been flown in to Shannon to repair the two SB-29s.

On Thursday, some pieces of wreckage, including a fuel tank from the Globemaster, were found fifty miles from where the duffle bag had been recovered. Fifty aircraft combed the area that day and the next, including several missions from Shannon but nothing further was found.

A journalist travelling back to the UK with the crew of one of the RAF Lancasters on Thursday almost met an untimely fate when flying over Waterford at an altitude of 4,000 feet. Mr Norman Ray stumbled against an emergency door and pushed it out. He nearly fell out himself but just managed to hang on. Luckily the door missed the residents of Dungarvan, Co. Waterford when it hit earth close to the town.

Searching destroyers picked up hundreds of small pieces of the plane 600 miles off the west coast of Ireland and it was announced that the giant Globemaster had been blown to bits by a catastrophic explosion in mid-Atlantic. This virtually ruled out all chances that any of the fifty-three men on board could have survived.

On Saturday, 31 March, eight days after it began, the search was called off. It was announced that the Globemaster had been blown to bits by an explosion in mid-Atlantic. No cause was given for what caused the explosion. Debris recovered was charred and showed signs of splintering.

The *Coral Sea* continued on its voyage and as the search aircraft arrived back at Shannon on the Saturday, the crews collected their belongings and returned to their home bases. Last to leave at 10 a.m. on Sunday morning was Major Horace Stephenson, with 14 others who formed his staff at the advance base at Shannon. They returned to their base at Lajes Field in the Azores.

However, no sooner were the search bases dismantled than in a highly unexpected move the following day the US third air C division announced that the search for the Globemaster would be resumed and continued 'indefinitely'.

An air force spokesman refused to elaborate on the brief official statement, leading to considerable speculation as to the reason behind it.

Colonel Lunde, the US air attaché arriving in Shannon on the Sunday to wind up the search process, was informed when he got there that the search was being resumed.

It was known that the search would not be started again without good reason and speculation was that the air force had either found some indication that survivors might still be alive – very unlikely – or that further clues to strengthen the sabotage theory were still being sought. Air force officers had said throughout the search that the question of sabotage could not be ruled out, although there had been no definite evidence to substantiate such a theory. However, most of the material turned up in the search to date had suggested sabotage.

The more powerful rumour was that the Globemaster had been carrying an atomic bomb and the US authorities, fearful that the Soviet government might find it and learn its secrets, was determined to ensure that any remains of the mighty ship were consigned to the Atlantic bed.

The search dragged on for some time and was then ended quietly. The Irish media in any case had already lost interest as the country was plunged into the mother–and–child controversy.

However, there was still another twist to the story. On the morning of Saturday, 28 April, over a month after the disappearance of the Globemaster, John Faherty, a sixty-year-old unmarried farmer, was out walking on the beach near his home at Tullybeg, Renvyle, Co. Galway. This beach was frequently strewn with driftwood and some years earlier an explosive mine had been found there, apparently washed in by the currents.

It was about 9.30 a.m. and high tide when Faherty, who lived with his unmarried sister, came upon a battered cylindrical tin can which had not been there when he walked the beach the previous evening.

The tin was about four and five-eighths inches in height by three and a half inches in diameter – a size which would usually contain about 2 lbs of paint. The lid of the tin was flat, with a lip all round which allowed easy removal and replacement and rendered the tin air-tight when pressed home.

When Faherty examined the tin he found the sides somewhat battered and slightly rusted. There were marks of scraping of a regular pattern on the outside such as might be made by a screwdriver or chisel in an effort to remove identification markings.

There were also traces of white adhesive paper such as that used for labelling and small patches of what appeared to be blue paint on the outside of the tin.

Faherty opened it without too much difficulty. Inside he found the following message: 'Cullen is worried when 300 miles west of Ireland, Globemaster alters course for no apparent reason. We are going north. Have to be careful. We are under surveillance. Pieces of wreckage will be found but are not of G-Master. A terrible drama is being enacted on this liner.'

The message was written by hand in blue-black ink with a ballpoint pen on a small scrap of thin white paper which appeared to have been carefully torn from a larger sheet. The message was written on both sides of the paper. The writing was quite clear and firm, suggesting that the author was accustomed to writing regularly or frequently and that he took some care in writing this message.

There was no signature, date, time, or position by latitude or longitude, such as might be expected if written by a person with military or technical training.

The paper was quite dry and crisp, suggesting that it was not long in the container, in which it should have otherwise become damp from condensation caused by changes in temperature.

Immediately he read the message Faherty went to the post office at Renvyle and telephoned the garda station at Letterfrack, where he reported his find to Sergeant Patrick Connolly.

Sergeant Connolly took possession of the tin and the message. He was due to go to Dublin for a few days leave later that day and while in Dublin the next day, Sunday, 29 April, he called into the United States embassy and left word about the finding of the message.

The following day Colonel Lunde, air attaché at the embassy, contacted Letterfrack station for further details of the discovery.

The tin and message were brought up to garda headquarters where Colonel Lunde inspected them. He asked that photographs be taken of them. He also suggested that they might be handed over to him when they were no longer required by the gardaí.

Colonel Lunde said he was going to Renvyle immediately to interview Patrick Faherty and he was accompanied from Dublin by Sergeant Connolly.

Reporting on the matter to the secretary of the department of justice the following day, Garda Deputy Commissioner Garrett Brennan said local police had reported that John Faherty was a very decent type of man who would not himself originate a hoax of this type nor lend himself to such conduct. He said enquiries were being made to discover if the tin and message were of local origin. Enquiries were also being made among paint manufacturers in the Dublin area to see if the source could be identified.

In a memo stamped 'Confidential' by the department of justice, Deputy Commissioner Brennan said it was to be noted that the loss of the Globemaster was fully publicised in the Irish and English daily papers for about eight days from 24 March. Brigadier General Paul T. Cullen's photograph appeared in Dublin papers of 27–28 March as one of the passengers on the missing aircraft.

The commissioner approved the handing over of the tin and the message to Colonel Lunde and they both disappeared into the keeping of the Americans.

And that, as far as officialdom was concerned, was the end of the Globemaster.

On 11 April 1951, the American ambassador to Ireland, George A. Garrett, wrote to the minister for industry and commerce, Dr T. F. O'Higgins, thanking the Irish government for its assistance in the Globemaster search.

He said that during the search, several US air force and RAF aircraft were operated from Shannon Airport. Obviously facilities at Shannon were not designed for concentrated efforts of this type; hence the personnel at Shannon were faced with new problems and a great amount of additional work.

Mr Garrett said the air attaché reported that every individual connected with the customs, immigration and other departments at Shannon Airport associated with the search was most cooperative and had added substantially to the operational success of that portion of the search directed from Shannon.

He said a number of people associated with aircraft control at Shannon were to be particularly commended for their wholehearted, friendly and energetic cooperation throughout the period 23 March to 1 April. Singled out were Lorcan Sinnott, officer-in-charge, air traffic control, D. H. Mitchelhill, senior control officer, Harry F. Carberry, control tower officer, Gerry Sammon, OAC control officer, Austin Davis, clerical officer, Michael Maloney, senior control officer, Ned Stapleton, senior control officer, and Len Vass, senior control officer.

Another spin-off from the massive search operation was that the potential of Shannon as an air base, and its great use for Atlantic operations, had been realised. This gave rise to widespread discussion at the time as to whether the airport might again be used as a base in the event of another war.

While the search for the Globemaster was at its height the US ambassador to Ireland, Mr Garrett, told reporters in a shipboard press conference before sailing from New York to Dublin that Ireland would be 'wide open' to an airborne attack if the Russian armies reached the channel ports. He emphasised Ireland's importance in the defence strategy of western Europe.

The officers billeted at Shannon were enthusiastic at what they saw as Shannon's tremendous strategic value.

They said that in 1949 it was common gossip at headquarters that plans were being prepared to present to the Irish government with the object of making Shannon available to the US in time of conflict, when civil aviation would be at a standstill. Apparently these plans were shelved on the advice of the US embassy.

It was argued that since that time there had been many advances in aircraft, their weapons and systems, but it could not be denied that Shannon must still retain much of its strategic value for operations in the Atlantic.

The search for the Globemaster was the most extensive and expensive search ever undertaken for a lost aircraft. (It cost the, at that time, enormous figure of £13,000 an hour.) The US government marshalled a virtual armada of planes, aircraft carriers, destroyers, a submarine and cruise liners but all that was ever recovered were some bits of scattered wreckage about 700 miles off the Irish shore.

Over fifty years later, the reason the US continued the search for days after there was no hope of finding survivors seems obvious: the Globemaster must have been carrying something they desperately wished to find or failing that to prevent others from finding.

At that time political relations between the Irish and UK governments were still fragile in the aftermath of Second World War tensions. It would be surprising if this virtual armada of foreign warplanes, including an RAF bomber, had been allowed to fly freely in and out of Shannon without the highest level clearance from the Irish government.

At the time a request from a single foreign plane to land in Ireland or to overfly Irish airspace resulted in a virtual deluge of paperwork flying between the minister for industry and commerce – who had responsibility for authorising overflies – and his cabinet colleagues. Yet despite extensive trawls of Irish government department records released since then there seems to be no mention of permission being sought or granted for any of the large number of warplanes and other craft that landed at Shannon during the search.

While there is no doubt that permission to use Shannon's facilities in this emergency was sought and granted freely not once but twice, it is surprising to say the least that no mention of this is contained in records which have been made public to date.

No mention of these landings is contained in the records of the military archives or in the papers from the Taoiseach's department dealing with requests for overflights or landings in that particular year.

Are these records of an accident which happened over fifty years ago still considered so sensitive that they have not been released by the government?

Many other questions are still unanswered. Did the Globemaster alter course for no apparent reason when 300 miles west of Ireland? Was a 'terrible drama' enacted on the giant aircraft? If so, what was it? Were the giant plane and its VIP crew the victim of sabotage? Was the message picked up by Patrick Faherty genuine and, most of all, did the Globemaster contain an atomic bomb? Was this the reason for the greatest search ever being mounted and for the absence of official records of the search from Irish government archives over fifty years later?

After the crash, did the US government succeed in virtually obliterating all signs of the giant plane which, with its VIP crew and passengers and possibly secret and sinister cargo, vanished in fog and rain into history and legend in the turbulent seas of the bleak Atlantic in Holy Week 1951.

CHAPTER 5

Rough over the Hills: The Loss of the St Kevin

'YOU'LL find it rough over the hills tonight. We were at five. Went up to six five. It seems to be right through.'

Within three minutes of sending this message to another Aer Lingus aircraft approaching the Welsh coast from Dublin on the hellish evening of 10 January 1952, Captain James Keohane, commander of the Aer Lingus DC-3, EI-AFL, fleet name *St Kevin* was dead. So too were his crew, First Officer William A. Newman and hostess Deirdre Sutton. Twenty passengers, including an off-duty Aer Lingus captain, his wife and their only child, died with them.

They died in a peat bog in Cwm Edno about a mile and a half from Lake Gwynant, 1,200 feet up Moel Siabod on the lee side of Mount Snowdon. The catastrophe was so sudden that there was no distress call. The *St Kevin*, on a scheduled flight from Northolt Airport, London, to the Aer Lingus home base at Collinstown, Dublin, suddenly went out of control and dived earthwards. As the speed of the dive built up to a terrifying level, a twenty-six foot section of the outer starboard wing broke off due to over stressing. Experts believe the aircraft hit the ground at an angle of eighty degrees and at a speed well in excess of 300 mph. (The Aer Lingus DC-3 manual gave the maximum speed for a dive or glide at 194 knots, or 226 mph.) On impact, the aircraft formed a crater in the soggy bogland. There was a brief and intense fire, which was quickly extinguished by the rising bog water – a typical case of what air crash investigators sometimes call 'smoking hole impact'.

Mercifully for the twenty-three people on board, death was instantaneous. Some bodies were thrown clear on impact. Others went into the crater with the forward part of the aircraft and were never found. The body parts that were eventually brought out of the crater were largely unidentifiable. The two engines and much of the forward fuselage also disappeared. As the aircraft went under, the port wing and what was left of the starboard wing folded inwards through the fuselage At the time of the inquest, four days later, thirteen of the twenty-three bodies had been found but only ten had been identified. The carnage was horrific. The inspector of accidents for the Irish government, R. W. O'Sullivan, told in his memoirs how he had found an index finger, neatly shorn off at the knuckle joint, to which was attached a playing card – the nine of diamonds.

As with every fatal air crash, this one was a huge tragedy for the families of the victims and the airline concerned. But the loss of the Saint Kevin was a tragedy which transcended the normal parameters of grief and desolation that distinguish all fatal air accidents. From the moment the first meagre details of the tragedy were broadcast on Radio Éireann on the night of the accident, the crash started to take on the proportions of a national tragedy. The next few days would see remarkable outpourings of national grief as the whole country seemed to go into mourning.

Across the divide of over half a century, it isn't easy to appreciate the degree of affection coupled with fierce national pride that Aer Lingus attracted at that period of its history. The infant national airline had caught the public imagination as the body that had shown the world that Ireland and its men and women were capable of matching the best in the world's most sophisticated industry. The award, in 1950, by the British Guild of Air Pilots and Navigators of the coveted Cumberbatch trophy 'for safety and reliability of operations', had instilled much self-confidence in Aer

Lingus personnel and was an occasion of great pride and rejoicing.

In a leading article the morning after the crash, the *Irish Times* said that while it was tragic that Aer Lingus had 'broken its fifteen-year-old record of immunity from death, and that all sensitive hearts should bleed for those who mourned the victims', it was fitting to point out that Aer Lingus had a history surprisingly free from blemish. 'Although – for a service belonging to a small country – it has flown a remarkable number of miles, it has flown them well and has had every reason to congratulate itself,' the leader writer continued. 'Yesterday evening's calamity is unlikely to impair, for any long time, its reputation for trustworthiness ...'

A diplomatic communication released by the British public record office under the thirty-year rule in 1986 shows clearly that the British embassy in Dublin was very much in touch with national feelings in regard to Aer Lingus. A letter written by the commonwealth office to the ministry of aviation strongly advises against penalising Aer Lingus because of its plans to start an Atlantic service.

The memo warned that 'our ambassador in Dublin has also pointed out that, politically, it must be borne in mind that Aer Lingus is the pride and joy of the average Irishman. Probably he does not know that BEA and BOAC have an interest in the company. He looks on it as a striking example of Irish achievement and efficiency – something that has put the Republic back on the map of the world after the long years of wartime isolation.

'The Ambassador says that a casual visit to Collinstown Airport is enough to prove the interest which Irish people have in their airline. On almost any day of the week one can see successive groups of people up from the country going on a conducted tour of the airport ...'

In an interview with me shortly after his retirement in 1967, the first general manager, Jeremiah F. Dempsey, spoke with some emotion about the struggle he and the other early pioneers of Aer

Lingus had in breaking through what he described as the 'rivers of prejudice formed by the stereotype of the fun-loving, feckless Irishman who spent most of his time fighting or drowning his sorrows.

'We had the precise image that was anathema to international air travellers and it was a huge struggle to shake it off and prove that not only were we responsible and efficient but that we were way above average in these virtues.

'What was being said at the time of our foundation was: "How the devil are the Irish going to run an airline?" Everything was against us. Scientific education in the country had been run down. We were a nation with an appalling reputation for punctuality and application. And these things, of course, were the very attributes which were vital to the task we were taking on.'

At the time of the *St Kevin* crash, Aer Lingus was still in the throes of a big postwar expansion made possible by the purchase – at bargain basement prices – of a fleet of ex-US air force C47s which had been converted to civilian DC-3s. Five months before the crash, Aer Lingus had carried its millionth passenger and in 1951 the airline returned a profit of £72,000 – its biggest to date. In 1952, it carried 277,000 passengers – another record.

Aer Lingus had already lost its original DC-3, EI-ACA, in a non-fatal crash-landing after an engine fire at Shannon Airport on 18 June 1946 (see chapter one). The *St Kevin* (EI-AFL) was bought by Aer Lingus in June 1950 and was placed on the Irish register on 15 May of that year. It received its certificate of air-worthiness from the department of industry and commerce on 9 June 1950 and the certificate was valid until 9 May 1952. Built by Douglas in the military C47B-35Dk version at their California plant in 1943, it was originally sold to the US air force where it had the serial number 44-77115. It then went to the RAF under a wartime lease-lend scheme and flew as KP-228. After six years it was transferred to Scottish Aviation Ltd, which converted it for civilian use and sold it on to Aer Lingus. At the time of the crash it had flown a total of 4,339 hours of which 2,343 had been under the Irish flag. As the British inspector of accidents acknowledged in his report, the number of flying hours didn't even approach the average life span of comparable aircraft. The two Pratt and Whitney Twin Wasp engines were also shown to be properly maintained and well within the approved engine life span.

Although it had been in airline service since 1936, the DC-3 was still the predominant short-range airliner on the world's air routes. Owing to its ruggedness and reliability, airlines queued up to buy it. Between 1936 and 1941 national passenger mileage in the US grew by almost 600 per cent – a growth which was largely due to the passenger appeal of the DC-3. By the end of the war, 10,692 DC-3s, in several versions, were built in the US and a further 2,000 or so were being built under licence in the USSR. It was the DC-3 that transformed Aer Lingus from being a minor peripheral carrier into an airline of substance.

The aircraft that awaited the twenty passengers for Dublin at Northolt on the blustery afternoon of Thursday, 10 January had left Collinstown on the outward journey at 2.43 p.m. It had been a long day for Captain Keohane. Having said goodbye to his wife and three young children at his home in Iveagh Road, Whitehall, he drove to Collinstown to prepare for his first flight of the day – the 10 a.m. scheduled service to Birmingham.

Flying conditions, which would deteriorate steadily during the day, were already rough and at one point during the flight to Birmingham Captain Keohane thought he might have to divert to Manchester. He touched down at Collinstown after an uncomfortable return flight from Birmingham at 2.03 p.m. As he was due out again within the hour, there was no time for lunch so a hot lunch was put on board for him for during the flight.

Whether he ever got round to eating his lunch will never be known. All day, a broad, deep and rapid stream of air from the middle of the Atlantic was spreading across the whole of Ireland

and across England south of a line approximately from Morecambe Bay to the Humber. The complex meteorological conditions created by this airflow resulted in gale-force winds, electrical disturbances, acute turbulence and hailstones. In such conditions there was a real danger of icing and, in mountainy terrain, severe downdraughts.

The strength of the winds and their impact on the *St Kevin* may be gauged from the fact that a tailwind enabled Captain Keohane to fly the Collinstown–Northolt sector in one hour thirty-six minutes, while in the teeth of headwinds varying from 60 mph to 75 mph, the return leg was estimated at two hours twenty-five minutes. Another Aer Lingus DC-3 over England on the way from Paris diverted to Liverpool as the captain feared he might run out of fuel. In the subsequent public inquiry into the loss of the *St Kevin*, the pilot of the Paris–Dublin DC-3, Captain Bill Wallace, gave a graphic account of battling to keep the airspeed steady as ice mounted up on the wings and the DC-3 pitched and rolled in the severe turbulence. The hostess described how, strapped to her seat in the rear of the aircraft, she could hear the chunks of ice bang off the fuselage as they broke away from the wings.

Captain Pete Little, who eighteen years later as chief pilot of Aer Lingus would fly the first Irish Boeing 747 into Dublin, was also on the Dublin–Northolt route that evening and was over the Irish Sea when the *St Kevin* went down. He reported very smooth conditions except for twelve minutes of extremely severe turbulence over the Welsh mountains when six of his thirteen passengers were sick. Captain Little reported two particularly severe bumps four or five minutes after passing Nephin Beacon, abeam (on a line at right angles to the aircraft's length) of Barmouth.

When he landed in Northolt earlier that afternoon, Captain Keohane had made three trips across the Irish Sea within a period of seven hours and could be under no illusions about weather conditions along the route. Not surprisingly, immediately he landed he started to study the forecasts for the return journey. Normally these forecasts were collected from the duty forecaster at the air ministry's meteorological office and then passed to the captain. But on this occasion Captain Keohane and First Officer Newman took the unusual step of going to interview the duty officer. The duty officer that day was Miss Joan McCay, a brilliant meteorologist and one of the very few women to reach the higher reaches of the service at that time. Captain Keohane had three separate routings available to him for the return journey and, under Aer Lingus regulations at the time, it was up to him as commander of the aircraft to make the choice.

He could have selected what was known as 'the Bristol route' which would take him westwards along airway Green One to Filton, just north of Bristol, then northwest across the mouth of the Severn and onwards to the Strumble beacon near Fishguard. The second choice was 'the Wallesey route' which would have taken him along airways Amber One and Green Two to exit the coast at Wallesey west of Liverpool and onwards across the Irish Sea to Dublin.

But despite any misgivings he might have had about the weather, Captain Keohane rejected these routings and opted for the more direct Daventry–Nevin route over the Welsh hills. The court of inquiry later accepted that it was the consensus of opinion of all the Aer Lingus pilots who gave evidence on this point that his decision was justified on the basis of the meteorological information available to him. Each of the pilots declared that, in similar circumstances, he would have taken the same routing.

On Thursday, 10 January 1952, sunset was at 4.11 p.m. Twilight was ending by the time the order was given at Northolt to start boarding flight EI-165. Although it was a wet and blustery afternoon, there was a full moon.

Northolt Airport in west London had started in 1915 as a royal flying corps base and was one of the first airfields used in the defence of London during the First World War. In the Second World War a number of Polish air force squadrons were based there during the Battle of Britain. Sir Winston Churchill landed there in July 1945 on his return from the Potsdam conference and in the following year the base was loaned to the ministry of civil aviation for domestic and European flights. Aer Lingus, which originally used Croydon for its London services, now moved them to Northolt. The base finally closed to civilian traffic in 1954.

With perhaps one exception, the twenty passengers awaiting the boarding call in the departure lounge that fateful afternoon were representative of the flying public in the early 1950s. Their ages ranged from four to fifty-five. Most were well off. Several were successful business people. There was the usual smattering of professional people: two doctors, a final year medical student, an accountant and an engineer. One was an off duty Aer Lingus captain, travelling with his wife and four-year-old daughter. Another was a sixteen-year-old girl coming to live with her grandparents in Dublin.

Inevitably, there were the cases of those who had changed their minds about travelling and lived or died as a consequence. A Michael J. Maguire of Manhattan House, Bird Avenue, Clonskeagh, Dublin, had been booked on the flight but a friend persuaded him to stay another day. Emile Stone, a twenty-two-year-old student at the Royal College of Surgeons in Ireland had been in London for the funeral of his grandmother. He too decided to stay an extra day and so took the fateful flight perished on the Welsh mountains with the twenty-two others.

Dr James Gaffney, a lecturer at Trinity College, Dublin, was returning from Cambridge having read a paper to the Pathology Society of Great Britain and Ireland on a new type of rare tumour he had discovered. A gifted pathologist and high-flier of the Irish medical world, he was still mourning the death of his eldest child in a drowning accident.

These were the kind of travellers who routinely flew the Aer Lingus London route in the early 1950s. An exception among the passengers of the *St Kevin* was John Stackpool, farmer and greyhound breeder from Kildorrery, Co. Cork. Mr Stackpool also operated a hackney, and when local boy made good, Thomas Carroll, returned to Kildorrery to spend Christmas and the New Year with his ninety-year-old mother and two brothers, he engaged John Stackpool to drive him around the Cork locality. Stackpool, whose father William was an internationally known horse breeder and first cousin of the murdered lord mayor of Cork, Tomás MacCurtain, was a busy man, engaged to be married and had no business in Britain.

Tom Carroll had done well in the US after he emigrated in the 1920s. He had been active in the IRA and, after the treaty, joined the Irish army. In New York he entered the saloon trade and made a substantial fortune with a string of saloons including 'The Tally-Ho' pub and restaurant in Lexington Avenue, Manhattan. Carroll, who was the youngest of nine children, had lost his father as an infant and he and his seven brothers and one sister were reared on a cottage on the Stackpool farm by their mother Peggy.

The eldest boy, Michael, somehow raised the money to go to the United States and then sent home the fare for the next son. One by one, with the support of those already there, the others followed and established successful businesses in the new world.

Locals still talk about how good they were to their mother, coming home to visit her and on one occasion during the war sending her a ton of coal by boat from the USA.

But while the sons were wealthy and successful their sister had disappeared. She'd been found walking out with a British soldier during the time of the Black and Tans, had her head shaved and was given twenty-four hours to leave the country. Mrs Carroll pined for news of her daughter and when he came home that Christmas Tom decided to go the England and hire private detectives to try and track her down.

He asked John Stackpool to go with him. Stackpool refused but agreed to drive him to Dublin – he didn't take a change of clothes with him in case he would be tempted to go. They put up in the Gresham for a few days and Carroll proved persuasive.

Stackpool, who lived on his own, decided to go for the trip – without telling his family in Cork.

The young air hostess who greeted the twenty passengers as they boarded the aircraft was Deirdre Sutton from Sandford Road, Ranelagh, Dublin. Aged twenty-three, she had joined Aer Lingus in May 1950 having worked as a sales assistant in Pimms department store in George's Street. Anna France (neé Greevy), the chief hostess of Aer Lingus, who trained her, remembers her as 'a lovely girl – gentle, caring and completely reliable. She was very pretty too – a natural blonde with a beautiful smile.'

By 5.15 p.m. all passengers had boarded and hostess Deirdre Sutton went to the cockpit to deliver the standard message: 'All passengers and ships papers on board; doors closed and ready for taxi.' Within ten minutes the *St Kevin* was at the threshold of the main runway. Just before 5.23 p.m. the tower controller gave the take-off clearance. At 5.25 p.m., having reached the V2 speed of 86 knots, Captain Keohane lifted off and joined airway Amber One which would take him to Daventry.

In the early 1950s, navigational aids were rudimentary and depended chiefly on a series of radio beacons, all of them low-powered in order to overcome the problem of overlap. The signals from these would be picked up by the automatic direction-finding equipment on the aircraft. But because of their low output, the signals could not be relied upon until the aircraft was almost directly overhead.

All Aer Lingus pilots of that era would have been familiar with the terrain over which they flew on the Dublin–London route and, in VFR (Visual Flight Rules) conditions, dead-reckoning was partially used to determine position; dead-reckoning is a way of calculating one's position by estimating the direction and distance travelled rather than by using landmarks or astronomical observations. Aer Lingus aircraft also carried what was known as a 'Gee Box' – a piece of navigational equipment capable of receiving high frequency radio pulses transmitted from multiple ground stations in an overlapping grid. The 'Gee Box' was simple to use and highly accurate. Its major disadvantage was that, in the absence of a radio officer, one of the pilots would have to leave his seat for a couple of minutes to take the 'fix'. In conditions of severe turbulence this was at best unsatisfactory and at worst hazardous.

The *St Kevin* did not carry a radio officer on its fatal last flight. Aer Lingus abandoned the use of radio officers on the Dublin–London route in 1950 on the grounds that the advance in R/T (radio transmission) communications and improved navigational aids made these crew members redundant.

The move was bitterly opposed by the Irish Airline Pilots Association (IALPA) and contributed greatly to the acrimonious industrial relations that existed between Aer Lingus and its pilots at that time. Not surprisingly, IALPA latched on to this aspect of the *St Kevin* tragedy and played it for all it was worth – a delegation of pilots went to the minister for industry and commerce and a submission was made to the chief inspector of accidents of the Ministry of Civil Aviation (MCA) in London. The main plank of the IALPA case was that in conditions of icing and turbulence which might result in a critical loss of airspeed which, in turn, could result in a catastrophic stall or spin, both pilots should be able to devote all their attention to flying the aircraft rather than having to bother with navigation as well.

The IALPA submission – which was rejected by Aer Lingus management – clearly stated that if a radio officer had been on board it would have been possible to use the 'Gee-Fix' apparatus and this would have ensured the aircraft was on course.

Management were even more resentful when the pilots raised the question of engine reliability. Discussing the possibility of engine failure, the submission to the MCA stated: 'In the Aer Lingus fleet there has been a history of an abnormal number of engine failures during the past three or four months.' (In fact, there had been ten DC-3 engine changes during the period January to December 1951 and in seven of these cases it had been necessary to shut down an engine in flight.) The assistant general manager (technical), Captain J. C. Kelly-Rogers, responded by insisting that this was an excellent record. The IALPA submission continued: 'The association regard it as significant that in May 1950 Aer Lingus increased from twenty-four hours to forty-eight hours the period of inspection of airframe and engine.' There was also a criticism of the new procedure whereby pilots, rather than licensed aeronautical engineers, were to carry out pre-flight ground inspections at all airports.

Whatever the merits of the argument in regard to the radio officer – and there are retired Aer Lingus pilots alive today who passionately believe that the occupants of the *St Kevin* would not have gone to their deaths if there had been one on board – it soon became clear that engine failure had nothing to do with the tragedy. And it goes without saying that Aer Lingus' commitment to the highest possible maintenance standards was as scrupulous in 1951 as it is today.

The *St Kevin*'s first communication after clearing Northolt was at 5.56 p.m. when they contacted Uxbridge (London Airways) by R/T with the message: 'Checked Daventry.' Up to this he had maintained a groundspeed of 97 knots (nautical miles per hour) but at Daventry (Northamptonshire) they had to turn on a course that brought the wind directly ahead. This, the experts calculated, reduced the *St Kevin*'s groundspeed to 89 knots. At 6 p.m. there was a further message confirming the time of passing Daventry as 7.56 p.m. There was a further call to Uxbridge at 6.41 p.m. saying: 'Check three degrees west.' By this, the crew meant that they had passed over the point where the track line cut the third meridian. Once they had passed that point they would be handled by the Northern Flight Information Region (NFIR). At 6.38 p.m. the first call to Preston (NFIR) said: 'Check three west now. Estimate Nevin one nine one zero (i.e. 19.10 or 7.10 p.m.) and Dublin one nine five one (i.e. 19.51).

At 6.54 p.m., about sixteen minutes before the estimated time of reaching the Nevin checkpoint, Captain Keohane radioed Preston asking for permission to ascend to 6,500 feet. He gave no reason for wanting to change his flight level and Preston immediately gave permission. Captain Keohane responded almost immediately with the message 'leaving four five now' and at an unascertained moment between 18.58 and 19.02 added the message: 'check six five'. The next signal came at just before 19.12 when the message was 'check Nevin'.

But the *St Kevin* was not over Nevin. It was approximately sixteen miles to the south of Moel Siabod on the lee side of Snowdon. Disaster was now only minutes away. It later became apparent, and the court of inquiry accepted, that from the time they had checked over Daventry, the *St Kevin* was always well behind the points which the pilots believed they had reached.

Preston now requested the *St Kevin* to change frequency to Dublin. As he acknowledged the instruction, First Officer Newman asked the Preston controller: 'Have you any news of any outbound aircraft from Dublin on the London route?'

The controller answered: 'Affirmative. Easy Charlie Item departed Dublin at one eight four eight. Estimating Nevin at two minutes past the hour.' (EI-ACI was another Aer Lingus DC-3, the *St Aidan*, piloted by Captain Pete Little and First Officer W. A. Mackay.)

First Officer Newman now called up the *St Aidan* and said: 'You'll find it pretty rough over the hills tonight. We were at four five. Went up to six five. It seems to be right through.'

Both pilots on the *St Aidan* heard the message. First Officer Mackay, who had operated the radio throughout the trip, acknowledged it. Neither detected any note of stress or concern in the first officer's voice.

Shortly after 7.12 p.m. and before 7.15 p.m. Dublin ATC received what was to be the last message from the *St Kevin*. This was: 'We checked over Nevin a minute ago flying six five IFR. We just passed Charlie Item. Request descent clearance please.'

The Dublin controller acknowledged and gave the clearance. Whether it was ever received by the crew of the *St Kevin* will never be known for nothing more was heard from them.

Moel Siabold is about two miles north of Dolwyddelan and two miles south of Capel Curig on the A5 from Holyhead. It is 1,200 feet above mean sea level. Snowden lies six and a half miles to the east, and Lake Gwynant is a mile and a half away.

On the evening of 10 January 1952, most of those who lived in this wild but beautiful area of north Wales had, in Thomas Hardy's phrase 'sought their winter fires'. As darkness fell that Thursday afternoon, the weather turned foul with strong winds gusting from the southwest. It was raining hard and a little higher up there was sleet.

Farmer Goronwy WIlliams was sitting in his kitchen in Nant Gwynant listening to the BBC at about 7.15 p.m. when, despite the howling wind, he thought he heard an aeroplane flying low over the house. Goronwy, along with millions of people around the world, had been following the saga of the courageous Captain Kurt Carlsen. Thirteen days previously Carlsen had ordered his crew and sixteen passengers to abandon ship but, in an effort to save the vessel, remained on board and was later joined by the mate of one of the rescue vessels, Kenneth Dancy.

The saga of Captain Carlsen and his *Flying Enterprise* had gripped the world. It came to a close at 4.10 p.m. that afternoon when, almost within sight of Falmouth, the *Flying Enterprise* sank in the English Channel minutes after Carlsen and Dancy had jumped from the disappearing funnel into the raging waters and were rescued.

Even though Mr Williams had heard no crash or explosion, when the noise ceased he went to the door. Through the swirling rain, he saw a fire glowing on the hillside. He alerted a man who worked for him on the farm and, having run almost a mile to the nearest public telephone, continued up the hillside to the crash site.

Even though the rising bogwater had put out the fire, the

wreckage was still smouldering. It was quite dark but the beam of Mr Williams' flashlight soon picked out pieces of wreckage. As he wandered around the site calling out to any possible survivors, the beam fell on the body of a victim who had been thrown clear on impact. Then it fell on a second body. Then on a third.

Profoundly shocked by the eerie spectacle, Mr Williams spent almost half an hour at the crash site hoping against hope that someone might still be alive. But the only sound was the wind howling through the mountains. With a heavy heart, Goronwy Williams left the scene of death and destruction and clambered down the hillside to the nearest road to wait for the rescue teams.

It was after 10 p.m. when the first of the rescue workers reached the crash site. Saturated by the driving sleet and frequently ankle deep in the marshy bogland, the stretcher-bearers were led by mountain rescue workers with flashlamps and lanterns. By midnight, almost 100 workers had reached the spot.

Fr Thomas Magee O.M.I., an oblate father working in the parish of Blaenau-Ffestiniog in north Wales was reading in his presbytery on the evening of 10 January when he got a phone call to say that it was thought a plane had crashed in the area.

Fifty years later, living in retirement at Inchicore, Dublin, he recalled: 'It was a very bleak, cold and foggy winter's night. I phoned a taxi and we set off in the direction of Bettwsy-Y-Coed. As we approached the village of Capel Curig, we saw a long line of rescue vehicles and ambulances heading in the direction of Bangor. We were told there was no point in going further as there were no survivors.'

As dawn broke the full extent of the devastation became obvious. The front part of the fuselage had formed a crater which would be the permanent resting place of six of the victims whose bodies were never found. The two engines had disappeared into two smaller craters alongside. A twenty-six foot section of the wing was lying 266 yards away. Other pieces of wreckage were found up to a mile and a quarter away.

And, inevitably, there were the pitiful reminders of the great human tragedy that has taken place: a child's shoe … a doll … a woman's wristlet watch … a playing card (the nine of diamonds) … numerous letters … a passport …

John Stackpool's sister, Agnes McCarthy, was also listening on the radio to the Captain Carlsen story in her home in Cork on the morning of 11 January when a neighbour rushed in and said that an Aer Lingus plane had crashed: 'I said 'shush, the *Enterprise* with Captain Carlsen is being towed into Southampton and shure we don't know anyone on the plane.

'She said "there's a Stackpool from Dublin" and I said "we must have cousins there that we don't know about".

'Within minutes John's friend, the horse breeder, Ruby Walsh, and his brother, Ted, came in to break the terrible news. John had obviously given his address as the Gresham.'

Agnes, her sister Maureen, Tom Carroll's nephew Jim, and Ruby Walsh, travelled to Dublin intending to cross over to Wales by boat.

Half a century later at her home at Martha's Vineyard, Rochestown, Cork, Agnes remembers: 'The weather was so bad there was no boat crossing. We met the general manager of Aer Lingus, Jerry Dempsey, who was very kind to us but said the only way he could get us over was by plane to Liverpool … I had never flown before and it wasn't the best time to start, but we had no choice.'

Flights for the families were arranged by Dr Garret FitzGerald, later to become Taoiseach and at that time working for Aer Lingus. They flew to Liverpool and then there was the long train journey to Caernarvon.

'When we got over, we were brought to a makeshift mortuary and I remember there was a pair of lady's high-heeled shoes and the top half of a crombie coat which I knew was John's. Then we found a piece of a shirt and a tie and Ruby opened his coat and showed his own identical shirt and tie.

'He said "We bought them together three weeks ago."

'The detectives said they could only release the body if we were absolutely sure and that wasn't sufficient identification.

'By this stage, my sister was hysterical with shock and grief and we left. We never got his body back. He was buried there ten days later and we heard the news on the radio. The fact that we never brought him home has haunted me ever since. The first real closure I got was at the memorial service held in Dublin Airport fifty years later.

'It changed all our lives. Mrs Carroll had to cope with the fact that her son had been killed trying to find her daughter. We lost our much loved brother. His fiancé, Mary, subsequently married his best friend. Peggy Carroll's daughter never came home.'

On the day after the crash, twelve bodies were recovered and brought to the morgue at Eryri Hospital. Eight were eventually identified and five, including that of the hostess Deirdre Sutton, were returned to Dublin for burial. Finally, on 29 January, nineteen days after the crash, nine unidentifiable bodies were buried in a communal grave. Six more remained in the crater, which was covered in and consecrated by a local roman catholic priest.

A team of Aer Lingus executives headed by the assistant general manager (technical), Captain J. C. Kelly-Rogers, and also carrying the chief aeronautical officer of the department of industry and commerce, R. W. O'Sullivan, had flown to Wales on the night of the crash and reached the scene early the next morning. The team included Michael Dargan, then staff and services manager; H. T. Williams, air safety officer; Patrick J. Brennan, assistant company secretary and company solicitor; and Captain W. J. Scott, operations manager.

In his memoirs, written thirty-six years after the event, Mr O'Sullivan recalled how several days after the accident he and the UK inspector of accidents, Michael Dargan, were lunching in a cave and 'laughing uproariously at nothing in particular' when they became aware of a man standing in the entrance to the cave. He explained that his brother had been killed in the crash and, as a doctor, he was worried in case his brother had died a lingering death on the bleak mountainside. The two experts felt confident in assuring him that this was most certainly not the case.

Michael Dargan, who fifteen years later would become the chief executive of Aer Lingus, recalls climbing the mountain to the crash site on the morning after the accident: 'The weather conditions were atrocious and we were soon bogged down in the soft ground. I did what I had often done as a child – I took off my shoes and tied them around my neck. It wasn't a good idea. There was snow on the ground and the terrain was rocky. I soon realised that if I went on like this I soon wouldn't have any feet.

'My task was to arrange the funerals and to do anything I could to ease the pain of the next of kin. It was a very difficult time, very sad and traumatic for all concerned. The Welsh authorities were marvellous and I am satisfied that the search was thoroughly done and done with dignity.'

Every air crash creates tensions within the afflicted airline. Regardless of how reputable the carrier or how committed it may be to maintaining high flying and engineering standards, doubts will almost inevitably be sounded on both scores. The crash itself will have attracted masses of unwelcome publicity – much of which may be insensitive, inaccurate and even irresponsible – which will put the airline under scrutiny, open old wounds and raise difficult questions. There is the inevitability of the official inquiry by the state inspector of accidents. A public inquiry involving high-powered lawyers eager and willing to bend the facts in order to suit their purposes, may follow. Reputations and livelihoods may be at stake. Many powerful interests ranging from the aircraft manufacturers to the oil company that refuelled the aircraft will be alert to the possibility of blame or misunderstanding.

The pilot corps, and its trade union, will be particularly tense and vigilant. And not without good reason. Even today, when the concept of natural justice has been highly developed by the courts, the temptation to blame the pilot – particularly if he or she is dead

– is occasionally resorted to. And, as every airline captain knows, there have been miscarriages of justice in this regard in the past.

These tensions are all the greater in the case of crashes which cannot be fully and definitely accounted for. All three Aer Lingus crashes involving fatalities fit into this category.

In the case of the *St Kevin*, the Aer Lingus pilots immediately went on the offensive. It was a period of rancorous industrial relations between Aer Lingus management and its pilots. The pilot corps mainly comprised men who had been trained either in the RAF or the Irish air corps. Some of the ex air corps pilots felt their RAF-trained colleagues looked down on them. The matter was complicated by the fact that many of the RAF men (Captain Keohane was a case in point) were Irish born. Both the RAF and the British civilian aviation establishment were heavily represented at management level.

The man who was ultimately responsible for running the technical side of the airline and who had most influence on the pilots was Captain J. C. Kelly-Rogers, who, though born in Dun Laoghaire, had spent practically all his working life in England and was a pillar of the British aviation establishment. The man with day-to-day responsibility for operations was Captain Bill Scott, who was ex RAF. In 1952, there were still two British directors on the board of Aer Lingus, Lord Douglas of Kirtleside and Conor Carrigan.

In their submission to the (British) chief inspector of accidents, the pilots, through the Irish Airline Pilots' Association, raised a number of points, several of which might be seen to have reflected poorly on Aer Lingus. While some of them were, no doubt, self-serving and grounded in good trade union practice, there is no doubt but that there was a great deal of genuine concern. Firstly, the pilots claimed that the hours worked by Captain Keohane on the day of the crash and during the previous nine days were, taken in the context of the atrocious weather that prevailed, excessive. They claimed that from 1 January until the time of the crash he had been on duty for at least forty-eight hours and that half these hours involved night flying. On the day of the crash he had come on duty at 9.15 a.m. and had completed a difficult round trip to Birmingham before setting out again for Northolt. The pilots made clear that they had the utmost confidence in Captain Keohane and would not accept that he might be guilty of any lack of judgement in regard to the crash. The words 'crew fatigue' were not mentioned but there was a clear innuendo that this could have had a bearing.

The second complaint concerned what IALPA claimed were inaccurate weather reports in regard to the Welsh mountains due to the lack of a meteorological reporting station in the area. It was also claimed that the Nevin radio beacon, being low-powered, was inadequate in conditions of electrical disturbance.

Then came a protest about the running controversy of the removal of radio officers. IALPA claimed that in conditions of severe turbulence and icing, with the consequent effect on airspeed, both pilots would be so totally immersed in flying the aircraft and ensuring that the airspeed didn't fall below 'critical speed', that they would not have been able to leave their seats and operate the 'Gee' apparatus to obtain a navigational fix. If there had been a radio officer on the *St Kevin*, they argued, he would have been able to ensure that the aircraft remained on course.

The IALPA submission also criticised the routing. While stating that they had no doubt that if Captain Keohane had been given a thoroughly accurate forecast of the weather conditions over the Welsh mountains on the night of the crash he would have taken a different routing, the pilots said they believed the proper IFR route from London to Dublin in the absence of a recognised direct airway was via Daventry, Dee estuary and Skerries Light.

There followed a suggestion that engine failure should not be ruled out and the claim that in the previous three months Aer Lingus aircraft had endured an abnormal number of engine failures. They felt it significant that in May 1950, the company had increased from twenty-four hours to forty-eight hours the period of inspection of airframe and engine. They were also dissatisfied with the new system whereby a pilot, rather than a licensed engineer, was made responsible for doing the pre-flight inspection at airports other than Dublin.

There was an additional complaint that the propeller de-icing controls were not standard throughout the DC-3 fleet and that the heating system in EI-AFL was capable of generating carbon monoxide as the detecting apparatus had been removed.

Not surprisingly, the management rejected these claims in their entirety. They produced records to show that in the period 10 December 1951 to 10 January 1952, Captain Keohane was on duty for twenty days of which seventeen were 'flying days' (including night flying) and three were standby. His total flying hours averaged four hours seven minutes per flying day. It was company practice, they said, to limit flying hours to 85 hours a month during the winter and to 100 hours a month for the three months, July to September. BOAC, they pointed out, did not limit the flying hours per month but had a yearly limit of 1,000 hours.

On the alleged inadequacies of the Nevin beacon, Aer Lingus claimed it had a published radiation range of 25 nm, although pilots said its radiation range was in excess of that. It also had the advantage of being remarkably free from interference. Further, the company's communications controller had received no complaints from pilots in regard to this facility.

Replying to the criticism regarding the absence of radio officers, the management outlined the phasing out of the radio officer grade from October 1948 when the (British) ministry of civil aviation announced that the progressive replacement of MF/WT aeronautical communications with VHF (very high frequency)/ RT over a two-year period. This was followed by exhaustive testing of the new equipment and meetings between the management and pilots to discuss the whole field of radio communications and navigation.

Answering the charges in regard to engine failures, the management replied that during the whole of 1951 there were ten unscheduled engine changes. On seven occasions pilots had considered it necessary to feather a propeller in flight. This was an improvement on 1950 and continued to show a downward trend.

Regarding the reduction of the inspection period of airframe and engine hours, Aer Lingus pointed out that this was in keeping with industry practice and that in BEA the time span was fifty hours as against forty-eight in Aer Lingus. The change in pre-flight inspections had been made because it was felt it was more desirable to have it done by a member of the airline staff rather than local staff at various airports whose interests would not lie with Aer Lingus.

But the greatest tensions by far were created, not by the pilots, but by the airline's safety officer, the executive who had responsibility for monitoring safety standards within the industry and ensuring that Aer Lingus kept pace with them. This post is normally occupied by a pilot, but H. T. Williams, the Aer Lingus safety officer in 1952, was an exception. He was neither a pilot nor an aeronautical engineer and in the aftermath of the crash of the *St Kevin* he found himself in such conflict with the management that it was with great reluctance that he was allowed to attend the public inquiry in London. He was eventually allowed to attend, but only on condition that he would make no statements and take no part in the proceedings without the sanction of the company solicitor.

Mr Williams had transferred to Aer Lingus from its sister company, Aer Linte, after the controversial government decision to abandon the Atlantic service on the eve of its inauguration. He was not popular with some sections of the Aer Lingus management and his initials, 'H.T', enabled his enemies to come up with the sobriquet 'High Tension Williams'.

After the crash, Williams raised questions about several aspects of Aer Lingus' operational procedures. He stated categorically that he believed it was not safe to operate a passenger-carrying aircraft over the Daventry/Nevin route in adverse weather conditions 'bearing in mind the limited facilities available to the pilot for positively identifying the flight's position under all circumstances'. In his report he also hinted that Captain Keohane and First Officer Newman may have been suffering from fatigue.

Williams was savaged for these views. In a memo dated 10 January 1952 to Kelly-Rogers, the general manager, J. F. Dempsey, reports on an interview he had with Williams on that date and how he had twice 'spoken sharply' to Williams in regard to his stance. Dealing with a complaint Williams had made about the use of anti-icing fluid, Dempsey wrote: 'He was quite open in admitting that he was on the circulation list for pilots' flight reports and I reminded him sharply that if he was, in fact, complaining that no action was taken, he must be included among the culprits and that he would have to account for his failure to do anything about it to his superior officer …'

Poor Williams. Whatever the merits of his complaints – and they may indeed have been misjudged – one wonders how, if they had such little faith in his judgement, the Aer Lingus management ever appointed him to such an important job in the first place.

The public inquiry opened in Holborn town hall, London, on Thursday, 17 April 1952. The court was headed by Mr J. Ronald Adams, QC, assisted by two assessors, Captain H. W. Caldwell, CB, a BEA pilot, and Mr E. Gold, CB, DSO. Desmond Bell, one of the leading senior counsel of the day, appeared for the Irish Airline Pilots' Association; Roger Winn, QC, (later Lord Justice Winn, and a brother of the writer Godfrey Winn) appeared for Aer Lingus; and relatives of four victims were represented by the Hon. SC Silkin, QC.

There were ten public sessions and nine private ones. Thirty-six witnesses were called. Finally, eleven questions, several of them routine ones such as whether the aircraft had a valid certificate of airworthiness, were put to the court by the attorney general.

Aer Lingus came out of it well. With the exception of one reply in which the court stated that the first officer was not properly licensed because he did not hold a radio/telephony licence (a claim Aer Lingus refuted) all the routine answers were in favour of the airline.

Most important of all, to the question 'Was the captain's decision to operate a service to Dublin via Daventry and Nevin a correct one?' the court answered: 'Yes.'

To the question 'In what respects, if any, was the navigation of the aircraft unsatisfactory?' they replied: 'The navigation of the aircraft was unsatisfactory in that it took the aircraft to a position close under the lee side of Snowdon at a time when the captain believed he was coming out over the Irish Sea.'

To the question 'What was the probable cause of the loss of the aircraft?' the answer was: 'The encountering of a powerful downcurrent of air on the lee side of Snowdon which forced the aircraft down into an area of very great turbulence where through one or another of several possible causes the pilot or pilots lost control.'

To the final question, 'Was the loss of the aircraft caused or contributed to by the wrongful act or default of any person or party?' the court answered: 'No.' The Irish experts who sat through the inquiry were amazed that nothing had been made of the fairly positive likelihood that the *St Kevin* had encountered sudden and severe icing conditions and that this was at least a contributory cause of the disaster. In his memoirs, the Irish inspector of accidents, R. W. O'Sullivan, says that neither he nor his British counterpart could accept that turbulence was the sole cause.

Once the enquiry ended the story of the *St Kevin* disappeared from the news pages. The crater had been filled in and trees were planted.

Amazingly, on the first anniversary of the tragedy, 10 January 1953, there was no recap in the three Dublin dailies. Ironically, there was a prominent story saying that weather conditions had closed Dublin Airport on the previous day causing the cancellation of all inbound flights and all but one of the sixteen that were outbound flights.

Two of the victims were remembered in that day's 'In Memoriam' column in the *Irish Independent*. One entry read: 'Belton (first anniversary). In cherished remembrance of Eveleen who departed this life on 10 January 1952, at Caernarvon, Wales …' The other, inserted by her former colleagues in Pimms department store, was for the hostess, Deirdre Sutton.

It would be several years before Aer Lingus designated another flight as EI-AFL. And up to the time of writing this chapter, no other Aer Lingus aircraft had been given the fleet name *St Kevin*.

But, as in all air disasters, though the names and faces of the victims recede from the public mind, they remain in the minds and hearts of those who knew and loved them. When I started researching this chapter I asked Anna France who, as chief hostess, was responsible for the training of hostesses in the early 1950s, if she remembered Deirdre Sutton. 'Remember her,' she said. 'I pray for her every night.'

CHAPTER 6

'Charlie Foxtrot' and the Fall of a Hero

IN the more leisurely days of piston-engined airliners, when airlines tended to be smaller and more personal than now, the pilot corps of practically every airline invariably included at least one hero – one outstanding airman who, by virtue of experience, skill and force of character, came to be regarded as the natural pack leader.

In the BOAC of the 1950s, it was the fastidious and demanding Captain O. P. Jones, the corporation's senior pilot on the Atlantic. In KLM, the mantle fell on Commodore Adriaan Viruly, who had achieved fame as an aviation writer as well as being a famous pioneering pilot on the Atlantic and West Indies routes and whose flying career would end tragically on the mudflats of the Shannon Eestuary. Pan American had Captain John Mattis, whom the airline used as the focus of a brilliant 1950s advertising campaign illustrated by Norman Rockwell.

The man who filled this role in the Aer Lingus of 1950 was Captain T. J. 'Tommy' Hanley, a former chief flying instructor of the Irish army air corps and the first air corps officer to join the newly-founded national airline. His airline career was soon interrupted by the outbreak of the Second World War and, after a couple of months, he returned to the colours to head an ill-equipped squadron charged with Atlantic reconnaissance and based at the Co. Clare townland of Rineanna, which would become known to the world as Shannon Airport.

As an air corps officer, Hanley was admired and respected by all ranks. His prowess as a sportsman – he had played in an All-Ireland football final for his native Mayo and he was an Irish squash champion – was only surpassed by his prowess in the air. As one of the air corps' top acrobatic pilots, he thrilled thousands at air shows every summer.

Captain Tommy McKeown, a brother officer from the Atlantic reconnaissance days who went on to become a Boeing 747 pilot with Aer Lingus, recalls the wartime days in Rineanna. 'Tommy Hanley was idolised by younger pilots like myself not only for his masterly acrobatic skills, but because of his fine intelligence and his tremendous leadership abilities.

'In all my years of flying, I have never met a more meticulous, a more serious or a more responsible pilot. Every acrobatic manoeuvre was planned in minute detail, over and over again. Every contingency was provided for, every possible flaw worked on.

'T.J. was obsessed with detail and a stickler for discipline. He saw to it that anyone who was flying with him in the morning kept out of the pub the night before. As far as flying was concerned, there could be no bending of the rules.'

The Aer Lingus to which Tommy Hanley returned in 1945 was, like the country itself, in the economic doldrums. The hostilities had all but closed the tiny airline. As the war ended, the Aer Lingus fleet consisted of one Douglas DC-3 D (in camouflage livery and with its passenger windows blacked out) and two wood and canvas DH86s. The DC-3 (EI-ACA) had been used on the airline's sole wartime 'international' service between Dublin and Liverpool. It was written off after a crash landing following an engine fire at Shannon Airport on 18 June 1946.

But there were prospects. Seán Lemass, Ireland's dynamic minister for industry and commerce, was aviation minded and had already been convinced that Aer Lingus should tap into the goodwill and commercial spin off from the Irish diaspora by operating an Atlantic service. The geographic position of Ireland as the last land mass before the long and arduous east–west crossing of the Atlantic had resulted in frenetic activity in the southwest of the country where a sea-plane base had been established at Foynes in the mouth of the Shannon estuary. Later, the land base at Rineanna, eight miles across the estuary, was opened with grass runways and became a base for the air corps. Ireland may have missed the industrial revolution, but there was a fierce determination to succeed in this new and sophisticated world of aviation.

Overcoming the prejudices and difficulties that stood in the way wasn't easy. The first general manager of Aer Lingus, Dr J. F. Dempsey, told me in an interview shortly before his death: 'What was being said at the time of our foundation was: "How the devil are the Irish going to run an airline?" Everything was against us – scientific education in the country had been run down; we were a nation with an appalling record for punctuality and application. And these, of course, were the very attributes that were vital to the task we were taking on.

'We had to overcome an appalling sense of apathy, cynicism even, born of a lack of confidence in ourselves; there was a feeling that air transport was alright for the high and the mighty, the imperial nations like Britain, France and Holland, but somehow, not for us ... Because of what they had been through, Irish people lacked that basic confidence in themselves and by the 1930s they had become sceptical and nervous.'

Scepticism, nervousness and a lack of confidence were attributes that found no place in the make-up of the young Tommy Hanley. He was born in the Co. Mayo village of Foxford on 11 April 1906, a mere three years after the Wrights had made the first sustained and controlled flights in a powered aeroplane and seven months before Alberto Santos-Dumont made the first public aeroplane flight in Europe.

A child of above average intelligence, he was carefully tutored by his parents, both of them teachers. In school he was fiercely nationalistic, carefully obliterating the word 'British' so that the title of his poetry primer read *Selected ... Poetry*. When he finished his secondary school course he went down to Dublin to study medicine at the Royal College of Surgeons in Ireland. But the premature death of his father ruled out a protracted and expensive medical course and the young medical student had to abandon his ambition to become a doctor. He sought and obtained a cadetship in the Irish army air corps.

Almost two decades later, in September 1947, Hanley was one of the captains who delivered the fleet of five Lockheed L-49 Constellations for the Irish airline's new Atlantic service. Most of the captains on the Constellation fleet were English. The serious frictions between the 'British' and 'Irish' sides that made up the board, management and pilot corps of the airline would play a major part in Hanley's future. He was the airline's best known and most respected pilot but his flying career would soon be terminated, suddenly, savagely and – many people still insist – unjustly.

Since 1946, when the minister for industry and commerce, Sean Lemass, negotiated an air transport agreement with Britain, forty per cent of the shareholding of Aer Lingus had been in the hands of the two British air companies, BEA and BOAC. Three of the seven Aer Lingus directors were nominated by the two British airlines. This arrangement enabled Aer Lingus and BEA to operate a cartel on all the cross channel routes.

It also attracted to the Irish airline a sizeable number of British management personnel and pilots, the most notable of whom was the late Captain J. C. Kelly-Rogers. Although Irish by birth, 'Jack' Kelly-Rogers had for most of his working life been a pillar of the British aviation establishment. He was a distinguished flying boat commander who had done valuable pioneering work in the area of in-flight refuelling. He had also flown Prime Minister Winston Churchill on hazardous and historic wartime flights across the Atlantic. The pilot and the prime minister, who had physical and psychological attributes in common, established an immediate rapport.

But the intensely formal and quintessentially British style which Kelly-Rogers and other British trained managers attempted to impose on the Aer Lingus pilots and general staff, were not always suited to the Irish temperament and often created serious tensions and problems. The British pilots – especially those who had come from the RAF – were, almost inevitably, more experienced than their Irish colleagues. The Irish pilots, though well trained and often highly talented, didn't have the same scope and opportunity within the tiny Irish air corps to put up the large number of hours required for the senior commercial licences.

There were wild men and prima donnas on both sides and the management had much difficulty in ensuring discipline. The Irish pilots complained of what they saw as excessive, British inspired formality. The sombre naval style uniform of navy blue and gold braid pioneered by BOAC was successfully introduced. But the pilots rebelled at the suggestion that they should formally salute members of the management when they encountered them within the airport boundaries. A direction that the pilots submit to psychological testing was met with the reply from the newly founded Irish Airline Pilots' Association (IALPA) that they would have no objections, provided all members of management submitted to similar testing. The offer was not taken up.

T. J. Hanley, captain first class, former chief flying instructor of the Irish army air corps and president of IALPA, was one of those who felt uncomfortable about the British presence and the British influence on the running of the airline. Intensely nationalistic, acutely aware of his superior talents as a pilot and with many years of distinguished service as an officer in the defence forces behind him, he was not readily impressed by ideas and procedures, many of which he regarded as suspect.

As president of the infant IALPA he had led an acrimonious strike by the pilots because of the refusal of the civil service to sanction a pension scheme in Aer Lingus. It is for these reasons that many of his contemporaries, and many younger pilots who never met him, still believe that he was scapegoated: the victim of savage and unyielding officialdom.

When Hanley's DC-3, EI-ACF, fleet name St Kieran, suffered a total power failure and crash-landed in a field at Spernall Ash, fourteen and a half miles from Birmingham Airport on New Year's Day 1953, the pilot was immediately hailed as a hero.

The DC-3 which Hanley was flying from Dublin to Birmingham had been delivered to Aer Lingus on 24 February 1946. In 1950, most of the Aer Lingus fleet comprised war surplus C47s, but 'Charlie Foxtrot' had been built as a passenger airliner by Douglas at Santa Monica, California. It was powered by two Pratt and Whitney Twin Wasp R-1830 engines, each of 1,250hp. At the time of the crash, 'Charlie Foxtrot' had logged 10,968 hours and thirty-five minutes flying time.

The aircraft was at 5,000 feet and in cloud when the tone of the starboard engine changed suddenly. Seconds later, and without further warning, it cut out completely and the aircraft lurched to starboard. Within ten seconds the port engine had failed in the same way, and the DC-3 with twenty-two passengers, a crew of three and a terrier in the baggage hold had been turned into a silent, cumbersome glider. Captain Hanley had been in several such scrapes before, but never in a passenger aircraft with twenty-four other lives in his hands. Coaxing a crippled airplane out of the sky was nothing new to him. As a young air corps pilot he had put his powerless fighter into a rocky field in his native Mayo and walked away from it.

In the eerie silence, and surrounded by cloud, his obsession with studying charts and his intimate knowledge of the terrain around Birmingham Airport would help save him. Even though he might be using IFR (Instrument Flight Rules), Hanley never took off without an intensive study of the route over which he would fly. He was, his daughter Patricia recalls, obsessed with charts. It was routine for him to spend up to an hour on the evening before a flight studying the charts of the terrain over which he would be flying the following day.

The site of the crash of Alitalia DC-6B in 1960.

All photographs © Irish Examiner

The KLM Super Constellation L-101049E, fleet name *Triton*, which crashed
into the Shannon mudflats in 1954.

Rescue services bringing ashore bodies from the crashed *Triton*.

Retrieving *Triton* wreckage from the mudflats at Shannon.

President Airlines DC-6B, fleetname *Theodore Roosevelt*, which crashed into the Shannon estuary just minutes after take-off in 1961.

Combing through the wreckage of the *Theodore Roosevelt* in 1961.

Some of the remains of the *Star of Cairo*, the TWA Constellation which crashed on Inishmacnaughton island in 1946.

Inside the cabin of the *Star of Cairo*.

Now, even though he could not see the ground, he had a mental picture of the power lines and other obstructions between him and the airport. He turned the DC-3 away from them and, in the words of the official inquiry 'demonstrated that he had chosen one of the few places – if not the only one apart from the airport – where he could hope to land with any degree of safety'.

Deprived of all power, he eased the DC-3's nose down and sought to maintain an airspeed of 90 knots – the minimum airspeed that would ensure the aircraft didn't stall and fall out of the sky. At 600 feet they broke through the cloud. To the left of him Captain Hanley saw a wood on a small hill. To the right were three small fields with trees and rising ground beyond. He aimed for the first of the three fields.

Hostess Philomena McCluskey, aged twenty-two, was sealing the tiny bar in the galley of the DC-3 when the starboard engine quit. A native of Claudy, Co. Derry, she had started as a hostess the previous April and all her flying had been in this type of aircraft. Like several of her colleagues, she had trained as a nurse.

As Miss McCluskey made her way to the cockpit to find out what was happening, most of the passengers were unaware of any trouble. It was precisely 11 a.m. and they had been in the air since 9.36 a.m. The captain had opted for a slightly longer routing than usual in order to save his passengers from the discomfort of flying through heavy cloud in the unpressurised DC-3.

But at least one of the twenty-two passengers was acutely aware of their difficulties. Roy Hudson, a Warwickshire man married to an Irishwoman, had over 100 hours flying experience in single-engined aircraft. He detected the change in engine sound before the first engine failed and thought it was a power reduction in preparation for landing. But when the aircraft lurched he knew instinctively that an engine had failed.

When the hostess entered the cockpit both pilots were deeply immersed in managing the emergency. After a brief look, the hostess decided not to bother them and returned to the cabin. She told the passengers to fasten their seat belts and made her way to the cockpit again.

At around 11.01 a.m., First Officer P. J. Whyte, a thirty-year-old Clareman from Miltown Malbay, with 2,668 hours flying experience, radioed Birmingham Approach with the message: 'Emergency – both engines giving trouble, may I commence immediate descent.'

Birmingham approved an immediate descent to 2,500 feet. At 11.05 a.m. the Birmingham controller anxiously requested the aircraft's altitude and Whyte replied: '"Charlie Foxtrot" now at 2,000 feet – will call you overhead.'

Captain Hanley's primary objective was to maintain sufficient airspeed so that the aircraft wouldn't stall. As well as this, he had to concentrate on trying to restart the engines and find a spot for an emergency landing.

The pilots' initial response to the engine failures was to treat the emergency as a case of carburettor icing. Neither thought of fuel starvation as the cause of the trouble. After the second engine cut, the booster pumps were switched on and this resulted in an immediate though erratic recovery of power, described as 'four surges' over a period of about thirty seconds.

When the first engine lost power, F. O. Whyte applied carburettor hot air. As the engine temperature reached over 50°C, he started to reduce it by moving the controls forward to the 'Cold' position. When the engine cut, the captain called for carburettor alcohol, which the first officer duly applied. Neither pilot felt he had any time in which to brief the hostess and, indeed, the co-pilot claimed at the inquiry that in her efforts to find out about the extent of the emergency the hostess had distracted him from carrying out a procedure which might have restarted one of the engines.

The hostess asked First Officer Whyte what was wrong. He didn't reply. She repeated the question and he replied: 'It's all right, go back to the cabin.' Captain Hanley – normally a most courteous man who never raised his voice – now shouted: 'Emergency – get out of the cockpit and into your seat.'

When Philomena McCluskey re-entered the passenger cabin there was no doubt in anyone's mind but that they were at grave peril. Children frightened by the spluttering of the engines and the eerie silence that followed started to cry. The adults, aware that something terrible was going to happen, sat petrified. The twenty-two-year-old hostess braced herself against the bulkhead between the cockpit and the cabin and demonstrated to the passengers how they should position themselves for a crash landing. Having finished the briefing, she suggested they should pray.

In his aisle seat at the front of the cabin, Roy Hudson felt a compelling urge to unstrap himself and rush to the back of the airplane where the hostess had taken his wife so that she could feed their infant son. Then, through the small, partly misted window he saw treetops and a hedge. Suddenly, the starboard wing dipped, and then rose again.

From the left hand seat in the cockpit Captain Hanley could see the first of the three fields looming. His undercarriage and flaps were retracted. With the airspeed down to 80 knots, he pulled back on the control column, raising the nose and inducing a slow, gradual stall which would bring the aircraft in contact with the ground.

There was a loud, grating bump as the DC-3's underbelly hit. As the aircraft careered across the field, Hanley saw a large tree looming directly in his path. He skilfully put on sufficient right rudder to send the aircraft skidding through a gap, across a road, and into the next field. In the skid that followed this manoeuvre, the tail of the St Kieran hit a tree and broke off. After what seemed to the terrified passengers as an eternity, what was left of the DC-3 came to a halt with its nose in a ditch. Along the trail of terror it had shed its port wing.

In the cabin, Roy Hudson had braced himself for the crash and thought of his wife and children. At the first impact he was thrown back in his seat, then as the aircraft skidded, the bolts holding his seat snapped and, still in the seat, he was thrown into the aisle. Now on his back, and still strapped to the seat, Mr Hudson saw a large hole form in the fuselage over his head. He undid the seat belt, righted himself and rushed to the back of the aircraft where he found his family unharmed and still strapped in their seats.

The pilots crawled from their seats. Captain Hanley, bleeding heavily from the head, face and hands, immediately took charge of the evacuation. Deeply shocked and in excruciating pain, First Officer Whyte was found stumbling across the field. A car appeared on the road and the driver urged him to get in and be taken to hospital. Whyte refused and insisted on going back into the aircraft in case passengers were trapped.

Having ensured that all passengers had been evacuated, the hostess went back into the rear of the aircraft, removed the small bar and set it up on the field where she administered welcome toddies of brandy to shocked passengers. By this time Sergeant John Thomas of the Warwickshire constabulary had arrived and presented himself to the captain. He told the subsequent inquiry that Hanley's first words to him were: 'It would happen to me on the first day of the year. But, thank God, no one has been killed.'

Philomena McCluskey slipped quietly back to Dublin and never flew as a hostess again. P. J. Whyte was detained in hospital in Stratford on Avon where he was treated for internal injuries and later discharged. After he had returned to Dublin it was found that his x-rays had been misread and that several vertebrae had been crushed. His flying career had also come to an end.

Captain Hanley came home to a hero's welcome. Passengers wrote to him to thank him for saving their lives. Miss Leticia Bowlby praised him for his marvellous skill. 'That we all of us are alive and none the worse except for bruises and some slight shock is, I feel all due to that skill,' she wrote. Miss Eleanor Morris said: 'I hope the next time I board an Aer Lingus flight for Dublin that it will be piloted by Captain Hanley.'

As the newspapers praised his brilliant airmanship, and his undisputed courage, Dublin corporation and Dun Laoghaire borough council passed motions of congratulations. There were moves to have him made a freeman of the city of Dublin. Colonel James Fitzmaurice, co-pilot on the historic first east–west crossing of the Atlantic and one of the most respected aviators of the day, issued a statement praising Hanley's superb airmanship and declaring that his skill and coolness had averted a major catastrophe.

What Colonel Fitzmaurice, the city councillors and the journalists didn't know, was that the airline and the official Irish investigators had already come to the conclusion that Captain Hanley had made a fundamental error in his fuel management procedures – an error so basic that a student pilot undergoing the flight test for the private pilot's licence test would be automatically failed for making it. And in the Kildare Street headquarters of the department of industry and commerce where a brilliant, iron-willed martinet named John Leydon had the final say in the licensing of pilots, the knives were already being sharpened.

Nearly half a century later, Captain Hanley's daughter, Patricia, recalled how during the internal Aer Lingus inquiry, Aer Lingus would not give their father the documents from the inquiry but allowed him to take them home each night after the day's hearing so that he could comment on them. 'We sent him to bed to be fresh for the morning and we sat up writing. My sisters, my mother, our friends, who called to the house, they all did a stint copying so that he would have a complete copy.' Forty-nine years later she still had the handwritten pages.

When the official court of inquiry placed the ultimate blame on Captain Hanley – a judgement he and many of his colleagues never accepted – John Leydon ordered that his airline transport pilot's licence be revoked and recommended that he be summarily dismissed from Aer Lingus. R. W. O'Sullivan, the department's chief aeronautical officer for many years and a contemporary of Leydon, says in his memoirs that Leydon quoted the archaic marine procedure whereby a captain was supposed to go down with his ship or else be dismissed with ignominy. 'It was only with great difficulty,' O'Sullivan wrote, 'that the secretary was persuaded that no such tradition existed in civil aviation and it was with great reluctance that he agreed only to limit the captain's licence to the transport of cargo.'

Even with this concession, the penalty was savage. According to Mr O'Sullivan, it was expected that the limitation was to have been relaxed after a few months, but Leydon resisted every attempt to restore Hanley's licence. As long as he remained head of the department of industry and commerce, he saw to it that Tommy Hanley never flew passengers again.

As there were then very few all-cargo airlines in the world – and certainly none in Ireland – Hanley's options were few. He received an ultimatum from Aer Lingus to resign with an *ex gratia* payment of one year's salary or to be sacked with no payment at all. He working as a dispatcher for the Belgian airline, SABENA, at Shannon for a few years and then emigrated to Honolulu where he got a ground job at the airport. He was forty-seven and, as his four teenage children were still at school in Dublin, he decided it was best to leave his family behind. To a devoted father who doted over his children who, in turn, adored him, it must have been a savage blow.

The court of inquiry that indirectly condemned Captain Hanley to a life of exile thousands of miles from home, was presided over by Thomas Teevan, SC, who in a few months would be appointed attorney general in the government of Eamon de Valera and, later, a judge of the high court. Mr Teevan, who had nothing to do with the penalty, regarded it as excessively harsh, Five years before his death in 1976 he revealed in a letter to Captain Hanley's family that he had made several efforts to have their father's licence restored – all without success.

But Mr Justice Teevan went to his grave believing that the findings of the tribunal were accurate; that Captain Hanley had suffered an aberration which resulted in the two engines of the Dakota being fed from the one tank until it eventually went dry. That view continued to be the official one in Aer Lingus and among others who believed that here was the classic case of a highly experienced pilot making an error so fundamental and so inexplicable that psychologically he could never bring himself to face up to it.

But so deplorable were the industrial relations in Aer Lingus at the time that practically every pilot who knew him and served with him insisted that he had been set up. Tommy Hanley, they claim, was another victim of officialdom's long tradition of finding a scapegoat fast – and, preferably, one who has been sitting in the left hand seat in the cockpit.

The inquiry – the first public inquiry into an air crash in the history of the state – opened at the Four Courts, Dublin, on Tuesday, 20 May 1953. Aer Lingus was represented by the forceful and acerbic, Mr George Murnaghan, SC, a high-profile barrister much associated with major criminal trials who was soon to be promoted to the bench. As Mr Justice Murnaghan he would earn a footnote in the history of Irish criminology by passing the last death sentence which was actually carried out in Ireland. (Years later, long after capital punishment had been abolished, Judge Murnaghan declared himself to be fully in favour of it.)

The fact that Aer Lingus had briefed a barrister with a reputation chiefly as a criminal lawyer was immediately seized upon by the pilots loyal to Captain Hanley and by a large section of the IALPA. This, they argued, was further proof that the airline was vindictively pursuing their pilot as though he were guilty of a criminal act.

The court of inquiry held eleven public sessions and examined thirty-seven witnesses. Its findings, issued on 9 June 1953 were devastating as far as Captain Hanley and First Officer Whyte were concerned.

The assessors stated unequivocally that 'the primary cause of the accident was the loss of power of both engines due to fuel starvation resulting from the inadvertent mis-selection of the port fuel selector.'

An even more damning indictment was to follow. 'Notwithstanding this,' the assessors wrote, 'the accident, in the circumstances, could have been avoided and was ultimately due to the failure by both pilots to diagnose the reason for the loss of power and to take proper remedial action …

'The captain was solely responsible for the initial error of inadvertently selecting the port fuel selector to the right main fuel tank prior to take-off. This error led to, but need not have resulted in the accident. Both pilots were equally responsible for the failure to observe a disparity of contents in the fuel tanks en route. This contributed to the accident.'

The inquiry also noted 'a failure by the captain to observe the company's regulation (prescribed in the Pilots' Handling Notes) for the use of carburettor hot air'. It criticised both pilots for failure to systematically check the instruments to ascertain the loss of power and for setting the pitch of the propellers to 'fine' which, they said, 'increased unnecessarily the rate of descent and could have endangered the aircraft had the engines picked up.'

Captain Hanley's defence was a complete rebuttal of the claim that he had mismanaged the fuel supply by wrongly selecting the fuel selector valves in such a way that both engines were running throughout the flight on the same tank, leaving the other main tank and the auxiliary tank full of fuel. He claimed under oath that he had correctly moved the selector on the port side to the left main tank and that he had made a fuel contents check at Wallesey, which indicated to him that the fuel consumption was normal.

The evidence for the prosecution was substantial. Calculations based on the actual conditions of the flight and the time from departure to when the first engine failed showed a fuel consumption of 115 gallons. This was the precise amount of fuel contained in the starboard (right hand) tank. The tank itself was empty when found, but as it had been badly holed on impact it could not have been otherwise. The other main tank, in the port wing, was largely undamaged but the fuel cock had been ruptured and by the time rescue workers arrived fuel was pouring from it.

Several rescuers said in evidence that they had seen petrol flowing from beneath the centre of the airplane. The main police witness, Sergeant Thomas, said he had seen and smelled petrol under the starboard wing. But the court concluded that the flow was from the left tank through the open drain cock and that, if this tank had been selected, there was sufficient fuel in it to continue the flight.

Mr Murnaghan, in his final address, was untypically apologetic. Aer Lingus, he said, had made their submission with some reluctance. 'But the company,' he added, 'realises that their first duty was for the safety of their passengers, and they must maintain the confidence of the public in their operations.

'I can understand how Captain Hanley, with his long experience as a pilot could not now believe he was capable of making such a mistake. But we are all human, and I have to suggest that Captain Hanley, despite what he now thinks, did make a mistake on this occasion.'

Captain Hanley's case was that the engines failed not because both were being fed from a single tank which had run dry, but because the fuel had been contaminated with water.

Mr Murnaghan made much of the fact that Captain Hanley had already claimed that each engine was feeding from a separate tank. 'Doesn't that necessarily mean that there was water in both tanks?' he asked. Captain Hanley agreed.

'And do you also put forward the theory that the water in both tanks reached the carburettors at the psychological moment?'

'Yes,' replied Captain Hanley, 'within an interval of five, six or seven seconds'.

He said he knew of a similar case in Zurich in 1946 and there was the strange case of another Aer Lingus DC-3, commanded by Captain Aidan Quigley, in Liverpool, where both engines cut out as the aircraft was being taxied to the runway for take-off.

The Liverpool incident had occurred two months prior to the crash of the St Kieran and, because sabotage had been suspected, it was investigated by Liverpool CID. One of the main conclusions of this report was that: 'As previously indicated from the results of tests carried out by Aer Lingus on one of their "Dakota" aircraft, it is not unreasonable to suppose that the aircraft EI-ACL could have flown from Éire to the United Kingdom with as much as three or three and a half pints of water in either main fuel tank (six or seven pints in all).'

Yet on Monday, 1 June 1953, a Shell executive told the inquiry that no petrol belonging to Irish Shell Ltd had ever, in his seven years' experience at Dublin Airport, been found to contain water.

Not only was the Liverpool CID report not considered by the St Kieran inquiry, but the court was told that it didn't exist. Yet it bears the date 5 March 1953, meaning it was written at least six weeks before the Hanley inquiry began.

The Liverpool police report eventually found its way into the hands of the Taoiseach, Éamon de Valera, who handed it to Mr Teevan – now his attorney general – and asked him to consider whether it justified reopening the inquiry. Mr Teevan summoned the two assessors resident in Ireland and, having jointly considered the report, came to the conclusion that it would not have led to any different conclusion.

In a letter to Captain Hanley's daughter, Patricia, who for many years has fought to clear her father's name, Mr Justice Teevan wrote: 'Now that I have read the report again, I regret that I must repeat that it could not justify the re-opening of the enquiry.'

The letter, dated 17 November 1972, continued: 'That is not to say that it would not have been relevant: it would have been both relevant and important. Without some such evidence, I personally would have thought that ALL water in petrol would collect immediately at the bottom of the tank or receptacle. The Liverpool police enquiry and experimentation demonstrated that indeed water may be held in suspension in petrol for long periods before precipitation by sufficient turbulence of the engines.

'This evidence establishes no more than the possibility of water being carried quite a long time in petrol before becoming effectively contaminative. It does not prove that the cause of the engine failure in your father's aeroplane.

'I have always felt that your father was too harshly treated. He had to concentrate on bringing down his aircraft and passengers as safely as possible without any power, in most difficult terrain and in difficult weather conditions … In fact, he achieved this with remarkable success, but in the punishment meted out to him he gets no credit for this.

'I think I may feel free to disclose now that I personally tried to have your father's licence restored: at least I interceded for him but (to my regret) unsuccessfully … I can assure you that my sympathies have been with your father and I therefore regret that there is nothing I can do to ease his misfortune …'

Another unusual feature of the Hanley case was the resignation of Eric Brereton, an inspector in the aeronautical section of the department of industry and commerce. Mr Brereton was convinced that the crash was not caused by fuel mismanagement and resigned because of the treatment of the two pilots. Until his death some years ago, he remained convinced that Captain Hanley and First Officer Whyte had been wrongly blamed.

On 16 February 1974 the *Irish Times* published an article by Geraldine Kennedy, then a features writer and later the paper's editor. This revealed the contents of the Liverpool police report on the DC-3 that suffered double engine failure at Speke Airport, Liverpool, previous to Captain Hanley's crash. The report recommended: '… that instructions be given immediately to Aer Lingus for water tests to be carried out on all aircraft under their control or supervision.'

In 1975, when Tommy Hanley was living in retirement in Sligo, the IALPA, headed by its president, Captain P. V. Donoghue made a fresh submission to the minister for transport and power, Gene Fitzgerald, claiming that a miscarriage of justice had taken place and that, even at this late stage, the inquiry should be reopened.

The main point of the submission was that the 'water in fuel' problem which, contrary to what had been suggested to the inquiry, was then a serious problem at Dublin Airport, had not been properly investigated by the inquiry. The committee of four senior pilots who drew up the submission made much of the fact that despite the denials by Aer Lingus and Irish Shell of water contamination hazards at Dublin Airport, more stringent precautions against water hazard were introduced by both companies after the accident.

The pilots further claimed that vital evidence from eyewitnesses at the scene, which was capable of refuting the fuel mismanagement theory, had not been called. They said that following their examination of all the evidence now available, 'a number of irregularities showed up in the method of investigation and relevant evidence of other incidents of water in the fuel of other aircraft at Dublin Airport'. They also claimed that the most important evidence to support the water-in-fuel theory – a Liverpool police report dated 5 March 1953 which the court of inquiry said did not exist – was not considered and that references to water in fuel were deleted from the verbatim report of the inquiry, thus preventing the court from coming to a just conclusion.

The submission made to the minister for transport and power, Peter Barry, was supported by a separate technical appraisal of the case carried out on behalf of IALPA by Eric Brereton.

Brereton told the *Irish Times* in 1977 that he considered it 'one hundred per cent certain that it (the cause of the accident) was not fuel mismanagement'. He said the evidence obtainable from the sketch of the accident, plus the evidence of eyewitnesses not called, indicated the engines were operating under power when the aircraft touched down.

The inquiry was not re-opened, but on 3 August 1977, the minister for transport and power, Padraig Faulkner, wrote to IALPA saying it had been decided to restore Captain Hanley's licence 'unconditionally'.

Captain Tommy Hanley died aged eighty-five in 1992. His family continued to campaign for the re-opening of the inquiry. In 2000, his daughters, Patricia, Aoife and Nuala applied to the minister for public enterprise, Mary O'Rourke, for an independent review of the case similar to that conducted into the crash of the *St Phelim* off Tuskar Rock. Mrs O'Rourke agreed to appoint Mr Patrick Keane, SC, to carry out the investigation with the assistance of two assessors. Their brief was to examine whether there was any new evidence that was not available to the original inquiry which might have led it to reach a different conclusion.

The results of the Keane inquiry were published in April 2003. To the grave disappointment of Captain Hanley's family it found that it had been reasonable for the 1953 inquiry team to conclude, as a matter of probability, that fuel mismanagement had been the cause of the accident.

While acknowledging the 'heroic achievement' of the pilots in landing the aircraft in difficult terrain without loss of life and accepting that there were flaws in the original investigation and its transcript it found that no new evidence had emerged to suggest that pilot error was not the probable cause of the crash.

And so, as far as officialdom was concerned, ended the saga of Captain Tommy Hanley and 'Charlie Foxtrot'.

The Hanley family have vowed to continue the fight and to explore further legal options to vindicate their late father's name and reputation.

The punishment meted out to Captain Hanley soured relations between Irish airline pilots and the accident investigation authorities to a huge degree and caused long-term damage to the accident investigation progress. Many experts now believe that the punishment was not only savage but illegal; that there was no clear provision for reducing rather than withdrawing his licence; and that the entire case did not meet the requirements of natural justice.

Throughout his years of exile, Tommy Hanley never gave up flying. His licence still allowed him to fly privately and, during his many trips home he would drive out to Weston Aerodrome in North Kildare and borrow a light aircraft from the owner of the airfield, his friend and former Aer Lingus colleague, Captain 'Darby' Kennedy.

Almost invariably, he would head westwards, across the Bog of Allen and the Shannon lakes over terrain that he had known intimately as a young pilot and where some of his best acrobatic performances were perfected. Then homewards again, skirting the Atlantic seaboard that he had patrolled as an air corps officer, and landing within sight of his old military base in Baldonnell.

What his thoughts might have been on on these occasions no one will ever know. T. J. Hanley was the kind of man who kept his thoughts to himself. Even his most vociferous enemies – and, mainly due to his work in IALPA, he had some – had to admit that he bore his misfortune with exemplary fortitude and dignity.

Not that he lacked friends. On the night his airline transport pilot's licence was restored he walked into the officer's mess in Baldonnell to a tumultuous welcome, which surprised him and touched him deeply. Young pilots to whom he might have been a distant and venerable figure took turns in shouldering him around the mess to the sound of 'For he's a jolly good fellow'.

The battered, petrol-soaked wreck of a DC-3 in a Warwickshire ditch must have seemed a long, long way off.

CHAPTER 7

'No Help from Fairyland ...'
The Demise of the Triton

AROUND 5 a.m. on Sunday, 5 September 1954 (All-Ireland Sunday) a team of Aer Lingus baggage handlers loading freight onto an airliner on the ramp at Rineanna (Shannon Airport), saw the figure of a man coming towards them in the semi-darkness from the direction of the ramp that bounds the estuary to the southeasterly side of the airport.

The man was covered in mud. When he started to speak, the voice was high-pitched and excited, the accent foreign. Gesticulating towards the embankment wall, the man shouted: 'There has been a crash out there. Are you doing anything about it?'

To the astonishment of the enquirer, the baggage handlers ignored him and carried on with their work. After a couple of quizzical glances, they decided that their mud-caked interrogator was either a drunk or an eccentric. Neither species was uncommon in the Rineanna of the 1950s where the combination of new-found affluence and opportunity had suddenly implanted a disparate and cosmopolitan community in what had, until recently, been a primitive and isolated corner of Co. Clare.

Incredulous, and in deep shock, the man plodded on until further up the ramp he encountered several members of a Swissair crew disembarking from their aircraft. He repeated his frightening message and, in anticipation of further rebuff, scraped the mud from the top left hand corner of his jacket to reveal the silver wings emblem of a KLM pilot.

Two and a half hours earlier, his airliner – a state-of-the-art Lockheed Super Constellation L-101049E, fleet name *Triton* – had taken off from Shannon towards the southeast from runway 14/32 on the second leg of its flight from Amsterdam to New York. The flight lasted less than forty seconds. Having crossed the embankment wall at a height of around 140 feet, the Super Constellation ploughed into the mudflats. Within half an hour twenty-five people were dead – asphyxiated by petrol fumes seeping through the cabin. Three others would die subsequently – two by drowning, the third from injuries received during the impact.

Although Shannon's air traffic controllers suspected the flight could have been in trouble within minutes of its take-off, no rescue attempt was made until 4.15 a.m. – three-quarters of an hour before one of the pilots, Second Officer Evert Webbink, having waded through the treacherous mudflats, clambered over the embankment wall and headed for the terminal buildings. The incredible series of blunders, miscalculations and administrative deficiencies had begun.

By 1954, KLM was well established as one of the great airlines of the world. The Dutch had been early into aviation. A young Dutchman named Anthony Fokker from the town of Haarlem had built his first aeroplane factory in 1913 – a mere ten years after the first sustained and controlled flight by the Wright brothers at Kitty Hawk. Fokker had established his business over the border in Germany where he built some of the most lethal early fighters of the Luftwaffe. With the collapse of Germany in the First World War, he cunningly diverted some of his plant and equipment back to neutral Holland.

One of his early associates was a former Royal Netherlands air corps pilot named Albert Plesman, a visionary and entrepreneur who recognised the great future that awaited the infant aviation industry. On 7 October 1919, Plesman registered a private company named Koninklijke Luchtvaart Maatschappij (KLM Royal

Dutch Airlines) and, on 19 May 1920, the airline flew its first service – from Amsterdam to London.

Plesman became the great father figure of KLM and remained in control until May 1954 – a few months before the Super Constellation *Triton* set out from Schipol on the fateful journey that would end in the Shannon mudflats. Building on the country's great tradition of ocean navigation, and insisting on the highest technical and flying standards, Plesman extended the KLM network beyond Europe into the Dutch West Indies. By the early 1930s, he had come to recognise the supremacy of the US built Douglas transports and, in 1932, KLM became the first European airline to introduce the legendary DC-3. In October 1934, this aircraft won the London to Melbourne air race for KLM.

The Second World War, when Holland was occupied by the Germans, had disastrous consequences for KLM. Most of its aircraft were either destroyed or seized and Schipol Airport had its buildings bombed and its runways cratered. But a limited KLM fleet was operated from outside the country. Plesman was first imprisoned, then exiled.

By 1954, KLM had been rebuilt and was once again a major force in world aviation. That year they carried almost one million passengers and had a turnover of about $77 million. The route network was now truly international and the North Atlantic services linking Holland with the great American cities of the east coast were already regarded as routine.

KLM had inaugurated its Amsterdam–New York service on 25 February 1945 with a C-54, the military version of the DC-4 Skymaster. At around the same time, a series of experimental C-54 flights were made over the South Atlantic under the command of one of KLM's most famous pilots, Captain Adriaan Viruly. It was Captain Viruly, now commodore of the North Atlantic fleet, who was rostered to take command of the Super Constellation *Triton* for its Amsterdam–New York crossing on the fateful evening of 4 September 1954.

Flight 633 was KLM's trice-weekly Amsterdam–New York service. This evening it had a crew of ten, with forty-two passengers. Four more passengers would join at Shannon. It was due to depart from Schipol in the early evening but a mechanical check had shown up a fault in the hydraulic brake valves and caused a substantial delay.

As he boarded the sleek blue and silver Super Constellation that evening, Captain Viruly looked a distinguished figure. Aged forty-nine, he had come to KLM from the Royal Dutch air force. Tall, blonde and slim, with searching blue eyes, in his dark blue uniform with four silver stripes on each sleeve, he looked every inch the urbane and confident international airline captain.

Unlike many of the senior airline captains of that time, Captain Viruly was neither a bully nor pretentious. In the words of a member of his crew that fateful evening: 'He was a kindly and a nice man. Unfortunately, as subsequent events were to prove and despite his reputation, he was not a great pilot.'

Employed by KLM since 1931, he had a total of 18,884 flying hours and held the most senior pilot's licence available, the airline transport pilot's licence, endorsed for the Lockheed Constellation, the Super Constellation, the DC-3, DC-4 and Convair 240. This was to be his eighty-eighth Atlantic crossing.

Not only was Captain Viruly a distinguished airline captain, he was widely known throughout the Netherlands as a writer of aviation books, both fiction and non-fiction. He had just completed his tenth book, which was due for publication that Christmas. He was married to a famous Dutch actress, the beautiful Mary Dresshuys.

For Adriaan Viruly, life must have seemed very sweet as he boarded his Super Constellation that mild autumn evening for the two hours and twenty minutes sector to Shannon.

It was to be his last flight as a pilot. Although Captain Viruly survived the crash and acted gallantly and courageously in the rescue of his passengers, his career as an airline pilot ended early the next morning in the Shannon mud. He severed all links with the aviation world, both as a pilot and an author.

There were two captains on the flight deck of the *Triton* that evening. Viruly's co-pilot, thirty-one-year-old Edward Parfitt, had been with KLM since 1949 and was a captain in his own right. The endorsements on his airline transport pilot's licence allowed him to fly as pilot-in-command of two twin-engined airliners, the DC-3 and the Convair 240. Here, on the four-engined Super Constellation, he was on his thirty-ninth Atlantic crossing as a co-pilot and could reasonably be expected to take command of one of the new Super Constellations in a relatively short time.

Parfitt was English, a native of Bristol. KLM had an international pilot corps made up of many nationalities. With the exception of the stewardess, Helga Lowenstein (who was stateless and a survivor of the Nazi concentration camps) the nine other crew members of the *Triton* were Dutch. Three of them – stewards Williem van Burenam and Robert Westergaard, along with Miss Lowenstein, were to perish.

Although some members of the crew knew each other by sight, and all knew Captain Viruly because of his formidable reputation in the airline, none of the ten had flown together before. Had Captain Parfitt, who was acting as co-pilot, previously flown with Captain Viruly, it is possible that the accident would not have happened.

The Super Constellation PH-LKY, serial number 4509, was only thirteen months old, the eighth of twenty-two Super Constellations delivered to KLM between 1953 and 1958. It was the leading aircraft for comfort and safety and had a typical unit price of $1.25 million – a huge sum for the time. It had been designed to fly the Atlantic between New York and most points in western Europe non-stop. In practice, however, none of the series was really a non-stop Atlantic aircraft (certainly not westbound) and it wasn't until 1957 – when the jet age was only weeks away – that the final version, the 1649A, achieved this capability.

Heavy headwinds on the night of 4–5 September dictated that the *Triton* would not only make its scheduled stop at Shannon, where it was to pick up four passengers, but would also stop at Goose Bay, Labrador in Canada.

The flight from Amsterdam was flown at an altitude of around 12,000 feet. Save for the failure of the aircraft's VHF transmitter on final approach to Shannon, the flight was uneventful. The weather conditions at Shannon were near perfect. A broken cloud existed at 8,000 feet and the horizontal visibility was twenty-five miles. Because of the wind direction, Captain Viruly was advised by air traffic control to land on the shorter of the two major runways, runway 14/32, which was 5,643 feet long.

The airport in which the *Triton* touched down was very different from the sophisticated and cosmopolitan Schipol, KLM's home base. The land base was established in the Co. Clare townland of Rineanna ('point of the marshes'), on the River Shannon estuary, midway between Ennis, the county town, and Limerick, the Republic's third city. Throughout the Second World War an air corps reconnaissance squadron was based there. The squadron leader, Captain T. J. Hanley, who later became an Aer Lingus captain, was now working at Shannon as an aircraft dispatcher and had been involved in the paperwork connected with the flight of the *Triton* on its fatal flight. The previous year he had lost his airline transport passenger licence after one of the most controversial crashes in the history of Irish aviation.

The land base had flourished during the era of the first generation long-range airliners such as the DC-4 and Lockheed 049 Constellation. The severely limited range of these aircraft, combined with the notorious prevailing headwinds on the east–west crossing, ensured that this unique airfield nestling on the edge of the Atlantic had a steady stream of aircraft availing of the opportunity to top up with fuel before attempting the long and arduous Atlantic crossing.

Although the original runways were of grass, by 1954 Shannon had four hard-surfaced runways, the main one (05/23) was 7,027 feet long. The runway used by the *Triton* on its last landing and take-off was 14/32, a 5,643 strip, one end of which was close to the embankment which forms the east/southeast boundary of the airport. This boundary takes the form of a dyke which is seventeen feet above mean sea level and fourteen feet above airport level. The Shannon's tidal waters extend to the base of this embankment and at low tide there is an extensive area of mudflats through which run many gullies and creeks. The airport was at that time serviced by: a low frequency radio range; an instrument landing system (ILS); ground control approach; control tower; and oceanic area control unit.

Despite its isolated setting, Shannon was technically well equipped according to the standards of the day and enjoyed a good reputation for safety and technical services. It offered considerable passenger comforts in the form of a good restaurant and in-flight catering service and a world-famous duty free shop. A number of wooden chalets known as the passenger hostels provided comfortable, if rather cramped, overnight accommodation for delayed passengers.

While their Super Constellation was being refuelled and having a new VHF transmitter fitted, the forty-two transit passengers and crew relaxed in the comfortable passenger lounge or inspected the range of high quality Irish and international goods in the duty free shop. The four passengers who were joining – all Irish-Americans – were checked in by Aer Lingus, KLM's handling agents, and escorted through immigration to the transit area.

Unknown to most of the passengers, a little drama was being played out. One US passenger, who had failed to get a first-class seat because the first-class cabin was full, was so vocal in making his displeasure known to ground staff that a Dutch passenger who overheard him offered to give up his first-class seat in the interest of good PR for his national airline.

Within a couple of hours all the first-class passengers, including the American who so badly wanted to avoid flying tourist class, would be dead. His benefactor, along with all but one of the tourist-class passengers, would escape.

At last, shortly before 2 a.m, came the departure announcement. At 2.30 a.m. precisely, Captain Viruly opened the four throttles slightly and started to taxi away from the terminal area. At the threshold of the 5,643 foot long active runway he pointed the nose of the big Super Constellation into the slight breeze and applied the brakes.

Now came the final procedures before committing the *Triton* to take-off. The captain ran up each of the four engines to its near maximum rpms, applied carburettor heat and monitored the fall in power to ensure it was within limits. As each engine was revved up, the passengers could see a long tongue of purplish flame trailing into the airflow from the exhaust pipes. Many passengers found this disconcerting, but it was normal for these large piston engines, especially at take-off when the rich fuel mixture and high power setting caused the flames to have a bright purple glow. Cabin crews always ensured that nervous passengers were made aware of these facts about the engine performance.

At 2.37 a.m. Captain Viruly and his co-pilot Captain Parfitt each checked for 'full and free movement of the controls', the final check before starting the take-off roll. Each pilot in turn manipulated the control column and rudder pedals to their maximum extremity thereby ensuring that the ailerons and elevators (hinged surfaces on the wings and the tailplane that control climb, descent and turning) were unimpeded. Now, in keeping with the procedures of the time, the flight engineer closed a pair of curtains that separated the two pilots from the other members of the cockpit crew. This was a routine procedure in night flights as the flight engineers needed to have their control panel brightly lit and the bright lights were likely to confuse the pilots.

At 2.38 a.m. Captain Viruly called for take-off power. Sitting at his control panel behind the co-pilot's seat, Flight Engineer

Hendrick Rademaker scrutinised the engine instruments carefully, alert for any sudden drop in oil pressure or evidence of any loss of power.

On the other side of the flight deck sat Second Officer Evert Webbink, who was navigating, and close to him Radio Officer H. E. Outshoorn. Second Flight Engineer Cornelius J. Kievits sat in a jump-seat directly in front of the door leading to the main cabin of the aircraft, and a third pilot, J. M. Tieman sat in the crew compartment which included three bunks directly behind the cockpit.

The passenger area of the 126 feet 2 inches (38.47 metres) Super Constellation was divided into three sections known as the forward, main and aft cabins. The rear or aft cabin was designated for first-class passengers and here Flight Stewardess Helga Lowenstein checked that the passengers were securely belted into their seats and that no one was having a surreptitious smoke. In the other cabins, her colleagues, Flight Stewards Robert Westergaard and William Van Burenam, performed a similar task. In due course Captain Viruly was informed that all forty-six passengers were ready for take-off.

As the four engines reached take-off power and their exhaust trails became longer and brighter, Captain Viruly held the Constellation on the brakes. He was operating from a slightly shorter runway than usual and wanted to make maximum use of the thrust available to him. Take-off power could be used for only two and a half minutes before reducing to METO power (climbing power).

At 2.38 a.m. Captain Viruly released the brakes and the *Triton*, its all-up weight (plane, passengers, crew, baggage and cargo) now standing at 131,930 lbs, surged forward to disaster.

In the left hand seat Captain Viruly was looking straight down the runway, his hands on the control column, his feet ready to make any necessary adjustments with the rudder pedals so that the airliner maintained a straight course along the centre line of the runway.

In the right hand seat Captain Parfitt watched for the ASI (airspeed indicator) to activate as the aircraft accelerated. As soon as it showed a speed of 120 knots he would call out 'V1' – the signal that the moment had arrived when a decision to abort or take-off must be made.

At this moment Captain Viruly sensed what he believed was a change in engine noise from the starboard side of the aircraft. He looked towards his co-pilot, but it was obvious from his expression that he sensed nothing amiss. Captain Viruly put the thought out of his mind. He eased back the control column. The nose-wheel lifted off and the take-off had begun.

The captain wasn't the only one to notice something odd as the *Triton* started to lift off. In the customs hall, looking directly on to the airfield, a young customs officer, Tom Kearney, just back from his honeymoon and starting a term of night duty, had been watching the aircraft since it left the apron.

Mr Kearney had no special knowledge of aircraft apart from an interest born of his three and a half years working at Rineanna. But his attention was attracted by what he thought was unusual noise and jets of flame which he thought were longer and brighter than usual. Turning to his colleague, John Fisher, Kearney said: 'I wouldn't like to be a passenger on that plane.' Curiosities aroused, both men walked out on to the ramp to follow the progress of the take-off.

As the airspeed reached 125 knots, Captain Viruly gave the order: 'Gear up.' From the right-hand seat, Captain Parfitt activated the hydraulic system that pulled the massive tricycle undercarriage into its three bays.

At 140 knots, Captain Viruly called for a reduction in power from take-off power to METO power. At 150 knots the captain ordered: 'Flaps up.'

At 160 knots he ordered the second power reduction calling: 'Climb power.' On the ground, the two customs officers watched as the Super Constellation strained to clear the embankment.

Then after a few seconds of what appeared to be a slightly steeper climb, Kearney thought he saw the aircraft veer to the right as it disappeared behind the fire station. He waited a few seconds for it to reappear. When it failed to do so, he said to his colleague: 'My God, they're going in.'

On the flight deck both pilots still believed the Super Constellation was climbing. It was, in fact, steadily heading towards the dark Shannon mudflats.

It was only after he had given the final command for climb power that Captain Viruly sensed something terrible was happening. Almost immediately there was a violent shudder followed by a swing to the right and a series of heavy bumps. As the aircraft struck the mudflat, Captain Viruly was knocked unconscious.

The *Triton*'s final flight had lasted a mere thirty-nine seconds. The airliner had travelled only 8,170 feet from the end of the runway from which it had taken off. Help was less than two miles away. Unbelievably, it would take almost four hours to reach them.

Within minutes of the take-off the airport authorities had two separate indications that the *Triton* was in trouble. Tom Kearney, the customs officer who believed it had crashed after crossing the embankment, immediately contacted the airport security services and made his fears known. His message was received with no great degree of alarm as such fears were often expressed by untrained observers.

If the airliner had crashed so close to the runway, it was argued, the control officer in the tower would undoubtedly have seen it. A distress signal would have been sent after the take-off. Besides, the take-off had been observed by a fire officer acting according to regulations and he had seen nothing unusual.

Even so, the fire and rescue station immediately set up a check, beaming out a searchlight from the balcony over the estuary. A white light was noticed, flashing low on the waterline at a point where no permanent light was sited. The light was so small that it was not thought to have anything to do with an aircraft. The belief was that it was a small boat which could have got lost on the river. It was, of course, a member of the *Triton* crew desperately trying to signal with a flashlight.

At 2.39 a.m. – less than a minute after the *Triton*'s lift-off – the control officer in the tower called the aircraft and, in accordance with normal practice, passed on the take-off time. There was no acknowledgement.

After two or three attempts to contact the aircraft, the control officer asked the separate area control centre to try and make contact on their frequencies. This also failed, and ground control approach were asked to watch out for the aircraft on radar. At 2.48 a.m., the *Triton* was due over the Kilkee fan marker, its first scheduled reporting point. As no contact was made, the air traffic controller phoned the area control officer to discuss the matter. Just as they started speaking they got news that the aircraft had been located on the radar screen.

The blip on the screen was outbound twenty-three and a half miles west. It was the news everyone wanted to hear. All were satisfied it was the *Triton*.

It wasn't. The 'blip' on the radar was a 'ghost echo'. The Super Constellation was already ditched in the Shannon mud with twenty-five of its passengers and three cabin crew dying of asphyxiation due to deadly petrol fumes.

Almost simultaneously, yet another erroneous report came in which helped convince the controller that the radar sighting was accurate. The pilot of a TWA Constellation who had been asked to listen out for any radio communications reported that he had heard another KLM aircraft which was approaching the Irish coast in contact with the *Triton*. This too was false. Shortly afterwards the KLM captain confirmed that while he had been trying to establish contact with the other aircraft, he had not succeeded.

Down on the mudflats, Captain Viruly and those of his crew who were still alive were striving valiantly to get the survivors into a dinghy to protect them from the rising Shannon waters.

No one had been prepared for the impact. The crew thought the aircraft was on a steady climb when, in the words of a survivor, it shook like a dog coming out of water. Captain Viruly looking out into the blackness said: 'Good heavens – what's happening?' Behind him, Radio Officer Outshoorn said to himself: 'This is the end.' Flight Engineer Hendrick Rademaker, fearful of a fire, pulled the main switch and cut the electrical power, plunging the flight deck and the three cabins into darkness. The screams of terrified passengers mixed with the grating of fractured metal.

Sitting in his jump-seat behind the door leading to the crew compartment, Second Flight Engineer Cornelius J. Kievits found himself being thrown forward towards the four throttles.

In the slide over the mud, one engine and its mounting was torn from the main spar. A second was partially dislodged. On impact, the fuselage fractured just in front of the main wing beam close to the seat occupied by New Yorker, Caroline Platz, who was travelling alone and was destined to be the last victim of the *Triton* crash. She received horrific multiple injuries from which she died the following day.

As the noise and the screams subsided, passengers heard the calm voice of stewardess Helga Lowenstein comforting her passengers. A New York surgeon, Ernest Bettman, who was seated near the emergency exit said later: 'In the darkness I could hear people screaming and praying. Everyone was knee deep in muddy water and although I couldn't see the air hostess, I could hear her trying to encourage despairing passengers.'

At that moment, Helga Lowenstein and her two male colleagues had only minutes of life left.

As the fuselage fractured, one of the seven fuel tanks ruptured. Gallons of high octane fuel poured out and were carried by the water flowing freely through the cabin. As the petrol rose to the top giving off lethal fumes and causing savage skin burns it proved to be a river of death. Within minutes twenty-three passengers and the cabin crew of three would be dead of asphyxiation.

The Constellation's emergency lighting system had failed as the batteries were under water. The emergency radio set from which an SOS could be sent was in a cupboard which had been damaged by the impact. And flares could not be used as they might ignite the petrol fumes.

As a torchlight beam passed over the face of the passenger beside her, New York advertising agency executive, Elizabeth Snyder, noticed a cigarette in the man's mouth and saw that he was about to strike a match. Miss Snyder, an amateur pilot, snatched the matches out of his hands. Had he succeeded in striking the match, it is likely that petrol vapours would have ignited, turning the *Triton* into a massive firebomb.

The petrol fumes in the main cabin were now so overpowering that Captain Viruly and his colleagues could only remain there for a few seconds before seeking fresh air. Two dinghies had been inflated and when eleven survivors had been boarded on the first, the captain ordered the first officer, accompanied by the two flight engineers, to take charge of it and make for shore. Twelve more survivors, including the second and third pilots, had boarded the no. 2 dinghy. The captain, satisfied that those remaining in the cabin were already dead, boarded the dinghy.

As the fumes rose in the first class cabin, the stewards and stewardess had attempted to open the main rear door. Unfortunately for them and for the twenty-five passengers who died with them, they either forgot that the emergency mechanism for opening the doors of the L1049 version of the Constellation was different to that of the older 049s with which they were far more familiar, or they became confused. One of the pilots had difficulty in opening the forward entrance door until he remembered that it was necessary to depress a device in order to unlock the handle.

A passenger who watched the cabin crew attempting to open the rear door told the official enquiry: 'The stewardess said to us that we should keep quiet and everything is all right. Then they were hammering on the door to open it. They were pushing with their shoulders against it and that is the last I heard.'

As the tide carried the first dinghy away from the wreck, shouts were heard coming from the tail of the area. In the darkness, Captain Viruly could see that two men had climbed on to the tailplane and were clinging to the rudders. He attempted to get the dingy back to them but the tide and wind made it impossible.

Hours later, as a consequence of an outrageous and still controversial piece of bungling, one of these men, a thirty-six year old American physician, Dr William G. Duller slid exhausted into the water and was drowned just as help had at last arrived.

The other survivor from the tailplane, David Ellis, a lecturer at the University of Maryland, gave a graphic account of their five hour ordeal. 'We sat there on the tail clinging to the rudders with the muddy water swirling around us. It was bitterly cold. My companion spoke for hours about his wife and children and how lucky he was to have survived.

'At first we just waited to be rescued. Then we consoled ourselves by waiting for dawn to break. We could see the lights of the control tower and the lights of the airport, like a fairyland in front of us. But no help came from fairyland …

'Daylight came and we could see trucks moving around the airport periphery. Time passed and my companion fell silent. The water seemed to be rising up against us and we had difficulty holding on.

'Through a haze I saw a launch approach. As I did so I looked towards my American friend. As I did so he slipped. He flung out his hands to get support but the current was too strong and swept him away. I saw only his look of despair. He didn't shout or cry out. I was numb with cold and fear and unable to help him …'

The drowning of Dr Duller was not only a tragedy but a scandal. The prospect of a disaster on the mudflats – which lay at the end of the two principal runways – was always a possibility and there was provision for a rescue operation on this difficult terrain. Two rescue vehicles called 'weasels', capable of travelling over the mud and slime were based at the airport. The sole rescue launch was based at Foynes eight miles and up to ninety minutes travelling time across the estuary.

On that morning, the coxswain of the launch was telephoned at 4.37 a.m. and told to muster the crew. At 5.13 a.m. he phoned the Shannon control tower to say the coxswain and crew were proceeding to the launch. At 5.30 a.m. the launch cast off from the pier at Foynes for a journey that could take up to ninety minutes.

As they left the pier the launch crew did not know the precise location of the wreck. This was to have been given to them by radio as they proceeded across the estuary.

The crew immediately attempted to reach the control tower on the designated frequency – 3032.5 kcs. They failed to make contact because, unbelievably, the control tower receiver was 'off tune'. The coxswain turned back to Foynes in order to make contact by ordinary telephone, thus adding to the already scandalous delay. Even more unbelievably, the official inquiry glossed over the incident and stated 'it was not considered necessary for the court to investigate fully the reason for the receiver being off-tune ...'

To do so might have unearthed a sensational fact which would have resurrected the severe criticism of the rescue services that surfaced at the time of the crash. The inquiry was told that a few months before, the head of air traffic control services had warned that the radio used for communicating with the rescue launch had been left off tune. The memo spoke of 'unauthorised use' of the radio. It had, in fact, been used for obtaining English football results from the BBC.

The veteran Shannon Airport reporter, Arthur Quinlan, who covered every disaster at the airport since 1947, describes the handling of the press during the *Triton* crash as 'utterly deplorable – the worst ever'.

'The civil servants were instructed not to speak to the Press and the KLM authorities adopted the attitude of trying to pretend the crash just hadn't happened,' Quinlan says. 'They indulged in every form of obstructionist tactics and tried to stifle every jot of information.

'Their technique was the exact opposite to that of Pan Am who, in the case of an accident, put every fact on the table at once in the belief that the quicker the facts got out the quicker the whole sorry business would fade from the front pages.'

The newly-appointed head of KLM, the formidable Lieutenant General Izakk Alder arrived in Shannon two days after the crash and publicly complained of what he described as 'the serious delay' in organising the rescue services. The Dutch press had already been highly critical of the Shannon authorities. The department of industry and commerce (which at the time had responsibility for civil aviation) continued with its wall of silence policy and a series of wild rumours which had begun to circulate in Shannon since the crash began to find their way into the newspapers.

The civil servants now changed tack and through the simple expedient of throwing the reporters a bone by way of unattributable, off-the-record briefings turned the situation round. Concurrently with these briefings, the government information bureau issued a statement pointing to the regulation throughout the civil service which prohibited 'unlawful disclosures'. The civil servants at Shannon, the statement said, had not been authorised to make statements about the crash 'because the circumstances connected with the crash are to be investigated at a formal public inquiry and the matter is therefore, sub judice'.

The hypocrisy of this stance may be seen from a report in the *Irish Times* of Thursday, 8 September headed 'Alarm quickly raised at airport'. 'While Shannon Airport was being criticised over the circumstances of the recent highly-publicised KLM crash,' it began, 'it is now known that the real picture was very different.' Quoting 'an airport technician' and 'a control tower expert' it said: 'It was disclosed for the first time yesterday, in an entirely unofficial way, that shipping, weather stations and Prestwick Airport were alerted twelve minutes after the take-off.'

Then, in a blatant distortion of what actually happened, the 'officer' was quoted as saying: 'I can say positively that there is no record in the log of anyone having informed the fire tower that the airliner was in difficulties immediately after the take-off.'

There may not have been a record in the log, but as the evidence at the subsequent inquiry was to show, the fire crew had indeed been informed of Mr Kearney's suspicion that the airliner had gone down. A senior member of the force acted upon that information, but failed to recognise the significance of the strange light he saw on the estuary and failed to pass the information to the control tower.

The inquiry, headed by Mr Justice Thomas Teevan of the high court and assisted by four technical assessors, opened in the King's Inns, Dublin, on 29 November 1954. It held a total of twenty-eight sessions.

The former chief aeronautical officer of the department of industry and commerce, R. W. O'Sullivan, who headed the investigation into the *Triton* crash, wrote in his memoirs that 'the outcome of the inquiry was nothing like so adverse to us as I had thought possible. There were, however, certain consequential internal "adjustments" made in the staffing arrangements of the air traffic control service at Shannon which were all to the good.'

The court acknowledged that 'a grave error of judgement' had been made by the ground control radar officer in positively identifying a 'blip' which had only remained on his screen for ten seconds as the missing *Triton*.

Noting that the tower control officer was operating alone during the take-off, the court found that while his failure to observe the aircraft for a longer period after its take-off, when he might have noticed it descend, was unfortunate 'he cannot be blamed for ceasing to watch it when he did'. This was because, owing to the layout of the control desk, the officer had been forced to turn around to reach a microphone to advise the area control downstairs of the time the aircraft became airborne and then to write that time in his own log. Following the crash an assistant to the controller was allocated to the tower for all further operations.

Dealing with the failure of the fire and rescue service to pass on the observations of the customs officer, Mr Kearney, to the control tower, the court recommended that it should be the normal practice to pass on all such reports. 'The recognition of the air traffic control tower as the nerve centre of the airport through his knowledge of minute to minute aircraft movements should be impressed on all airport personnel,' they wrote.

The court accepted the evidence of the technical experts that the *Triton* crashed because its undercarriage had failed to lock up and possibly came down again after the flaps had been raised. This caused a catastrophic lack of 'lift' and the aircraft simply hadn't enough power to continue its climb.

Inevitably, the captain had to bear the responsibility. The court found that Captain Viruly 'had failed properly to co-relate and interpret his instrument indications during flap retraction, resulting in the necessary action not being taken.

'This failure was partly accounted for by the effect on instrument indications of inadvertent and unexpected landing gear re-extension.'

During the take-off, Viruly had been concentrating almost exclusively on maintaining airspeed and failed to pay sufficient attention to vital altimeter readings.

Flight Engineer Kievits, who survived and went on to fly with KLM for a further thirty-two years clocking up a total of 21,217 flying hours, remembers the Shannon crash as vividly as if it were yesterday.

'When you see people die like that you never forget it … It was a great tragedy, principally for those who died and for their families. It was also a tragedy for Captain Viruly who was a decent man, even if he was shown to have had limitations as a pilot.

'Although it was never mentioned by the court of inquiry, within the airline there was some criticism of the junior captain sitting in the right hand seat. Some people said that he should have realised that Viruly wasn't up to it in these particular circumstances and that he should have taken over.

'This, of course, is the age-old question of the co-pilot overruling the captain. It is very easy to make such criticisms but, at the time, people like Adriaan Viruly were gods within their airlines.

'Suppose Parfitt had forcibly taken over and the accident had been avoided – would he have succeeded in explaining his action? There were only the two of them there and my own view is that he would have had a very hard job in having his word accepted against that of the famous captain in the left land seat who was already something of an aviation legend in the Netherlands.'

After the inquiry, Captain Viruly immediately resigned from KLM, thus ending a long and illustrious career in Dutch aviation. He also ceased to write about aviation. He died, aged eighty-nine, in 1994.

In retrospect, one of the most puzzling aspects of the inquiry was the failure to investigate fully the reason for the tower receiver being 'off tune'. The unfortunate Dr Duller, who clung valiantly to the rudder until his strength finally failed, would almost certainly have lived were it not for the fact that vital minutes had been lost when the rescue launch had to return to Foynes to make telephone contact after failing to get through on the radio-telephone.

In 1954, Ireland was still a young player in the world's most sophisticated industry and the sensitivities of the age were acute. Facing the fact that on a previous occasion the tower radio had been used for getting the football results, and the headlines that such a revelation would produce, was more than officialdom could bear.

Only one happy story came out of the crash of the *Triton*. During the official enquiry, several members of the crew stayed at the Russell Hotel in Dublin. As the weeks dragged on, the *Triton*'s second flight engineer, Cornelius Kievits, persuaded one of the hotel receptionists, Kathleen Dowling from Tullaroan, Co.

Kilkenny, to go to the cinema. In due course they were married. Forty-three years after the tragedy on the Shannon mudflats, they live in happy retirement in Amstelveen, near Amsterdam.

CHAPTER 8

The Theodore Roosevelt: the Death of an Airline

AT 2.49 a.m. on Sunday, 10 September 1961, Captain Edward Tonnesen, commander of President Airline's flight 773 to Chicago, via Gander and New York, lined up his Douglas DC-6B, fleet name *Theodore Roosevelt*, on Shannon's 10,000 foot main runway to begin his second crossing of the Atlantic in fifteen hours. It was his fortieth birthday.

Tonnesen was a controversial figure in a small peripheral carrier which was already in deep financial difficulties. He had landed the DC-6B at Shannon at 12.40 p.m. the previous afternoon after a flight of ten hours and twenty-seven minutes from New York (six hours of it through the night and all without benefit of autopilot). In the interval, he had a rest break of eight hours in the Old Ground Hotel, Ennis, fourteen miles from the airport; the US federal aviation administration specified rest breaks of sixteen hours for President Airline's pilots. Another crew had taken over the aircraft, flown it to Dusseldorf and returned it to Shannon with a new load of passengers.

At the time of the *Theodore Roosevelt*'s departure from Shannon, weather conditions were bad. An incoming aircraft, having descended to 300 feet on an instrument approach, had pulled up and diverted to Prestwick. The weather forecast for the time of take-off was: wind variable – visibility 330 yards in fog with clear sky. Company regulations required a ceiling of 300 feet and visibility of one mile. While he was taxiing, Tonnesen asked the controller to increase the brilliance of the high intensity lights on the runway.

The *Theodore Roosevelt* was six years old. It was one of fifty DC-6s ordered by American Airlines and was built by Douglas as DC-6B N90773 (maker's serial number 44085). It was delivered to American Airlines on 7 May 1953, with the fleet name *Flagship Delaware*. Seven months later, its fleet name was changed to *Flagship Phoenix*. Having served on America's domestic network for over six years it was sold to a brokerage company which disposed of it to Los Angeles Air Service Inc. On 1 December 1959, this company became Trans International Airlines and, on 18 July 1960, N90773 was leased to President Airlines and given the fleet name *Theodore Roosevelt*.

By any standards, the DC-6 was a great airliner. Its forerunner, the Douglas DC-4/C-54 Skymaster had played a huge role in military transport in the Second World War and, along with the Lockheed L-49 Constellation, was one of the great pioneering long-range civil airliners on long-distance routes. One of the chief attractions of the military C-54 version of the DC-4 was its outstanding safety record on these long ocean crossings. Of nearly 80,000 wartime ocean crossings of the Pacific and Atlantic oceans, only three aircraft were lost.

Unlike its predecessor, the DC-6 had a pressurised cabin which enabled it to fly at much higher altitudes, thus avoiding the turbulent conditions often found below 10,000 feet. The DC-6B was the third development of the type which provided standard airline seating capacity of fifty-four, although high-density layouts of up to 102 passengers were not unknown. The DC-6Bs were powered by four 1865-kW (2,500hp) Pratt and Whitney R-2800-CB17 Double Wasp radial piston engines. They had a cruising speed of 507 km/hr (315 mph) with a service ceiling of 7,620 metres (25,000 feet) and a range with maximum payload of 3,005 miles.

The seventy-seven passengers on the *Theodore Roosevelt* were made up of German farmers and agriculturalists bound for a two-week educational tour of farms and agricultural plants in the American mid-west. They touched down at Shannon at 8.47 p.m. after an uneventful flight of two hours and thirty-eight minutes from Dusseldorf. They now faced a delay of six hours at Shannon while Captain Tonnesen and his crew of five completed their rest period.

Delays were part of the territory with President Airlines and by their standards, one of six hours was minor. An irate cardiologist from Hartford, Connecticut, who had taken his family on a trip to Lebanon on this same aircraft two months previously, had written to the director of the federal aviation administration, Najeeb Halaby, complaining of a nine hour delay on the outbound charter and a thirty-six hour delay on the return. The pilots, he wrote, seemed to be overworked; the stewardesses were inefficient; and there was no water on the aircraft.

Also delayed at Shannon on that fateful night of 9–10 September 1961, was the second of President's three aircraft, another DC-6B, chartered by students of Cornell University, New York. Already delayed for twenty-four hours in Paris, the aircraft then developed engine trouble on the way to Shannon and landed with one of its four engines shut down. The students spent three days at Shannon while a spare engine was flown in and on the evening of 9 September they were told that their departure was imminent.

During their delay at Shannon, the Cornell students had been hearing stories and rumours about President Airlines. They were told that the airline's credit facilities had been withdrawn and that everything now had to be paid for in cash. One of them, a young engineering physics undergraduate named Ron Poggi, had spent the summer in Germany. Later, as a fifty-seven-year-old computer programmer living in Warren, New Jersey, he recalled those three dramatic days in the autumn of 1961:

'It had been a great summer for me. After completing my junior year at Cornell I had a bit of a row with my family and got work with a firm in Hanover. It was my first trip to Europe. When I turned up for the return flight from Le Bourget, Paris, I was told we were to be delayed for a day, but President kindly put me up in a hotel for the night.

'During the take-off the next day someone across the aisle from me told the stewardess that he had heard a loud 'ping' in one of the starboard engines. He was told not to worry as the pilot knew what he was doing. Later I learned that the engine had blown a piston and had to be feathered.

'One of the stewardesses was a very attractive and very cordial young lady of German descent … This was back in the days before cockpit doors were locked during the flight. I can still remember the pilot joking about wondering what Shannon looked like as he had never seen it before.

'So we spent three days at Shannon, sleeping on the floor in the passenger lounge and dropping in and out of Limerick to the pubs and to the cinema. I remember seeing *The Guns of Navarone*.

'When the German farmers arrived on the second President aircraft I talked to several of them in the duty free shop as I had become fairly fluent in German and they were a friendly group. I learned that our attractive cordial stewardess was swapping with another from their flight as she had an uncle on the Chicago charter and wanted to be with him. I remember feeling a bit annoyed at this and the fact that the farmers' flight would be taking off before ours.'

Poggi's friend and fellow student, David Lifton, was returning after a magical summer in Europe and Israel during which he had bought a Volkswagen Beetle at the factory in Wolfesburg, arrived in Berlin just days after the wall had gone up and drove on to Venice and Rome before taking a student charter to Israel. Then, after several weeks in Paris, he joined the President charter for home.

The farmers spent their six hour delay sitting in the lounge. eating in Shannon's celebrated restaurant and browsing in its famous duty free shop. One of them, strolling around the concourse in front of the terminal building came across the life-sized statue of the Blessed Virgin that still stands there. A devout roman catholic, he was much impressed. Back inside the terminal he bought a postcard featuring the statue and posted it to his family with a message saying he had offered a prayer for them in Ireland.

Captain Tonnesen had checked in at the Old Ground Hotel in Ennis at 3.30 p.m. on the previous afternoon and left for the airport at 11.30 p.m. Upon arrival at Shannon he went to the offices of Seaboard and Western Airlines (handling agents for President), ordered 4,550 gallons of fuel and then went to the restaurant for a meal while his aircraft was being refuelled. In the restaurant, he met the captain of the other President Airlines aircraft who, jokingly, asked him if he had been drinking. Tonnesen replied that he had, but within the legal limits.

Captain Tonnesen had been receiving half hourly reports on the weather and knew that it was not improving. The latest report said there was mist with fog patches. Vertical visibility was down to 150 feet and lateral visibility was at 220 yards. This was below company minima for President Airlines but Tonnesen decided to press on. At 2.52 a.m. air traffic control cleared the *Theodore Roosevelt* for take-off and told Tonnesen to take a right turn out. The captain acknowledged the clearance by advising that he was 'rolling'.

Because of the foggy conditions, no one saw the take-off. But one pilot on the ramp and two others resting in the nearby airport hostels heard the DC-6B get airborne. All thought it sounded normal.

The air traffic controller entered the lift-off time at 02.52 hours. Then, approximately one minute later, he heard the noise of engines which appeared to him to be coming back over the airfield. There was a loud thud followed by silence. The controller immediately declared an emergency by activating the crash siren. Some 7,000 feet away, the *Theodore Roosevelt* had plunged nose first into the Shannon estuary. Its fuselage had broken into two pieces; the nose section disintegrating in the treacherous mud. Most of the eighty-three people on board were already dead or dying. One would survive her horrific injuries for just over two hours.

Back at the airport, Cornell student David Lifton was in the bathroom. 'I was actually sitting on the pot when I heard this frightful thud and the eerie wail of the siren,' he recalls.

Mrs Sarah Donlon, who lived in Rineanna South, close to the main runway, was awakened by what she thought was an unusual take-off noise. She got out of bed to look out and after the aircraft had passed over went back to bed. As she lay down she heard what she described as 'a terrible thud'.

Unlike the KLM crash on these same mudflats seven years previously, when rescuers didn't reach the crash scene until nearly two hours after the event, the rescue operation for the *Theodore Roosevelt* was under way within seconds. After that crash, Shannon's security, fire-fighting and rescue services had been amalgamated. Several members of the security and rescue services lived in the airport hostels for a notional rent of 2/6d a week on the understanding that they would turn out whenever the emergency siren went off. Although there was no 'disaster plan' in place in 1961, an impressive contingent of rescuers and medical personnel was soon assembled and set off in boats down the estuary. Several of the Cornell students, including David Lifton and Ron Poggi, joined them.

They found that the *Theodore Roosevelt* had come to rest in the estuary 5,000 feet to the left of the southwesterly end of runway 24 and 2,400 feet from the foreshore. The wreck was in twenty feet of water. The nose was buried and the left wing had completely disintegrated and separated from the fuselage. The starboard wing had also broken off and had come to rest on the left side of the wreckage path, indicating that the aircraft had continued a left roll after hitting the water. All four engines had separated from their nacelles and one of them would never be found.

Ron Poggi still remembers the eerie scene: 'I was in one of the handful of boats that had cast off and I can still see the tail sticking up from the water in the eerie pre-dawn light. I watched as a bundle wrapped in a blanket was removed and put on one of the boats. Later I learned that it was our beautiful stewardess who had transferred to the flight in order to be with her uncle.

'Coming back from the boat ride we were a sombre crew. Our minds quickly turned to the possibility of confusion as we began to hear broadcasts claiming the victims were students from Princeton. I tried to call home to let my family know I was safe but to no avail. I later learned that my parents and family had been called up and told I was on the fatal flight and were beside themselves.

'Much to my amazement, everyone including myself got on to that other President Airlines charter flight when it was called a few hours later. We just desperately wanted to get away. The experience had a lasting impact on me. I am a private pilot with an instrument rating and I learned a lesson about safety, attitude and life in general from this accident. Cornell learned something too as they never again allowed a charter flight to use their name.'

Within days of the tragedy it was becoming obvious that, even by the standards of the supplemental carriers of the time, President was a peculiar airline. After the cardiologist, Dr Robert M. Jreissaty wrote to complain about his trip to the Lebanon, the FAA director, Najeeb Halaby, replied on 13 October 1961, stating that 'President Airlines have been doing a good job and met our safety standards'.

In the light of documents I have obtained under the US freedom of information act and state papers released in Dublin under the thirty-year rule, it is difficult to understand how Mr Halaby could have been so sanguine. To begin with, President was on the verge of bankruptcy. And, just under a month previously, George G. Prill, the FAA's inspector in Shannon at the time of the crash, had cabled Mr Halaby with the message: 'Present indications are that he crashed while trying to return to the field after engine failure or worse. Wreckage examination badly hampered by incredible mud. Appears possible violation of weather minima ...' Add to this the fact that the commander had only half the required rest period prior to the flight, that the aircraft was 313 lb over the maximum allowable weight and that other members of the crew may also have been suffering fatigue and the picture scarcely adds to a well regulated airline.

FAA documents also show that on 26 November 1960, the licence of a President Airlines captain was withdrawn after violation proceedings. In June 1961 there had been another investigation of President when its other DC-6B flew in a restricted area and failed to conform to control tower instructions. Because of these and other shortcomings and the fact that it was a relatively new supplemental carrier, President Airlines had been investigated by two maintenance inspectors and two electronics inspectors of the FAA to determine whether their certificate of public conveyance should be continued. In a memo to the FAA's chief of operations, the inspectors wrote: 'The operations conducted by President Airlines are considered safe and within the operations limitations as prescribed in the company operations manual. There is no reason to believe that the carrier will not continue to operate safely.'

After the Shannon crash, President was again investigated by the FAA. This time the report read: 'This investigation has shown that President Airlines is in condition to continue operations and action to suspend their certificate is not indicated ... Although several discrepancies were noted, none were regarded of such serious nature by the investigating group as to require certificate suspension ...'

President Airlines was one of many small 'supplemental' carriers which sprung up in the US in the decade following the ending of the Second World War. The availability of lucrative military transportation contracts knows as MATS charters, an increasing amount of civil charter work, and the ready availability of cheap serviceable piston engine airliners, such as the DC-4 and DC-6, created an environment favourable to the establishment of new airlines. Some of them were progressive, well-run outfits which, like Seaboard and Western, Transocean and Flying Tigers, were started by highly experienced military pilots determined to make a name for themselves in civil aviation. Others were under capitalised and under resourced and often skimped on operational requirements, including safety.

President originated in 1949 as a Delaware Corporation with authorised capital of 10,000 shares of common stock with a par value of $10 per share. Operations didn't start until 1960 when a DC-4 was acquired for charter work. Later, another DC-4 was added and these were soon replaced by two DC-6Bs and a DC-7.

At the time of the Shannon crash, President's financial situation was critical. On 27 October, Mr T. Nally of Shannon Airport management wrote to the finance branch of the department of transport and power in Dublin saying he had been informed by the Bank of Ireland, Shannon Airport, that cheques drawn on the airline in respect of landing fees totalling $3,854 had been bounced. A cash payment of $1,215 had been made by a President Airlines captain leaving an unpaid balance of $2,639. 'I should be glad if you would arrange for the matter to have early attention as the sub-agent at Shannon is anxious to have the adjustment made as soon as possible,' he added.

Worse financial news was to come. Frank Thompson, the Limerick undertaker who had embalmed and coffined the eighty-four bodies found that not only could President Airlines not meet his account for $11,315 but he had been required to reimburse the Shannon Airport branch of the Bank of Ireland for a $250 cheque which he had endorsed for a President Airlines executive and which subsequently bounced. Having contacted President he received a telegram which read: 'Have verified balance due to you as negotiated ... Payment forthcoming upon completion of reorganisation audit. Sorry for delay. Will square at earliest opportunity – President Airlines.'

Mr Thompson invoked the assistance of his friend, Donough O'Malley, mayor of Limerick and parliamentary secretary to the minister for finance who, on 27 October 1961, sent a copy of Mr Thompson's letter to Frank Aiken, minister for foreign affairs. 'I should be obliged,' O'Malley wrote, 'if you would have the matter looked into to see if there is any possibility of having the amount due to Mr Thompson recovered.' Through the vice consul in San Franscisco, Michael Drury, the department obtained a sizeable amount of information on the financial status of President Airlines. Drury engaged the services of the Crocker-Anglo National Bank of San Franscisco which, on 11 December 1961, supplied an extensive two-page report. This showed that during the previous September the entire stock of President had been acquired by a Glen H. Taylor who was now secretary-treasurer and sole proprietor of President.

Mr Taylor had had a varied business career. Born in 1929, he had served with the US air force in 1945–46, attended the Pacific Bible Seminary in Long Beach and the Pepperdine College from 1946–50. He operated an airline called Republic Airlines from 1951–52 and for the next four years was engaged in the production of audio-visual educational materials through his company Taylor Enterprises. He owned and operated a general store until 1957. Mr Taylor, the bank reported, was also involved in educational publishing and was the dominant principal of Taylor Building and Development Co. Inc. which was involved in real estate tract development in sSouthern California.

The report added that Mr Taylor had been 'well and favourably known for several years' to the President Airlines bank of account and they were pleased to continue loaning him medium four figure amounts for the financing of particular flights.

The Crocker-National report went on: 'Our banking friends could not divulge financial statement information which is given to them in strict confidence, but from outside sources we learned that as of 30 April 1961, the company had available current assets of $1,206,000, current liabilities of $156,000, and a deficit net worth of $77,000. Operations for the seven months ended on the statement date resulted in a net loss of $120,000. The company's financial difficulties were compounded, naturally, as a result of the September crash at Shannon Air Port and the later stranding of passengers there which received considerable adverse publicity. Therefore, it has been estimated that the company's liabilities at the present time are well in excess of the amount shown in the above statement.'

On 24 March 1962, the secretary of the department wrote to Mr O'Malley stating that the acting pro consul in San Franscisco had reported that Mr Thompson had received a payment of $10,000 on behalf of President Airlines which had reduced his claim to $1,403.

President limped on until February 1962 when an official named Lyle W. Ballard issued a circular to all creditors announcing a temporary suspension of operations because of 'the harassment of a few creditors who have selfishly resorted to entangling legal action rather than providing us with the cooperation required to work out an arrangement to satisfy all creditors – not just a preferred few'. The suspension, Mr Ballard wrote, was not entirely without merit for it would give them time to present their plan for revitalising the airline. According to contemporary reports in the aviation press, Taylor had ambitious plans for buying up a large fleet of ex-Pan American Boeing 337 Stratocruisers and converting them for cargo and charter work. In the event, the fact that President never flew again surprised nobody – least of all the long-suffering creditors.

The inspector of accidents' report on the President Airlines disaster, although painstaking and thorough, was not conclusive. It found that there was 'a strong possibility' that the captain, co-pilot and flight engineer were suffering from fatigue due to long duty periods and short rest periods prior to the flight and in the previous ninety days.

It acknowledged – but didn't attach much significance to the fact – that the take-off was made in conditions below the company minima and that the aircraft was 313 lb over the maximum allowable weight.

More importantly, it found that there was a possibility that the artificial horizon on the captain's side of the flight deck may have been defective and that there was an unexplained failure of the outboard aileron push-pull rod of the starboard aileron, but it had not been possible to determine what contribution this may have made to the uncontrollability of the aircraft as it climbed away from runway 24.

Attributing the cause of the disaster to the failure of the captain to maintain control of the aircraft after take-off because of: (1) defective artificial horizon and/or (2) a fault in the right hand aileron tabs, the inspector added: 'As far as can be determined, the aircraft maintenance may not have been up to industry standards, as evidenced by the condition of the tab-rod assembly and the manner in which the artificial horizon was handled.'

The report failed to satisfy many of the victims' families. Soon rumours began to circulate about a secret document (known as 'Appendix H') which had been prepared by two FAA inspectors and which contained serious allegations against Captain Tonnesen. The existence of 'Appendix H' was acknowledged in the official report of the inspector of accidents but, in accordance with a convention of the international civil aviation authority which allows for witnesses to make statements in secret, it was not published.

On 23 November 1964, the German embassy in Dublin made a formal request to the department of transport and power to provide them with a copy of 'Appendix H' together with permission to release it to 'persons who have a bona fide interest in the matter'. On 15 December 1964, the Irish ambassador in Washington, wrote to the secretary of state informing him of the pressure being brought to bear by the German government in their efforts to obtain a copy of 'Appendix H'. The ambassador wished to be informed whether the appropriate US authorities had any objection.

The reply took over six months, but when it came it was thoroughly decisive. 'The Civil Aeronautics board,' it stated, 'has given careful consideration to the questions in the ambassador's notes and regrets that it cannot, consistent with its statutory responsibilities, the terms of its own regulations and the public interest, consent to the release of Appendix H to private persons.

'It is the United States government policy,' the letter went on, 'that all reports prepared by official United States government accident investigators which contain analysis and opinions shall be withheld from public disclosure.'

Why the secrecy in regard to Appendix H? The documents of which it is formed contain grave and largely unsubstantiated allegations against Captain Tonnesen made to the FAA and CAB inspectors by another President Airlines captain. It was alleged that Captain Tonnesen was a heavy drinker who frequently flouted company regulations in regard to abstaining from alcohol in the hours immediately prior to flying. It also alleged that he was a belligerent and irresponsible pilot with poor flying standards.

Writing to the secretary of the department of foreign affairs on 24 November 1964, R. C. O'Connor explained that Appendix H consisted of statements made by the other President Airlines captain as well as a number of allegations of irregularities by personnel of President Airlines. 'The allegations are expressed in rambling and, in places, rather incoherent language,' he wrote. 'Some of the allegations are trivial, but others would be regarded as very grave … The report is in certain respects inconclusive.'

Many of the allegations are indeed inconclusive and rambling. But some are a matter of public record and indisputable. For example, prior to one of his eastbound crossings of the Atlantic, Captain Tonnesen had been 'rolled' while socialising in Harlem. He reported the loss of $1,000 of company money to a Detective

Keenan at the 123rd precinct. On the morning of his last crossing of the Atlantic, a stewardess who consistently refused to fly with him tried to persuade the flight engineer not to travel. She later insisted that this had nothing to do with Tonnesen's flying abilities but because she had a premonition about him.

In his official report, the inspector of accidents acknowledged the remark about drink made by the second President captain and added that no evidence had been found to suggest that Captain Tonnesen had partaken of alcohol during his stay at Shannon. The autopsy report on Tonnesen gave the alcohol content of the blood samples as 65/70 mg per ml. This would have brought him well within the 1998 driving limit of 100 mg per ml. Added to this is the fact that the test on Captain Tonnesen was done using the 'Kozela and Hine' method which could not distinguish between alcohol ingested and alcohol produced in the body as a consequence of decomposition. It had long been accepted that decomposition produces alcohol and four days had elapsed between Captain Tonnesen's death and the autopsy.

Even so, the inspector of accidents concluded that there was a strong possibility that Captain Tonnesen was suffering from fatigue. 'Coupled with the bad visibility that existed at take-off and the possibility of taking some alcohol, it is possible that his reactions would not be good enough to cope with an emergency,' he wrote. The inspector also found that on the basis of the hours flown leading up to the disaster, First Officer Richard Budenich and Flight Engineer Alvin Krueger, could also be suffering from fatigue.

Edward Tonnesen was born in Evanston, Illinois, in 1921, but grew up in Chicago. Having graduated from Lake Forest College, he attended Wentworth Military Academy and then joined the US air force where he achieved the rank of captain. Demobbed in 1948, he joined Slick Airways in Chicago as a co-pilot and soon had ratings for the DC-2, DC-3 and DC-4. After two years he joined the cargo carrier Seaboard and Western. He resigned from Seaboard in 1955 and for the next two years was self-employed. He resumed his flying career in 1959, flying with various non-scheduled carriers. In September 1959, he joined Overseas National Airways as a co-pilot, remaining only for six months. His next move was to World Airways of Oakland, California. Six months later he resigned from World Airways although it appears that he had no other appointment. On 15 May 1961, he landed a job as a captain with President under a contract which said that his employment 'may be terminated at any time without advance notice and without liability for wages or salary except such wages and salary as may have been earned at the time of such termination'.

The agreement went on: 'I thoroughly understand that the company will not tolerate or be subject to any annoyance or expense because of any action of mine such as bad checks, garnishments, wage assignments, insults, etc. I also agree that any complaints or criticisms I may have towards any crew member or company employee will be submitted to the company in writing.' He named his mother, Mrs Ruth Tonnesen of Costa del Mal, California, with whom his two teenage daughters lived, as the person to be informed in case of accident.

Soon after the crash, his mother told the *Los Angeles Times* that she and her husband, Victor, had driven their son to the President Airlines maintenance base at Burbank to collect the *Theodore Roosevelt* which was undergoing maintenance and which he then flew to New York and subsequently to Shannon. She added that as they parted he said to them that for the first time he hated leaving his two teenagers, Kay, aged sixteen, and Kerry, aged fifteen. The paper carried a photograph of the bewildered teenagers holding a large photograph of their father in his US air force uniform.

The President Airlines crash was at the time the worst disaster concerning a US civil airliner abroad. At the time of writing, it remains the worst air accident in Irish aviation history. In human terms, the suffering it caused was enormous. A high proportion of the victims were enterprising and progressive farmers and agriculturalists at the peak of their careers and with young families. Over 100 children lost a parent.

The autopsy reports revealed horrific injuries. By the time the rescuers arrived, all but one of those on board was dead. The sole survivor, a twenty-six-year-old woman from Griesbach-in-Rottae, was discovered standing up in the muddy waters. As the rescue workers extricated her they found that both her feet had been severed. She was placed in a rescue boat and the airport medical officer, Dr William Flynn, administered morphine. She was given several blood transfusions and the doctors began emergency surgery. Two hours after she had been found she died on the operating table in the airport medical centre.

The beautiful stewardess whom the Cornell student admired on the Paris to Shannon flight and who left the student charter in order to join her uncle on the *Theodore Roosevelt* was twenty-two-year-old Erica Urban, a native of Linz. It was to have been her last flight as a stewardess as she was embarking on a course in hotel management. The second stewardess, Lasia Jackson, was Finnish and was also about to resign in order to marry.

As always, the diplomats and the civil servants fretted over the unwelcome international publicity which Ireland's transatlantic airport was again attracting. On 12 September the Irish ambassador in Stockholm, James A. Belton, reported to his headquarters in Iveagh House that: 'It is disturbing to find that reports in each of the principal Stockholm papers contain a passage in almost identical words saying that Shannon had been the scene of many of the bad crash disasters in recent years and going on to list the crashes which took place in 1954 and 1958 (both KLM) and in 1960 (Alitalia). The secretary at the Bonn embassy sent a bunch of press clippings with the comment: 'It should be noted that despite a few sensational questions in the cheaper type of papers, there has been no adverse comment on the Shannon Airport. In an interview on the local television from Cologne, the manager of the

Dusseldorf Airport praised conditions at Shannon Airport and said, in effect, that it was not conceivable that the accident would have arisen from any fault there.'

He was right. This time the fault lay squarely with a small, dubious and financially troubled airline which, despite all its shortcomings and difficulties, had the support and carried the imprimatur of the licensing authority of the most technologically advanced nation in the world. Seventy-five innocent and unsuspecting passengers had cheerfully submitted their lives and well-being to an airline that clearly didn't deserve such trust. Once again there had been another tragic demonstration of the fatal flaw in having regulatory bodies such as the FAA and the CAB responsible for promoting air travel as well as policing it.

The DC-6Bs had no black box and no cockpit voice recorders. So no one will ever know now what unexplained emergency caused Captain Tonnesen to make a steep left turn soon after taking off in the Shannon fog rather than turning out right as he had been instructed. Was he, as seems likely, making a desperate attempt to return to the airport?

Had the turn continued, the *Theodore Roosevelt* would have lined up with runway 05 which was 7,000 feet long? But runway 05 was in darkness and Tonessen made no request for runway lighting.

Did a combination of pilot fatigue and disorientation aided by a faulty artificial horizon result in the deaths of eighty-four people in the Shannon mud? Or does the secret of the *Theodore Roosevelt* lie in the defective aileron tab push-pull rod which caused the starboard wing to dip immediately after take-off? In his effort to correct, did Tonnesen, depending on faulty instruments, cause a lethal roll to the left?

The President crash soon faded from the headlines. President Airlines rapidly went the way of numerous other supplementals and faded into oblivion. Apart from the Shannon crash, it gets no mention in the numerous histories of US airlines. In his memoirs,

Crosswinds, published in 1978, Najeeb Halaby (the man who, as head of the FAA, assured the irate cardiologist that the airline was safe and doing a good job), makes no mention either of the airline or the crash.

But the name of President Airlines still lives on in the minds of the loved ones of those who died in the fog on the Shannon mudflats on All-Ireland Sunday, 1961.

More than thirty years after the tragedy, an elderly woman got off a flight at Shannon and asked to be taken to the office of the airport manager. In broken English, she told the officer who dealt with her that she was making a pilgrimage which she had planned for many years but which her children had persuaded her against making. Now, she explained, her children had all left home and she was, once again, a free agent.

She produced a faded postcard showing the statue of the Blessed Virgin that stands in the concourse outside the terminal. Her husband, she explained, had posted the card on the night of 10 September 1961, before embarking on President Airline's flight 773 for Chicago. For all those years, she explained, she had desperately wanted to visit the spot where he died and say a prayer for him there.

They drove her to the estuary and left her to her thoughts. After several minutes she thanked them and said that she was now ready to go home.

CHAPTER 9

Flying Tigers

THE Gander–Frankfurt leg of Flying Tiger Line's military air transport service (MATS) charter from McGuire air force base, New Jersey, was just another routine assignment for the commander of the L-1049H Super Constellation N6923C, Captain John D. Murray, from Oyster Bay, New York.

At forty-four, and with 17,500 flying hours to his credit – 4,300 of them in L-1049s – Murray was at the peak of his airline career. His airline transport pilot's certificate rated him to fly six other types of heavy transports as well as single engine privileges in helicopters and seaplanes.

Murray and his crew of three men and four women had arrived in Gander the previous day. The Super Constellation, with its complement of sixty-eight passengers made up of US service personnel and some twenty women and children from their families, arrived from New Jersey in mid afternoon. None of the children was to survive the forthcoming ordeal. Murray met the incoming crew and meticulously reviewed the records of the first sector of the flight. As the aircraft was relatively light, he ordered an additional 3,000 lbs of fuel and had it put in the no. 5 tank. He then studied the weather forecast of the Canadian meteorological service and, confident that all was in order, signed the weight and balance manifest that had been prepared by his co-pilot, Robert Parker.

The pre-flight inspection was done by the flight engineer, James Garrett, and at 5.09 p.m., the Super Constellation, with seventy-six souls on board, took off. Captain Murray was given an instrument clearance to Frankfurt-Rhein Main Airport and was asked to maintain flight level 110, 11,000 feet. The navigator, Samuel T. Nicholson, estimated the flight time to Frankfurt at nine hours and twenty-two minutes.

The first of several routine position reports from 923 'Charlie' came fifty-six minutes after take-off when they reported at 51°00' north latitude, 50°00' west longitude, at flight level 110 (11,000 feet) in cloud and experiencing slight icing. Another position report came forty-five minutes later and a third, at 7.32 p.m., gave their position at 52°50' north latitude and 40°00' west longitude. Three minutes later the flight asked Gander area control centre (ACC) for permission to ascend to 13,000 as their icing problems, though still slight, were continuing. This was granted and, at 7 p.m., Captain Murray reported that he was at flight level 130.

But the icing problem continued and, having reviewed the meteorological forecast folder and discussed the situation with the crew, Murray requested permission to go up to 21,000 feet. At 7.51 p.m. Gander cleared them to climb to flight level 210. At 8.10 p.m. Murray told the centre they were at flight level 210.

They were now three hours and one minute into what was still a normal Atlantic crossing. Despite the moderate icing that they had encountered almost from the start of the flight, Captain Murray's crew had no reason for concern. Flying Tiger Line and its crews were still reeling from a highly publicised double tragedy seven months previously when, on 15 March 1962, two of their Super Constellations crashed in separate accidents with the loss of 108 lives. Nor was the tragedy about to unfold to be the last for Flying Tiger Line in its *annus horribilis* of 1962.

Of the many 'irregular' or 'supplemental' carriers that had their origins in the surplus of men and machines that followed the Second World War, the Flying Tiger Line was one of the most famous and most successful. In the eyes of aviation enthusiasts, it was also one of the most romantic. It was founded as the National Skyway Freight Corporation on 25 June 1945, by veterans of

General Chennault's 'Flying Tigers' who flew C-46s in the far eastern theatre of Burma and China. Unlike many fledgling airlines, Robert Prescott and his fellow veterans had the right mix of cavalier spirit and commercial shrewdness.

The name 'Flying Tiger Line' was adopted in 1946, the year in which Prescott secured his first military contract for twenty-eight flights per week across the Pacific supporting US bases. In 1955, Flying Tiger Line ordered ten Super Constellations with a view to retiring its fleet of DC-4s and DC-6s. In that year the CAB reduced the restrictions on group passenger charters and Flying Tiger Line immediately entered this sector of the business by offering fifty round trips to Europe at $250 less than the IATA fare.

In 1949, Tigers helped transport 35,000 Yemenite Jews from the Arabian desert to the newly founded state of Israel. They participated in the Berlin airlift and, in 1956, transported thousands of Hungarian refugees to the US. The airline and its crews also played a major role in transporting military personnel and civilians to and from Vietnam during the Vietnam War. In 1966, Flying Tiger Liner ordered ten Douglas DC-8-63F jet freighters at a cost of $105 million. Even with turnover of this magnitude, however, the airline failed to survive as a separate entity and was taken over by the Federal Express Corporation in 1989.

The L-1049H Super Constellation being flown by Captain Murray and his crew on that fateful day in September 1962, was four and a half years old. Model 1049H was designed for use as a passenger and/or freighter aircraft. It followed the 1049G major upgrade and was the final production version before the Super Constellation gave way to the Starliner. N6923C was bought directly from Lockheed. As it lifted off from Gander on 23 September, it had logged 15,800 flight hours. It was powered by two Wright 988TC18-EA3 and two Wright 988TC18-EA6 engines, each with Hamilton Standard 43H60-363 propellers.

Within minutes of reaching the new altitude of 21,000 feet,

a fire warning sounded, signalling that there was a fire in no. 3 engine. Murray feathered the propeller and ordered the flight engineer to shut down the engine and discharge one fire extinguisher bank. While the engine was being shut down, the senior stewardess, Elizabeth Sims, came into the cockpit to advise that the fire was visible from inside the passenger cabin. Captain Murray then instructed Flight Engineer James Garrett to go to the passenger cabin and check the engines visually.

At 8.19 p.m. the co-pilot called Gander Radio to report the loss of the no. 3 engine and to request immediate clearance for a descent to flight level 90 (9,000 feet), the maximum altitude which could be maintained on three engines at the computed aircraft weight. Gander responded with permission for the descent and asked whether the flight needed escort. Parker replied: 'Stand by.'

Flight Engineer Garrett had just returned to the cockpit when there was a further serious complication. Without warning, the no. 1 engine now started to overspeed. Murray pulled all throttles back, raised the nose in order to slow down and ordered no. 1 propeller feathered.

As he looked back, he saw to his horror that Garrett had set the no. 1 engine emergency shut-off lever to the 'off' position and was now re-setting it to 'on'. Captain Murray told the inquiry that at this stage the flight engineer said: 'I'm sorry, John, I goofed.' Instead of cutting off fuel, oil and air to the crippled no. 3 engine, Garrett had shut down no. 1. Murray called for METO (maximum except take-off) power on engine numbers 2 and 3 so as to maintain a minimum rate of descent. He was now left with two functional engines, one on each wing. The flight engineer checked the performance charts and estimated that at their current weight flight above 5,000 feet would not be possible.

Repeated attempts were made to restart no. 1 engine but all failed. A major emergency with the strong possibility of ditching now existed. The crew requested a descent to flight level 50 and an escort. Gander asked whether they wished to return or to proceed to Shannon. Murray thought that he might try Keflavik, Iceland, and asked for a weather report. On being told that winds were gusting to 58 knots with rain and stratocumulus clouds at 1,800 feet, Murray decided that his only hope was Shannon.

Meanwhile, the crew started to consider the prospect of putting down in the ocean. Garrett read the ditching procedures in the operations manual and computed the ditching airspeed. He then reviewed the ditching stations and procedures required for the co-pilot and navigator. Senior stewardess Elizabeth Sims was summoned to the flight deck and briefed on the procedures to be followed in the cabin. Radio contact with Shannon, Gander and the other aircraft that were now diverting towards them was maintained by the co-pilot, Robert Parker. Ironically, one of the diverted aircraft was an eastbound DC-7 of Riddle Airlines. For many years Riddle had been the deadly rival of Flying Tiger in the cargo field. Another aircraft sent to the area was a sister ship of 923 'Charlie' piloted by Captain Dick Rossi, one of the original Flying Tigers under General Chenault in Burma.

Although he was given a run-down on the prevailing sea conditions – wind from 260° at 28 knots with primary swells eight to twelve feet high and secondary swells of eight feet – Murray still believed that he could make it to Shannon. In response to a query from Gander, the flight reported: 'do not intend to ditch.' They reported their position as 54°05' north latitude; 30°30' west longitude. The ETA (estimated time of arrival) for Shannon was given as 2 a.m.

It was now 8.45 p.m.

For a further twenty-six minutes the big Super Constellation lumbered eastwards in the moonless sky towards the Irish coast, its crew tense and fearful for the sound of yet another warning device which would spell catastrophe. At 9.15 p.m. their worst fears were realised.

The engine fire warning bell rang and the light signifying trouble in the no. 2 engine came on. The message now was that a fire had occurred in no. 2. As soon as Murray reduced power on the engine the bell stopped ringing and the light went out. Murray ordered all passengers and crew to don life-jackets. He then changed course away from Shannon and aimed the nose of the Super Constellation towards the position of weather ship *Juliet* which lay a few hundred nautical miles away at 52°30' north latitude and 19°54' west longitude. Co-pilot Parker called Shannon and told them of developments. They would not, he said, be able to maintain 5,000 feet.

Within minutes the Super Constellation was a mere 3,000 feet over the ocean limping along with an airspeed of around 150 knots produced by METO power on engine no. 4 and reduced power on engine no. 2. At 9.54 p.m. the diverted Seaboard flight sent to intercept 923 'Charlie' reported that he had the stricken aircraft in sight. Three minutes later the Riddle Airlines captain advised that he too had arrived overhead.

Just as these messages were relayed to Captain Murray, engine no. 2 quit. He immediately turned on the public address system and said: 'Ladies and gentlemen, we are going to ditch.' A ditching heading of 265° magnetic was decided upon and Murray initiated a left turn into the heading. The final decision was so sudden that Murray still hadn't put on his life-jacket. Now, because he couldn't divert his attention from the controls, the co-pilot put it over the captain's head and tied him into it.

Then, as he was halfway into the turn for ditching, the controls froze. Murray attributed this to a loss of hydraulic pressure and started to disengage the hydraulic control boost. The flight engineer suggested that the use of the hydraulic crossover switch might be more effective. Murray took his advice and to his great relief found that the controls were responding normally. As the aircraft was lined up on a heading of 265° Murray reduced power on the no. 4 engine so as to maintain directional control and started to put out the flaps. He first selected 60%, gradually dropped them into the 80% and, finally, the 100% positions.

Watching the scene from overhead, the captain of the Riddle Airlines DC-7 reported that there were scattered clouds over the area with bases of around 2,000 feet and tops near 3,000 feet. Weather, he reported, was good but there was no moon.

In the left hand seat of the Super Constellation, Captain Murray was relieved to find that depth perception and visibility during his final descent were better than he had hoped for. There was, he reckoned, a considerable distance between the waves – as much as 200 feet. Immediately prior to impact he switched on the landing lights and cut the power so as to land just past the top of a swell. He then raised the nose to bring it parallel to the face of the approaching swell.

There was only one impact, but it was extremely severe. Although all passengers and crew had been warned that ditching was imminent, no final 'brace yourselves' order had been given and several passengers and stewardesses found themselves in the upright position as the deceleration occurred. At impact, Captain Murray's head shot forward and struck the instrument panel causing a two and a half inch gash on his forehead. He remembered the co-pilot, Robert Parker, leaving his seat and asking: 'Are you all right, John?' Murray replied that he was and, with blood streaming down his face, followed the co-pilot and flight engineer out of the cockpit and into the passenger cabin.

For nearly two hours the passengers had known with varying degrees of perception that this fate awaited them. They ranged in age and experience from middle-aged senior officers and their wives to teenage rookies just out of jump school. One of the former, forty-eight-year-old Captain Robert C. Eldred from Cape Cod, Massachusetts, held his wife's hand as they agreed that for the sake of their children they would leave through separate exits. Captain Eldred survived, his wife was drowned.

One of the most poignant descriptions of those terrifying minutes before the ditching came from eighteen-year-old Private Willie Smith of Atlanta, Georgia who, with his friend, was sitting to the extreme right front of the aircraft. 'As we were coming down towards the water,' he told reporters, 'my buddy sitting beside me was crying and praying. I was trying to stop him acting that way and kept telling him not to worry and that we would make it.' Tragically, he didn't.

Army Paratrooper Fred Caruso recalls that when he first thought there might be trouble ahead 'the sun was setting deep on the horizon behind us and we were flying into the darkness.

'Step by step, little-by-little, we went through the ditching procedure. It was spread over a couple of hours. Everyone was in their life vests and stripped of all sharp medals and jewellery. Then to make our drill just a little more realistic, we were told to take our shoes off. A stewardess collected our footwear and locked it up in a toilet room up front to keep it all from flying around when we ditched.

'There we sat in our life vests and in stocking feet, waiting for what might come next. While we were doing the ditching procedure I had written a letter to my folks and I put it in my shirt pocket, after carefully writing on the envelope, 'If recovered, please deliver to my parents at …' I assumed there would be a recovery operation.

'The army major sitting to my left and I decided that if we should finally ditch, it would be awfully cold out there, so we helped each other in putting on our wool uniform jackets under the life vests.

'Finally, nearly two hours after the first two engines went out, a third engine sputtered and died from the strain. Only one engine remained. The pilot calmly called over the speaker system, "It looks like we're going to have to ditch."

'We were some 500 miles west of Ireland's Dingle Peninsula, somewhere southeast of Iceland.'

During the five minutes between the captain's announcement that he was ditching and the aircraft making contact with the water, the cabin lights were turned down so that the passengers may accustom their eyes to darkness. The four stewardesses positioned themselves at the emergency exits, senior stewardess Elizabeth Sims occupying the right rear seat opposite the main cabin door.

The Super Constellation carried five inflatable life rafts, each capable of holding twenty-five people. One was stowed in the crew compartment, two were in the passenger cabin and two were held in special compartments in the wings aft of the main spar. A cable control placed over the wing exits was designed to sequentially unlatch the cover doors and open the valves of the CO_2 cylinder of each raft. As the raft inflated, it was designed to eject automatically from its compartment.

Just prior to ditching, Navigator Sam Nicholson seated himself in an aisle seat in the last row of the left side, forward of the main cabin door. A life raft had been tied down there and in the final moments Nicholson removed the tie down strap. Soon Nicholson would perform a feat of outstanding bravery which almost certainly saved the lives of all the survivors.

As the Super Constellation hit the water the starboard wing broke off and several rows of seats from the wing root to the most rearward row on the opposite side failed, trapping many passengers.

One of them was a twenty-one-year-old serviceman, Art Gilbreth, just out of jump school and on his way to taking up a posting in Germany. Thirty-nine years after the event, he still remembers it with total clarity.

'I was in a window seat, about two rows from the back,' he recalls. 'When we hit, the seats to the back of me and my row broke away, I thought I was going to be cut in half by my seat belt and that my back was going to break from the pressure.

'I'm not sure if I passed out. Things happened very rapidly. I remember I was sitting in water up to my chest and when I tried to move I thought my back was broken. I did, in fact, have three cracked vertebrae.

'I tried to get up but was unable to. I decided to give up. Then, when the water reached my chin, I changed my mind. I discovered that I was still in my seat and had my seat belt on. I unbuckled it and found I could just about stand. It was very dark. I couldn't see anyone. The only exit I could remember was the door at the back where I entered the airplane. By this time the water was about chest high and I had to move floating objects out of the way to get to the door. When I got there I could see about 18 inches from the top of the door and the water was rushing in through it.

'I held my breath and started out of the door. Then I was struck in the face by something. My reaction plus the force of the water caused me to go back several feet and by the time I got back to the door it was under water. I felt around until I found the sides of the door and then I went out like a torpedo.

'Once outside I inflated by life-jacket and started to look around for a raft. I remember everyone yelling for the raft and thinking "why don't they shut up and go look for it". Then I discovered I was yelling too.

'I bumped into someone and heard a woman's voice saying: "help me, I can't swim". I turned her around and inflated her life-jacket. She said thanks and I told her to hang on to me and we would find the raft. Then a wave hit us and I lost my grip of her. When I looked around I couldn't see her. I swam a couple of strokes but couldn't find her. It has bothered me to this day that I didn't try hard enough to find her.

'It was around this time that a really weird thing happened. I left my body. I had two planes of vision, one from about 30 feet up in the air from where I could see everything – myself, the raft, the airplane, everything. The other view was from my body at water level and my body person did not know the other person in the air was there. The person in the air was giving advice to the one at water level.

'I could now see the raft and I started to swim towards it. All of a sudden I saw three fins coming towards me. I thought they were sharks. Just as I started thinking that, the person in the air told me they were the airplane. Which they were – I was swimming over it as it was sinking. All of a sudden one of the fins caught my right leg. It suddenly got real dark and cold and all I could see was a silver shimmer down by my leg. My leg felt like it was on fire. A jagged edge of the fin had caught my leg and now it was taking me down with it. I started to kick at the fin with my left leg and tore it loose. I didn't know which way was up. Then I felt myself drifting up. I started swimming again. Eventually I located the raft and swam over to it. I laid my arms over and waited for someone to help me in. No one was helping me, so I launched myself up and in …'

Although all five life rafts on 923 'Charlie' were later recovered, only one was found by the evacuating passengers. This was the raft launched by the navigator and it was only through his great courage that it too hadn't been lost. Samuel Nicholson had difficulty in opening the main cabin door and when he eventually succeeded he was knocked over by the force of the water. He managed to throw the raft out, but the lanyard attaching it to the aircraft snapped and it floated away. Nicholson, a strong swimmer, jumped into the turbulent seas and succeeded in retrieving it.

The one hope of survival for the seventy-six souls who had survived the ditching and evacuated during the ten minutes the Super Constellation remained afloat, was a single life raft designed to carry twenty-five people. And because of the accident at the time of its launching, the raft was upside down in the water, its emergency lighting system now worthless. Some of the passengers who had exited on the left hand side suffered wounds from the jagged edges of the fractured wing. Although there was no fire, all would suffer severe petrol burns from contact with the fuel which had poured from the ruptured tanks.

Caruso recalls: 'The life rafts carried emergency kits, which included a flashlight and flares. Unfortunately there was only one access to the emergency kit and that was through the floor of the rubber raft. The first frantic passengers climbed into the raft and helped others in as fast as they could, not knowing the raft had inflated upside down. The emergency lights that ring the top of the craft were under water along with the zipper to the emergency kit. Fortunately on their way out someone had the presence of mind to grab the emergency flashlight hanging near the back door of the aircraft, so we had one light.

Fifty people reached the raft designed for twenty-five. Conditions on the raft bouncing about in twenty-five foot waves for over five hours about 500 miles west of the Irish coast were horrific. Some sang 'Glory, glory, hallelujah'. Others recited the Lord's prayer in unison. Three people died on the raft, either through suffocation or drowning. Two of these were women who died almost as soon as they got aboard.

Art Gilbreth recalls the ordeal. 'I was stretched out on the bottom,' he said. 'I was on my back and someone was sitting on my chest. The back of my head was on someone's legs. As the raft would reach the bottom of a trough and start to go up the other side, all the water would go over my head. I couldn't move with the person sitting on my chest so I had to hold my breath.

'Once I could see again I could tell that the person sitting on my chest was in shock because whenever the moon would come out from behind the clouds that person looked as white as a sheet. I yelled and started hitting him to get off me. I don't know how many times I went under. In the moonlight, I saw a friend with whom I had gone through jump school. I started to yell at him, then holding my breath, then yelling again. He said he couldn't see me, so I started waving my arm. The next time I went under I felt the weight move off my chest and arms pulling me up. I scooted up until I was sitting up but it was so cold I sank back down in the water in the raft which was warmer.

'I turned round and I could hear Carol, the stewardess, passing on Captain Murray's instructions as she was wrapping something around the wound on his head. We were told that we were not saved yet and that we would have to bail out with anything we could find. I don't remember much after this, just a lot of waiting. I kept passing out because of loss of blood ... I remember coming to and seeing the lights of a ship.'

Caruso takes up the story: 'The navigator, Sam Nicholson, who had made it to the raft told us he had managed to make contact with a ship before the aircraft ploughed into the sea. However, it was twelve hours away.

'After nearly three hours in the water, we were able to catch an occasional glimpse of a light on the horizon. Sometimes we would lose sight of it for ten minutes or more. It took almost an hour to make certain it was a ship and not just drifting flares or the rising moon.'

That ship was the 9,000 ton Swiss-registered cargo vessel *Celerina* on its way to Antwerp in Belgium. It had been only six hours away when it received Sam Nicholson's call for help, but was unable to radio back. When it reached the ditching site, the fifty people had been in the life raft for almost six hours. 'By this time the wind had blown the raft some 22 miles from the point of impact.'

Equally fortuitously, the Canadian aircraft carrier HMCS *Bonaventure* was also in the general area. It had several helicopters on board which were dispatched to ferry the more seriously injured, including Art Gilbreth, to the carrier for medical treatment and later to a hospital in England.

Caruso remembers: 'Captain Murray got on the ladder. The boat pitched upward and jerked him out of the raft. He fell backwards into the water.

'I grabbed him by his shirt and pulled him back into the raft. He made it up on his second attempt.'

Art Gilbreth remembers 'climbing up a rope ladder and just reaching the top. Then nothing. The next memory is of lying on a table in what looked like a mess hall drinking what I think was hot rum and milk. After a couple of those I was still thirsty and when someone told me to hold on to this bottle I drank about three inches of it. I was feeling no pain. To this day, Scotch is my drink of choice.

'The next day a group of men came into the room with a wire stretcher and after wrapping me in blankets, put me into it. They took me up on deck and I could see the cold grey seas again. I was yanked off the deck and went swinging out over the ocean. It looked bad. I looked up and saw a helicopter about 150 feet above me. I was running a high temperature. At the hospital in England I had four operations on my leg because I had developed gangrene from the water, gasoline and rubber burns. From this remove it all seems like a dream …'

The CAB board of inquiry found that the probable cause of the accident was 'the failure of two of the aircraft's four engines and the improper action of the flight engineer, which disabled a third engine, thereby necessitating a ditching at sea.'

In its report, the board of inquiry acknowledged that 'under the circumstances of darkness, weather and high seas which prevailed in the North Atlantic at the time of this ditching … the survival of 48 occupants of the aircraft was miraculous.'

Even so, neither the Flying Tiger Line nor the manufacturer of the survival equipment came out of the inquiry unscathed. In the case of the airline, the board found that, apart from the major error by the flight engineer, there was a lack of proper crew training which led to confusion in regard to the position a passenger should assume before ditching and the fact that no final 'brace yourselves' instruction was given by the captain. They also found that the captain was not aware that there was a lever in the cockpit which would release one of the rafts stowed in the wings. Another serious flaw in the preparations for ditching was the failure of the aft over-the-wing exit panels. 'Performance and testimony by surviving crew members,' the report stated, 'indicated a lack or a low degree of proficiency having been gained from the training program designed to meet emergencies such as were encountered on this flight.'

The board also cast doubts on the adequacy of the means of inflating the life-jackets carried on the aircraft and called for improvements in the basic design of these jackets. They also recommended that an automatically actuated light be fitted to all life-jackets and that the lighting systems on life rafts should be improved.

One of the most fascinating aspects of this ditching was that Captain Murray's way of doing so was in total contravention to the directions given in the Flying Tiger Line manual or with the procedures recommended by the US coastguard. Instead of ditching parallel to the anticipated primary swell, as recommended, Murray pointed the nose straight into the face of the swell. According to the prevailing wisdom, this could easily cause the immediate destruction of the aircraft. But Murray reckoned that the interval between swells as based on the latest forecasts offered him a better chance. The procedure he used was, in fact, warned against in the manual.

Although the inquiry noted that the considerable impact force encountered because of landing into the swell caused the wing to fracture, thus depriving the survivors of one life raft, and that it also caused several rows of seats to fail, it was careful to make no criticism of Captain Murray or any other members of the crew involved in the actual ditching.

On Wednesday, 26 September, the *Celerina* anchored thirty-one miles off the Cork coast and a fleet of RAF helicopters ferried eight of the more seriously injured to Cork Airport from where they were transferred by air ambulances to England. The remaining survivors stayed in the *Celerina* until it docked in Antwerp the following Friday. Twelve bodies were repatriated to the USA for burial. Thirteen others were never found. Thus ended the saga of 923 'Charlie'.

Caruso adopted the nickname O'Caruso and became an Irish citizen buying a home in Glengarriff in Co. Cork.

Three weeks after the public hearings of the inquiry had finished, Sam Nicholson, the navigator, was working on another

Super Constellation over the Atlantic. He wrote later: 'We were in the middle of the ocean when suddenly we had an engine failure. The crew shut it down and feathered the propeller. I sensed that it was unusually quiet in the cockpit. When I looked up, every crew member was staring at me as if I was hexed or something.'

John Murray continued his flying career with Flying Tigers and was one of the first captains to be checked out on the new DC-8-63 jets. Seven years after his ordeal in the North Atlantic he was on a lay-over in Wake Island west of Honolulu and was drowned while swimming in a quiet lagoon. He was fifty-one.

CHAPTER 10

'Age Shall Not Weary Them …' The Tragedy of the Aer Lingus Cadets

THE early morning weather forecast for the Dublin region on Thursday, 22 June 1967 was, for a midsummer day, unpromising. At 8 a.m. a weak warm front lay from Arklow to Limerick, moving northwards at a rate of between 5 to 10 knots. During the preceding five hours, Dublin Airport reported intermittent light rain and drizzle with similar conditions extending northwards to Drogheda. The meteorologists reckoned it was going to be a grey misty morning with little or no sunshine, negligible wind and a low cloud base.

This was not the kind of forecast that should trouble any experienced professional pilot. And Hugh O'Keeffe, at thirty-seven, an Aer Lingus senior captain and flying instructor, was both. He was one of the most accomplished and talented pilots in the airline, noted for the high standards he demanded of himself and his subordinates and for his outstanding technical knowledge of the Vickers Viscount airliner. Like most Aer Lingus captains of that era, Hugh O'Keeffe had come to the airline by way of the military. Originally from Birr, Co. Offaly, he joined the army in 1949 after completing the leaving certificate course at the Patrician College, Ballyfin. He transferred to the air corps two years later where his flying skills so impressed his superiors that he soon became an instructor. In 1958, he joined Aer Lingus as a second officer. Promotion was rapid. Within three years he had gone through the first officer rank to acting captain. He was given a full command in 1962 and, two years later, he was invited to join the select band of company pilots who were taken off line duties to act as instructors.

He lived with his wife, Alison and his two young daughters, Nicola and Alison, at a comfortable home in Offington Park in the north Dublin suburb of Sutton. Having said goodbye to his family, Captain O'Keeffe set out for Dublin airport on that fateful morning where he was to put two young cadet pilots through the routine of coping with an incipient stall in a Viscount 803.

It was to be his second exercise with the cadets, Ruairí de Paor, a twenty-year-old from Home Farm Road, Drumcondra, and nineteen-year-old John Kavanagh, from Falcarragh Road, Whitehall. Both, along with an ex-RAF pilot who was infinitely more experienced that either of them and was also converting to the Viscount 803, had already flown together ten days earlier.

In 1967, Aer Lingus was experiencing substantial difficulties in recruiting suitable trainee pilots. Recruitment of pilots had long been a formidable personnel problem for the airline. In the early days, the pilots were mainly recruited from the military with both RAF men and Irish air corps men forming the main body of the pilot corps. As seen in chapter six, this created much friction.

In his memoirs, *Green is My Sky*, a former chief pilot of Aer Lingus, Captain Aidan Quigley, wrote scathingly of this system where the key credential to obtaining a civilian flying job was the logbook – usually a service one. 'Such a facile method of qualification,' he wrote, 'produced from time to time a highly mixed result – forged logbooks or genuine qualifications confirming pilots of immense experience but who could occupy no place in domestic flying.' This system, he wrote, had produced 'some cookies in the guise of pilots and assorted ground personnel, and it took some time to filter them out.'

Although the cadet pilot scheme had, by then, been in operation for six years, it still wasn't operating satisfactorily. From the start, psychological testing of applicants had been undertaken in co-operation with UCD. But no psychologist can foretell with complete accuracy how anyone, young or old, is going to perform when confronted with the challenge of flying an aeroplane. Talents vary enormously. Sometimes even quite unlikely candidates turn out to be 'natural pilots' blessed with extraordinary skills in airmanship and rapidly and almost effortlessly moving forward to the vital 'first solo' stage. Others encounter difficulties ranging from a poor sense of balance and co-ordination to an inability to measure distances at speed. Some never adjust to the cramped, noisy and often unstable cockpit of a light aircraft. A few may discover that they harbour an unsuspected fear of flying. Many find it difficult to master the art, vital in flying, of being able to concentrate on more than one problem at the same time. Ireland's most experienced flying instructor, the legendary Captain Darby Kennedy, is on record as saying that he could teach practically anyone to fly – provided he was given the time. To an amateur, time is of little consequence – provided he has the wherewithal to continue paying for the lessons. But to a would-be professional embarking on a course which is going to cost an airline or an air force large sums, time is of the essence. In the commercial and military worlds, failure to reach the 'first solo' stage within a respectable and economic time frame will almost inevitably lead to exclusion.

In 1961, forty-nine applicants were sent for psychological testing and only ten passed. In 1966, forty-eight were sent and thirty were selected. The class of 1966 – of which Ruairí de Paor and John Kavanagh were members – comprised thirty cadets, selected from 600 applicants. Of the thirty selected that year, eleven cadets had failed before the accident that was to kill Ruairí de Paor, John Kavanagh and Captain O'Keeffe. In the first draft of his report on the accident, the inspector of accidents of the department of transport and power, Captain Robert M. Reidy – himself a former

Aer Lingus pilot – suggested that the Viscount training programme may have been rushed because of the urgent need for new line pilots. This comment was objected to by Aer Lingus and was subsequently erased following representations by the general manager of Aer Lingus, Michael J. Dargan, to the secretary of the department of transport and power. But the inspector refused to tone down or remove other specified criticisms which included his belief that: 'there are indications, such as an increase in the average failure rate of cadet pilots on conversion courses ... that the company's training policy, while not unsafe, is not of the optimum ...'

Ruairí de Paor and John Kavanagh had come through the stringent psychological testing of the UCD academics and the Aer Lingus staff psychologists. They had also come through the equally stringent physical examinations at the Aer Lingus medical centre. Both were well-adjusted, intelligent, honourable and likeable young men.

Kavanagh had carried out his basic flying training at the Oxford Air Training School at Kidlington and de Paor at another training school in Perth. Both had succeeded in passing the independent written examinations and practical flight tests of the UK department of civil aviation. Both gained a UK commercial pilots licence enabling them to carry passengers for hire or reward in single-engine equipment not exceeding 12,500 lb. Although both had received some instruction on flying by instruments alone, neither had obtained the instrument rating. John Kavanagh graduated in February 1967 and Ruairí de Paor the following month. When they returned to the Aer Lingus training centre, John Kavanagh had a total of 226 hours in the air, 143 of them as pilot in command; Ruairí de Paor had 203 hours, 151 of them as pilot in command. All of these hours were in light aircraft. The next hurdle in their task of converting from relatively simple, low-speed light aircraft to the large and complicated Viscount 803 was a course of lectures in the ground school where the intricacies of the Viscount were explained.

This was to be followed by forty hours on a rather primitive Viscount flight simulator which was designed principally to assist the student in gaining an instrument rating. The simulators of those days were not sophisticated enough to be a substitute for the kind of emergency training which the two cadets were receiving on the day of their deaths. Both Ruairí de Paor and John Kavanagh had experienced difficulties with the simulator and neither had completed their simulator course at the time of their deaths.

Their instructor, Captain O'Keeffe, was a brilliant pilot but, temperamentally, he was unsuited to instructing. His gruff exterior and lack of patience with those who were less than first rate intimidated many of his charges – particularly those who were in most need of encouragement.

Internal communications within the training school were far from perfect – they were tightened up after the crash – and when Captain O'Keeffe took the two cadets for their first Viscount training session on 12 June 1967, he was not aware that both had encountered problems on the simulator. Ruairí de Paor and John Kavanagh had known each other as schoolboys when they attended St Patrick's National School, Drumcondra. Later, their paths diverged when Ruairí went to Coláiste Mhuire and John went to Chanel College in Coolock. Then, after the completion of their secondary education, they were to sit in the same classroom again in the Aer Lingus flight training school.

Now, Ruairí de Paor confided in his father that he was unhappy about the fact that he was rostered for flight training before finishing his simulator course. On the night before the fatal accident, Mr de Paor was so concerned about his son's worries that he urged him to call in sick. On the morning of 22 June, Mr de Paor drove his son to the airport. He noticed that he was very quiet. After Ruairí got out of the car a terrible sense of foreboding overcame Mr de Paor. He parked the car, went up on the viewing balcony and took three snapshots of the Viscount as it started to taxi.

At the Kavanagh household over in Falcarragh Road, Whitehall, the atmosphere was also fraught. James Kavanagh had been unable to sleep until about 2 a.m. and had been vomiting. Many pilots are extremely tense before a check and it is not uncommon even for senior captains not to sleep the night before. James Kavanagh's mother said later that as he left the house that morning she had a clear premonition that something was going to harm him.

By 7 a.m. both cadets had checked in for their second Viscount conversion flight. Captain O'Keeffe assigned Ruairí de Paor to the co-pilot's seat. As was customary practice, John Kavanagh strapped himself into the 'jump' seat behind his two colleagues. As neither of the cadets were proficient in the operation of the Viscount's radios, Captain O'Keeffe did the R/T work himself. At 7.34 a.m. he called the control tower for the first time that morning saying: 'Dublin tower – this is Echo India Alpha Oscar Foxtrot.'

Told by the controller to go ahead, Captain O'Keeffe said: 'Oscar Foxtrot is starting up now for training and I'll be looking for the northwest sector between flight level 50 and 100 (5,000 and 10,000 feet)'.

The controller asked for the number of souls on board, the elapsed time and the endurance. To this Captain O'Keeffe responded: 'Roger, we've got three on board, endurance is four hours, duration of detail is three hours – two hours in the northwest and one in the circuit.'

Viscount 'Oscar Foxtrot' was then cleared to taxi. Captain O'Keeffe was offered runway 17 but said he would prefer 35. This was agreed and he was given permission to taxi to its holding point. After a brief discussion about the availability of VOR (a navigational aid known as Very High Frequency Omnidirectional Radio Range) during the exercise, Captain O'Keeffe called out: 'Oscar Foxtrot is ready.' He was immediately cleared for take-off.

As Ruairí de Paor opened the throttles the clock in the tower read 7.44 a.m. Two minutes later, Captain O'Keeffe called again to report that they were climbing out on course to the northwest. Dublin Tower now handed him over to Dublin Centre.

The next communication from 'Oscar Foxtrot' came to Dublin Centre at 7. 55 a.m. when Captain O'Keeffe asked for an alteration in his clearance so that he could operate at flight levels 6 to 12 (6,000 to 12,000 feet) rather than the earlier 5 to 10. This was granted.

At 8.06 a.m., Captain O'Keeffe called again asking for clearance to up to flight level 150 (15,000 feet). The controller asked him to stand-by while he checked the clearance and almost immediately came back with permission. Captain O'Keeffe replied: 'Affirmative 100 to 150.'

The controller responded: 'That's it and just ... in case you have radio trouble – expected approach time 0900, flight level 110, back to Rush ADF, let down for Runway 17.'

Captain O'Keeffe responded: 'Flight level 110, 0900 to Rush ADF let-down to runway 17.' The controller replied: 'That's it,' to which Captain O'Keeffe responded: 'Roger.'

It was 8.08 a.m.

Nothing more would be heard from 'Oscar Foxtrot'. In the words of the inspector of accidents: 'During a period of probably two to three minutes after that time something happened which caused the aeroplane to descend, without requesting or getting air traffic control clearance for descent, to an altitude very much lower than that for which it was cleared or at which, during any of the training exercises scheduled, the aircraft would normally operate.'

During the twenty-seven minutes between its last call to Dublin Centre and its plunge into a cornfield in the Co. Dublin townland of Ballymauden on the Dublin–Meath border nine miles northwest of the airport, there were numerous sightings of the Viscount flying at perilously low levels. The first was at Rathdrinagh, four miles southeast of Slane when, at 8.10 a.m., a twelve-year-old boy, attracted by the high-pitched whine of the Viscount's turbo-props, looked out of a window and saw the aircraft, undercarriage down and engines under power, flying past and travelling approximately northwards.

Within the next five minutes it was heard by four separate witnesses as it flew low in cloud in the vicinity of Collon, nine miles from the first sighting. At 8.20 a.m. another witness saw it flying just below the cloud base (believed to have been a mere 200 feet). There was no further sighting until soon after 8.30 a.m. which convinced the investigators that in the intervening ten minutes it had climbed, under control, to an altitude where it no longer aroused particular attention on the ground.

Then, at 8.30 a.m., two young farm workers in Adamstown, two miles northeast of the crash site, were so startled by the noise of aircraft engine power going on and off erratically that they rushed from their milking shed to see a large four-engined aeroplane flying so low that it barely missed roofs and telegraph poles. One of them noted the telegraph wires swaying and vibrating after it passed. Both youths – they were aged seventeen and fifteen – insisted that when the aircraft appeared the two inner engines were stopped. This conflicted with the evidence of other boys who claimed that it was the two engines 'on the right hand side' that were stopped.

Another witness told how she ran from her cottage having heard the roar of the engines. She could smell the fumes of the burnt kerosene. There were forty-two witnesses in total and all who observed the final minutes were unanimous in saying that that the aircraft was 'twisting and tumbling' before impact. A witness who saw it about one mile from the crash site said that 'it barely missed one of the high trees'. The last witness, who was on the road beside the field where the Viscount eventually crashed, said that it passed over him at a height of about thirty feet. In its final desperate moments, its engines throttled back, yet with occasional spurts of power. 'Oscar Foxtrot', appears to have approached Mangan's cornfield at Ballymaudin from a northwesterly direction. There was evidence that its port wing was 'drooping' in what investigators believed to be an attempt at a turn. Having crossed the field for about 900 feet, the Viscount appeared to go into the initial stages of a spin.

There was a sudden burst of power followed by silence. Then came the terrifying noise of the impact and the roar of the flames as the fuel tanks containing nearly 1,400 gallons of kerosene ruptured and caught fire. It was 8.35 a.m.

At 8.43 a.m., Dublin air traffic control received a phone call from the Ashbourne post office to say that an aircraft had crashed nearby. In keeping with normal procedure, ATC had not initiated any contact with the Viscount while on its training session. The radar controller had been monitoring 'Oscar Foxtrot' but at that time the radar display equipment was not capable of showing changes in altitude so the aircraft's descent from its cleared altitude was not apparent to him.

A few seconds after this, Dublin Centre put out the message: 'Echo Oscar Foxtrot – Dublin, how do you read.'

Eleven seconds later the controller called for the second time: 'Echo Oscar Foxtrot – Dublin.' The resultant silence was confirmation that his efforts were in vain and that 'Oscar Foxtrot' had crashed.

A few miles from Dublin Airport, in the same estate from which Captain O'Keeffe had earlier that morning set out for Dublin Airport, the Aer Lingus chief safety officer, Captain Gordon Black – himself a veteran Viscount pilot – was enjoying a day's leave when the call from head office came at 9.03 a.m. He reached the accident scene at 10.20 a.m.

By the time he arrived, the firefighters had put out the flames but the wreckage was still smoking furiously. The aircraft was on its back in a nose-down position near the centre of the forty-acre field of ripening corn. Each of the four engines was buried to a depth of approximately four feet. Virtually all parts of the wreck were contained within an area equivalent to that of the aircraft itself.

Driving through O'Connell Street, Dublin, that morning, Matthew de Paor, Cadet de Paor's father, switched on the car radio for the 10 a.m. news bulletin. It started with a news flash saying that an Aer Lingus Viscount had crashed near Ashbourne. In one petrifying moment, Mathew de Paor's earlier fears were crystallised and amplified. He knew that, barring a miracle, it was the Viscount carrying his son. He parked the car near a public telephone box and with a heavy heart phoned the Aer Lingus head office. He was put through to the company secretary. His immediate aim now was to locate his wife, Ann, who was shopping, and to get her home under some pretext where he would break the devastating news in private. As the couple pulled up outside their house, they found officials from the Aer Lingus personnel department waiting in a car. Mr de Paor waved them away as he took his wife inside. Another management team had arrived at the home of Cadet Kavanagh in Falcarragh Road, Whitehall. Mr John Kavanagh, John's father, had taken early retirement from the department of posts and telegraphs having suffered two heart attacks. As well as his heartbroken parents, John Kavanagh left a brother and six sisters, five of whom were abroad.

After the relatives had been informed, the chief press officer of Aer Lingus, Captain Jack Millar, put out the following statement: 'Our Viscount airliner EI-AOF crashed while on a training flight near Ashbourne, Co. Meath, at approximately 8.35 this morning. There were no passengers aboard but the crew of three pilots were killed.' After flying over the wreckage in another Viscount, the general manager of Aer Lingus, Michael J. Dargan, made another statement. 'We deeply regret the deaths of Captain O'Keeffe and cadets Power and Kavanagh, and I offer my heartfelt sympathy to their relatives,' he said and added: 'They gave their lives to maintain the safety of scheduled airline flying.'

As always in the case of civil airliner disasters, two inquiries immediately got under way. Aer Lingus set up its own internal inquiry, headed by its assistant general manager (technical) Captain W. J. ('Bill') Scott which heard evidence in private, and later issued a set of recommendations. The minister for transport and power, Erskine Childers, appointed Captain Robert J. Reidy of the department's aeronautical section to conduct the official inquiry and to issue a report in due course. Unlike the cases of the DC-3 crash in Wales and the crash-landing of another DC-3 in Birmingham, there was to be no public inquiry. There is evidence that because of its experiences in the earlier public inquiries, this formula had become anathema to the airline and to sections of the civil service.

Both inquiries invited and obtained assistance from the British aircraft corporation (which, having taken over Vickers, was now the manufacturer of the Viscount), Rolls Royce Derby Ltd (the engine manufacturers), and BEA, the original and largest operator of the type.

And so the two sets of experts started the exhaustive process of teasing out the clues, human and mechanical, which could lead to an understanding of the catastrophic event. It was soon established that the aircraft had been properly maintained and was airworthy. 'Oscar Foxtrot' – fleet name *St Cathal* – was one of a fleet of eight Viscounts (803 series) which had been bought from KLM between December 1965 and October 1966. Another of these aircraft (EI-AOM *St Phelim*) crashed off Tuskar Rock on 24 March 1968 with the loss of sixty-one lives (see chapter 11). Even before these crashes, these aircraft had proved troublesome and were disliked by Aer Lingus technical staff. A senior engineer had described them as 'a bad buy.' But there is no doubt that 'Oscar Foxtrot' was in an airworthy condition and had been properly maintained and serviced as it took off for its final flight. The inspector of accidents was entirely satisfied on these points.

'Oscar Foxtrot' had been built for KLM by Vickers at their Weybridge plant. It first flew on 11 September 1957 and was delivered to the airline's Amsterdam base on 19 October 1957 with the registration PH-VIE and the fleet name *Jan Olieslagers*. It was sold to Aer Lingus in November 1965 and, after conversion by Scottish Aviation Ltd (which included the installation of weather radar), it was put on the Irish register as EI-AOF and given the fleet name *St Cathal*. None of these Viscounts had either a 'black box' or cockpit voice recording equipment. At the time of the crash, EI-AOF had flown a total of 17,447 hours (3,064 with Aer Lingus) and made 15,346 landings. As the aircraft had struck the ground at a relatively slow speed, a large proportion of the wreckage was sufficiently intact to enable the investigators to rule out any form of mechanical or structural failure. The investigators were able to prove that all four engines were turning at the time of impact and there were no indications of any pre-impact engine failure. There was no evidence of control surface malfunction or of over-stressing in flight. Neither was there evidence of explosion or fire prior to impact, and it was shown that electrical power had been available and all radio aids were functioning. There was no evidence of malfunction in hydraulic or fuel systems.

There was, however, severe damage to the flight deck and the official report acknowledged that because of the damage caused by the impact and subsequent fire, it was not possible to exclude the possibility of 'a localised explosion affecting the flight deck and hence the flight crew'.

During the early afternoon of the day of the crash, the bodies were recovered. Captain O'Keeffe had been occupying the left hand seat where the commander of a commercial airliner is required by law to sit. Ruairí de Paor was in the right hand seat, and was therefore the pilot under instruction at the time of the crash. John Kavanagh was at the back, behind the two other pilots, but it wasn't possible to determine whether he had been standing or was strapped into the jump seat. The investigators believed that these deductions narrowed the field of the investigation dramatically and placed the emphasis squarely on the human factors involved. The severely limited Viscount experience of both cadets (each had only forty minutes training on the type) laid the foundations for the possibility of human limitation or error. On the evidence available, most of the investigators were strongly inclined to believe that in an emergency neither cadet would have been capable of managing the Viscount without assistance. Captain Reidy's final report stated: 'The two cadet pilots under instruction had probably not reached a stage of proficiency in training at which they would have been able to maintain control of the aircraft, in the flight conditions existing at the time of the accident, without assistance from a more experienced Viscount pilot.'

The next question to be faced was: had Captain O'Keeffe, through injury or illness, become incapacitated, leaving two inexperienced cadets to manage a large, highly complicated airliner and get it back to base?

Like all airline pilots licensed in Ireland, Captain O'Keeffe was subject to stringent medical examinations at regular intervals and his tests had always been clear. But earlier that year he had suffered a severe kidney infection which caused him to run a very high temperature. He was admitted for tests to a nursing home by his family doctor and, after the appropriate antibiotic had been prescribed, he made a rapid recovery. Even so, colleagues noted that he had been shaken by the illness.

There were, however, no precise records of this illness in his Aer Lingus records. A medical certificate had been submitted and Captain O'Keeffe also took leave at this time. The medical certificate, however, did not state the nature of the illness. This was contrary to staff regulations but it was a commonplace occurrence at the time.

The post-mortem examination made no link between this illness and the crash. After the accident a directive went out insisting that the cause of illness would have to be stated or the certificate would be deemed invalid.

The pathologist was unable, because of damage to the body, to determine the condition of Captain O'Keeffe's heart. No solid proof of an incapacitation either through illness or injury was ever brought forward. But Captain Reidy in his report gave considerable prominence to what he described as 'a hypothesis which would be reasonably consistent with the ascertained facts' and went on in the unemotional language of official reports to outline the nightmare scenario which could have ensued.

'If this occurred, either through injury or sudden illness,' he wrote, 'the cadet pilot left in control would not, especially in the extremely difficult circumstances of having a disabled man in a pilot seat beside him, be able to maintain control of the aircraft above (and possibly in) cloud.

'Being unable (through lack of familiarity with the aircraft's radio equipment) either to communicate with air traffic control or to use radio-navigational aids for a return to Dublin Airport, his most likely action would be to descend through cloud, fix his position by sight of the ground and so get back to base visually ...

'In view of his very limited experience in such a large and complex aeroplane, his capacity would have been strained to its limits even if there had been good visibility under a cloud base allowing visual manoeuvre ... The task of trying to keep the aeroplane under control and beneath cloud whilst trying to find out where he was may have proved so much beyond him at this stage that the decision to attempt a landing was forced on him ...'

This was a perfectly valid hypothesis. When plotted from the statements of the various witnesses, the movements of the Viscount during the final few minutes all seemed to point to an approach to the cornfield with engines throttled back and then an attempt to overshoot as the pilot became aware either that the field was too small or that electrical or telephone cables lay in his path. All the conditions for the incipient stall and spin were here present, hence the sudden burst of power as the nose dipped and control was being lost. There were several serious questions to be addressed by Aer Lingus and the crash led to several recommendations which wrought wholesale changes in the pilot training programme.

Firstly, there was the suitability of flying instructors. The internal Aer Lingus inquiry dealt with this problem and acknowledged that the practice of selecting training captains on the basis of their superior flying prowess and experience but without serious consideration of the personality and temperament was potentially hazardous and needed immediate attention. It recommended that steps be taken to ensure that 'adequate teaching ability and acceptable personality traits' existed in those selected as flying instructors and that a quality control system be introduced to monitor training captains. This recommendation was never fully implemented.

A major investigation was launched into the selection procedures for cadet pilots. There was a thorough examination of why such a large percentage of applicants were failed at the first interview. Weakness in the communications machinery between those sections of the airline dealing with pilot training were identified and eliminated. The responsibility for monitoring the progress of cadets was placed on a single official who was charged with ensuring that the training of cadets who were not achieving satisfactory standards should be discontinued at the earliest opportunity. Revised stalling procedures for Viscount training flights, including the banning of all 'power-on' stalls, were devised in consultation with the air registration board and promptly implemented. There was an admission by the committee of inquiry that the conversion from the aircraft flown at the flying schools to the kind of airliners used by Aer Lingus was asking too much of cadets and an intermediate stage in which students flew smaller twin-engined aircraft was introduced.

And while the committee acknowledged that the presence of a flight recorder or even a cockpit voice recorder would have been of great assistance to the investigation, it would not because of the big financial cost recommend the installation of same in an aircraft fleet which was soon to be phased out.

But the most radical recommendation by far was the insistence that, in addition to the instructor, every training flight would have to include as a crew member a pilot, fully qualified on that type of aircraft, capable of handling the aircraft in the event of the instructor becoming incapacitated. This was implemented.

The report of the inspector of accidents contained a number

of criticisms of the Aer Lingus training scheme. When the draft report was – as is customary – submitted to the airline for its comments, the general manager, Michael J. Dargan, wrote to the secretary of the department of transport and power, Mr D. O'Riordan, seeking amendments.

'Individually,' he wrote, 'these criticisms are not necessarily damaging but, collectively, they could create the impression of an underlying unsatisfactory state of affairs ... The report states that there is no evidence that these minor deficiencies contributed to the accident. Why then should these criticisms be made public where they will damage the airline? We would know and understand that your department must take them up with us direct to ensure that we make any improvements found to be necessary. Publication is the problem.

'I suggest to you that publishing the report in its present form is not only unnecessarily damaging to the airline, but also could provoke pressure for a public inquiry ...'

The secretary responded on 3 July with a letter to Mr Dargan informing him that the inspector 'has been able to accept most of your suggested amendments and has amended his text accordingly'. He added that the inspector could not however see his way to accepting three of the suggested amendments and added: 'I feel, however, that the amended text will allay your concern to a very large extent.' Curiously, although Mr O'Riordan's letter is dated 3 July 1968, the published report bears the date 14 June 1968.

Two months, almost to the day, after this crash, Aer Lingus lost another Viscount when EI-AKK, fleet name *St Aidan* crashed after an abandoned overshoot while attempting to land in poor weather conditions at Lulsgate Airport, Bristol. The aircraft – a Viscount 808 – was written off with one passenger and one hostess suffering serious injuries and six passengers and another passenger suffering minor injuries.

Six months later came Tuskar rock when EI-AOM, the *St Phelim* went down in the sea off the Wexford coast with the loss of sixty-one lives. As was the case in all the fatal Aer Lingus crashes, its cause would remain a mystery – in this case, one of the great mysteries of civil aviation.

The huge advances in flight simulator technology during the 1970s meant that fewer and fewer pilots were lost in training accidents. In the 1960s training accidents were almost a monthly occurrence and usually merited no more than a column inch in the newspapers, distinguishable always by the fact that the numbers killed were nearly always three or four. Today, all dangerous emergency procedures are perfected on the flight simulator. There has been much study, too, in regard to the relationship between airline captains and their subordinates and great emphasis is given to human relations in the cockpit. Every database of fatal air accidents is replete with examples of how co-pilots went meekly to their deaths knowing full well that the man in the left hand seat was botching things but unable, because of the existing culture regarding command and seniority, to countermand or even appraise him.

Michael Dargan was demonstrating a sweet tooth for rhetoric rather than cool objectivity when he said that the three pilots of 'Oscar Foxtrot' had given their lives to maintaining the safety of scheduled airline flying. It is true that as a result of their deaths training standards were greatly improved and some major pitfalls removed. But the fact that these improvements were made only after their deaths will always be the real tragedy of 'Oscar Foxtrot'.

The official hypothesis of the cause of the crash was not queried for the next thirty-five years. Then, in 2002, three international aviation experts, the French air investigator, Rear-Admiral Yves Lemercier, his colleague, aeronautical associate expert, Manuel Pech, and Colin Torkington, the Australian nominee on the ICAO air navigation commission compared similarities between the periods of disabled flight of 'Oscar Foxtrot' and the Aer Lingus Viscount Alpha 'Oscar Mike', which crashed off the Tuskar Rock with the loss of all sixty-one on board. In light of their examination, they felt that the conclusions of the 1968 accident report into 'Oscar Foxtrot' should be re-assessed.

At the time of writing, no action has been taken on this and it remains to be seen if a future investigation will throw new light on the tragedy.

Ruairí de Paor and James Kavanagh were not, alas, the only Aer Lingus cadets to lose their lives in training accidents. Twenty-two years later, in far-off Vero Beach in Florida, two other youngsters who were only toddlers when 'Oscar Foxtrot' crashed, were to die with their instructor in another training accident which had little in common with the first one except its mystery.

The Piper Crash, 9 May 1989

On the evening of Friday, 4 May 1989, Aer Lingus cadet, Michael Murphy, was in jubilant form when he telephoned his parents, Detective Chief Superintendent John P. Murphy and his wife, Betty. He was in Florida with seventeen other Aer Lingus cadets all doing their flight training at the Flight Safety Academy in Fort Pierce. He had received his US flying certificate with single/multi engine ratings and all he had to do now was some more flying on a twin-engined aircraft, he told his parents.

He had enjoyed Florida. He and his close friend, James Byrne, who he had met while both were doing their medicals for Aer Lingus the previous September, had bought a volkswagen car between them and so had been able to get about a bit.

However, he was looking forward to returning to the family home 'St Elmo's' in Fairview in Dublin, in a couple of weeks and meeting up again with his family. Murphy, who had qualified as an accountant before joining Aer Lingus, was one of ten children. One brother, Martin was an army captain while another, Sean was a garda detective.

His friend, James Byrne, from Shanganagh Grove, Shankill, Co. Dublin, was aged twenty-four. He was an honours graduate of Trinity College, Dublin, where he had studied micro-electronics

CLEARED FOR DISASTER

215

and electrical engineering before deciding to become a pilot. An only son, he had one sister, Louise.

The following Wednesday, 9 May, Cadets Murphy and Byrne boarded a twin-engined Piper, registration N2231M, at Fort Pierce with their instructor, Richard Lockerman. It was a lovely sunny day and all three anticipated a good, if taxing, session. The task for the day was crew co-ordination training and the take-off into the blue sky was routine.

The Piper climbed to about 3,500 feet when without warning things began to go wrong. It turned east and those watching on radar noticed that its ground speed slowed to 53 knots. It then began to turn east and its speed slowed further to 37 knots. There was no apparent reason why the speed slowed so dramatically but the inevitable result was that it went into a spin.

At 3,000 feet or more it should have been possible to pull out of the spin but in this case disaster was rapid. The Piper began to fall out of the sky at a rate of 8,000 feet per minute, then spun left before crashing into the sea about two and a half miles off shore and twenty miles south of Vero Beach Municipal Airport.

There were no survivors. Cadets Byrne and Murphy and Captain Lockerman died instantly. Their bodies were recovered shortly afterwards as their shocked colleagues began to gather round.

A local priest, Monsignor Irvine, celebrated a special mass which was attended by the remaining sixteen cadets, as the terrible news was broken to those at home.

James Byrne's father, also James, had just returned from London when the news was broken to him and his wife. In Fairview the Murphy clan began to gather.

In Florida, investigators from the US national transportation safety board backed up by two US coastguards began a sweep of the seabed around Vero Beach in a bid to locate and salvage the aircraft. Kevin Humphries, the investigator for the department of transport and power in Ireland flew to Florida to take part in the investigation.

Members of the two bereaved families, colleagues and friends from Aer Lingus, as well as a group of senior Aer Lingus personnel, led by the chief pilot, Captain Donal Foley, were at Dublin airport when the bodies of the two young men were flown in on an Aer Lingus flight from New York a few days later. Ironically, the flight was over two hours late, due to technical difficulties.

The investigation found that there was no pre-impact part failure or malfunction. There was evidence that during impact neither engine was operational, flaps were extended ten degrees, the main gear was extended and the nose gear was in transit.

The aircraft manufacturers reported that a spin might cause an interruption of fuel to the engines. Intentional spins were prohibited.

The national transportation safety board determined the probable cause of the accident was inadequate supervision by the instructor pilot and failure of the crew to maintain sufficient airspeed which resulted in an advertent stall/spin and subsequent loss of engine power from possible interruption of fuel.

CHAPTER 11

'Five Thousand Feet Descending – Spinning Rapidly'

THE Tuskar Rock crash remains one of the great mysteries of civil aviation, on par with the disintegration of TWA flight 800 over Long Island more than a quarter of a century later, and the disappearance of two Avro Tudor airliners of the British South American Airways Corporation within the Bermuda Triangle more than twenty years before.

All three disasters have common basic themes: excruciating human tragedy and the unexplained destruction over the sea of trusted airliners operated by reputable airlines on routine flights.

The crashes have yet another element in common: all resulted in conspiracy theories and gross sensationalism verging on paranoia.

In the case of Aer Lingus Viscount *St Phelim* (call sign 'Echo India Alpha Oscar Mike') which went into St George's Channel east of the Tuskar Rock around 11.14 a.m. on 24 March 1968, the sense of paranoia assumed clear-cut nationalistic lines which spilled not only into the media but also the civil service.

Within hours of the crash, the rumour machine had it that the Viscount had been downed by a British missile or drone aircraft. Later, the royal navy would be accused of frustrating the search for the wreckage.

It was the most widely investigated Irish air crash ever, with no less than four official investigations: separate investigations carried out by Aer Lingus and the department of transport and power; an official review ordered in 1998 by the minister for public enterprise, Mary O'Rourke; and, most recently, a review by an independent international team of aeronautical experts, again ordered by Mary O'Rourke. Each of these investigations threw up new and often contradictory conclusions.

The mystery is further compounded by the fact that the official Shannon air traffic control tapes of its last communications with the Viscount were taped over and the Aer Lingus maintenance records relating to the aircraft have vanished.

It has also now emerged that the initial department of transport and power investigation carried out between 1968 and 1970 did not take into account the stories of crucial witnesses which would have dramatically changed the scenario it painted of the last flight and crash of the *St Phelim*.

Also inexplicable to many was the refusal to allow victims' families or their legal representatives access to the recovered wreckage on the basis that under departmental regulations, the investigation was private to the minister. This was followed by the strange decision by Aer Lingus to remove and destroy the wreckage of the *St Phelim* which it had re-assembled in Baldonnell.

There is also the eerie silence surrounding the last seventeen or perhaps even more than thirty minutes flight of the disabled craft when nothing was heard as the crew appear to have fought desperately to achieve sufficient control to manage a landing.

What is probably most amazing of all is that a team of international experts have now concluded that the 'catastrophic event' which led to the fatal crash may have occurred at least thirteen and possibly fifteen minutes earlier than previously believed. If this is so, it means that in an almost unparalleled feat of airmanship – for which the international investigators believe they should receive a posthumous citation – the crew managed to recover the aircraft from an initial spin into which it was flung by a 'catastrophic event'.

The investigators believe that in this scenario they tried and failed to get back to Cork Airport and then flew the aircraft around the southeast coast in a disabled condition for up to half an hour, desperately trying to put it down safely while they increasingly lost control as it disintegrated around them.

During this time, watched by horrified mass goers, they narrowly avoided crashing into a church steeple and at another point were so close to the ground that the grass beneath was bent as the plane hurtled forward at 200 miles per hour.

Witnesses on the ground could plainly read the plane's call sign EI-AOM and poignantly, a number recall watching the passengers through the windows of the plane as they crouched forwards in their seats during that last dreadful flight.

Thirty-eight years later we still do not know either what caused the crash or indeed what happened in that last fateful fifteen minutes or half hour in the life of the disabled *St Phelim* and her doomed crew and passengers. Nor do we know why during this long time they failed to make any outside radio contact.

It was just 10.32 a.m. GMT* (11.32 a.m. local time) on the spring morning of Sunday, 24 March 1968 when the *St Phelim*, operating as EI Flight 712 under the command of Captain Bernard O'Beirne, took off from Cork Airport en route for London.

The 100 minute flight was a routine one for O'Beirne, an experienced pilot with over 6,000 hours flying time. One of the airline's most popular pilots, he had served in the air corps for three years before joining Aer Lingus in March 1956.

Before he left his newly renovated home at Briar Lodge in the north County Dublin seaside village of Portmarnock the previous Wednesday (he was to work out of Cork from Wednesday to the following Sunday) he had said goodbye to his young wife Bega, his ten-and-a-half-year-old daughter, Sally, and his son, David, who at one year and ten months, would never remember his dashing father.

Thirty-five years old Barney O'Beirne was born in Tralee, in

* For convenience all times used are GMT; local time was GMT + 1.

Co. Kerry and educated at Clongowes. A keen golfer, he was a member of the prestigious Portmarnock Club and was due to go to Palm Springs later in the year with his wife to take part in the third World Airline Golf Championship.

His first officer was twenty-two-year-old Paul Heffernan who had joined Aer Lingus in 1966 and had over 1,000 hours flying experience. Heffernan, who was single, and from Cork, was in buoyant mood that morning having just been told that he had got his senior commercial pilot's licence. He told officials in the department of transport and power that he'd collect it when he returned from the flight to London.

The two air hostesses on the flight were twenty-one-year-old Ann Kelly from Dublin and Mary Coughlan, also twenty-one, from Ballykisteen, Tipperary.

Both had joined Aer Lingus in 1967. Ann Kelly was the youngest of three daughters of Michael and Stella Kelly who had originally lived in Wexford but by then had moved to St Laurence's Road in Clontarf. Mary Coughlan, a former beauty queen, was the only daughter of Mr and Mrs William Coughlan.

It was a sunny spring morning, weather conditions on the route were favourable and O'Beirne expected to make good time to London.

Hoping to make good time also on the first leg of their long flight to Russia and the Siberian wastelands were flocks of Irish whooper and bewick swans who had taken to the air that weekend from their wintering sites in the south, east and west of the country. These were the same swans that had achieved record heights on their inbound journey to Ireland and had been involved in an 'air miss' above the Outer Hebrides.

There now seems little doubt that as they lumbered into the air they were on a collision course with the track of the *St Phelim*.

About half the fifty-seven passengers on board were from the Cork area and, for one reason or another, many had good reason to be happy as they boarded the London flight.

Rev. Edward Joseph Hegarty, the chaplain at Cork Airport waved goodbye to friends as he left on his way to attend an annual reunion for emigrants from Ballyphehane, Co. Cork, which he helped to organise each year.

As he crossed the tarmac to the waiting plane, Mr William Cox-Ife was in euphoric form, waving the silver tankard with which he had been presented for his production of Gilbert and Sullivan's *Oliver* at the Cork Opera House. The night before, friends had tried to persuade him to stay an extra day, but he had decided against it.

As he boarded the flight, Dr Noel Mulcahy (a science lecturer at University College Cork, and the son-in-law of the former University College Cork president, Dr J. J. McHenry) was thinking of his wife, Maire, and of the second child they were expecting.

A Swedish couple, Svenhans Gahlin and his wife, Karin, of Compass Hill, Kinsale, were excitedly looking forward to the wedding in London that week of their only son, Svenhans.

Two Swiss anglers, Dr and Mrs Roland Wrreckerling had enjoyed their fourteen-day holiday at the Towers Hotel in Glenbeigh. The previous day they considered staying on longer but made a split second decision to go home.

The *St Phelim* had been built by Vickers Armstrong (Aircraft) Ltd for KLM and Aer Lingus purchased it from them on 2 November 1966. It was the 178th Viscount built and it went into service for Aer Lingus on 14 February 1967. Aer Lingus had been operating Viscounts since 1954 and was the second airline in Europe – apart from BEA – to buy them.

The take-off at 10.32 a.m. of flight 712 was reassuringly normal. At 10.38 a.m., when the aeroplane had passed through 7,000 feet, Cork ATC gave clearance on course to Tuskar and advised them to change over to Shannon ATC. Flight 712 responded with a breezy 'Cheerio'.

At 10.40 a.m the flight reported to Shannon in a clear message advising that it was by Youghal at 7,500 feet, climbing to 17,000 feet and estimating at reaching Tuskar at 10.57 a.m. The fact that the Viscount which at this stage should have been climbing at the rate of 1,000 feet a minute appeared to be climbing at only half this rate shows a 'timing' problem.

Air traffic control suggested that if desired, the flight could route direct to the Strumble beacon. There is some confusion as to whether the instruction came from Cork or Shannon but it would have had to be approved by Shannon. The initial reply from flight 712 was unreadable but following a further query from Shannon it confirmed it would accept a direct routing to Strumble.

At 10.41 a.m. another clear message 'Passing FL 90' was received at Shannon.

At 10.51 a.m. the flight reported to Shannon that it was level at 17,000 feet. The message was slightly weak but readable and *St Phelim* was advised to report at Bannow.

The controller on duty at Shannon changed at 10.55 a.m. and, at 10.57.07, EI 712 reported that it was 'by Bannow, level at 17,000 feet estimating Strumble at 03'. The air traffic controller in Shannon pointed out to EI 712 that the time was actually 10.56.50 rather than 10.57. While quibbling about a few seconds in the Bannow time there is no record that ATC in Shannon queried the fact that for the *St Phelim* to travel the forty-four nautical miles between Bannow and Strumble in six minutes implied a ground speed of 440 kts, which was impossible for a Viscount.

The discrepancy in the Strumble estimate would also have been of major importance to London ATC in its management of the flight into Heathrow traffic.

Neither this discrepancy nor the earlier one where the Viscount appeared to have climbed 500 feet in one minute was commented on in the initial official inquiry.

At 10.57 a.m. Shannon instructed flight EI 712 to change to the London Airways frequency of 131.2 and this was acknowledged to Shannon by the laconic reply '131.2'. The time was now 10.57.29.

At 10.58.02, London radar intercepted a garbled call: 'Echo India Alpha Oscar Mike with you.' The message was unusual in a couple of ways. It was not in the form generally used by Aer Lingus flight crews, in which the call sign used was the flight number. Nor did it begin with the usual preamble which would give the call sign of any ground communications station.

But neither was it in the recognised form of a distress or urgent message, which would have been 'Mayday! Mayday! Mayday! Echo India Alpha Oscar Mike! Echo India Alpha Oscar Mike! Echo India Alpha Oscar Mike!' followed by the nature of the emergency. However, if the flight was already in trouble the crew might not have been in a position to relay a full message. It was subsequently concluded that this was probably the first sign that something was amiss, that the message was intended to convey an element of urgency or distress and that the aircraft was in difficulties at the time of transmission.

Eight seconds later London intercepted – through two other aircraft – another and infinitely more alarming message: 'Five thousand feet descending spinning rapidly.' Subsequently, Captain Felim Cronin, of the well-known Cronin aviation family, and a colleague and close friend of Barney O'Beirne, identified the voice on the tape as that of the captain and not First Officer Heffernan.

These were the last words ever heard from the doomed *St Phelim*.

This message was intercepted through another Aer Lingus Viscount, Flight 362 en route from Dublin to Bristol and by BOAC Speedbird, Flight 506, both of which immediately relayed it to London ATC where it was recorded.

There was considerable background noise in the recording and following expert research the first official inquiry into the disaster concluded that the message was actually: 'Twelve thousand feet descending spinning rapidly.'

The logic for believing the aircraft was at 12,000 feet was that as the flight seems to have been at 17,000 feet at 10.58.02, it would have had to plunge downwards at an impossible speed of over 1,000 mph to have reached 5,000 feet eight seconds later. If it had dropped at this rate the wings would have fallen off and the plane would have broken up in the air.

However, over thirty years later, it was to emerge that there could have been a very different explanation.

At the time nobody seemed to have given consideration to the fact that the final message should have been intercepted directly by London if the *St Phelim* was flying at over 12,000 feet but not if it was flying in the region of 5,000 feet.

The Aer Lingus flight 362, piloted by Captain John Knox with co-pilot Joe Molloy, was immediately requested to search west of Strumble. It descended to 500 feet in good visibility, circling low for over an hour. The weather in St George's Channel was fine with brilliant sunshine but nothing was seen by Knox or his crew.

However, there were a number of strange and dramatic sightings on land and sea which added to, rather than throwing any light on, the mystery of what occurred.

A British tanker reported to Ilfracombe radio station that she had sighted a green and white coloured airliner about fifteen miles off Strumble Head in Pembrokeshire, It was circling and appeared to be heading towards the mainland. It appeared to be an Aer Lingus Viscount.

At times, given as between 10.45 a.m. and 11.15 a.m., six people in the Fethard-on-Sea area of Wexford, twenty-eight miles west of the crash, saw an aeroplane which they said flew in approximately a northwest to southeast direction. They described it as coming out of three small black clouds with a sudden sharp turn 'as if fired out of the clouds'. One spoke of seeing an aeroplane with the nose and portion of the wing enveloped in a small dark cloud which travelled along with the aeroplane 'swirling'. They described the cloud as looking 'the size of a large hayshed' and said it went in the direction of the Saltees and shortly afterwards there was a bang which sounded like thunder.

Four people in the same area described seeing an aeroplane going in a southeasterly direction with a very red colour on part of the wings and the tail 'as if on fire' but no smoke was seen. The colour of the aeroplane was not green or white.

A twenty-year-old Spanish seaman, on board a passing ship, the M.V. *Metric*, caught a fleeting glimpse of what he first thought was a large bird but subsequently realised was an aeroplane falling into the sea with a big splash, near the Tuskar Rock and in line with it.

Ten people in the area between Greenore Point, Carnsore Point and the village of Broadway, about three miles inland from the coast, heard a loud noise which they described as like a very sharp roll of thunder. One heard a double clap, like thunder, from the direction of the Tuskar Rock.

Another on the coast four miles further to the north heard a sound like 'a very loud whoosh' while two others on the coast near Greenore Point heard a loud sound which one described as 'a loud boom, like a jet coming out of cloud'.

A fifty-four-year-old farm worker, Joseph Auglim of Saltmills, Fethard-on-Sea, was feeding cattle in a field near his home at about 10.52/53 a.m. when he saw a plane enter a small black cloud which he estimated was five to six times the size of the aircraft. He then heard a queer drone from the plane and watched for it to come out but it was a considerable time before it emerged:

'When it did emerge, it had dropped considerably in height and had changed course. It now seemed to be travelling south. Then it suddenly turned at right angles and was almost facing in the direction from which it had come. It seemed to be drifting to its left and falling away out to sea.'

A young Co. Wexford man, Martin Donahoe, on his way to a football match near Greenore Point saw a large splash in the sea near the Tuskar Rock at 11.15 a.m.

By 11.25 a.m. a full alert was declared and Rosslare Lifeboat was dispatched to the area. By 12.36 p.m. Haulbowline received a report that wreckage had been sighted and the air corps sent a Dove aeroplane and a helicopter to search. Within minutes there were ten aircraft from the UK in the search area.

Back at Cork Airport, shocked families and friends began to gather. Then a strange Mayday call was reported four times accompanied by an automatic alarm radio distress signal. It was picked up at Rosslare Harbour and at Ilfracombe and Land's End radio stations and it was thought it might have come from a lifeboat or a dingy.

People began to hope again. The lord mayor of Cork, Alderman Pearse Wyse, and the bishop of Cloyne and Ross, Most Rev. Dr R. D. Perdue, went to the airport to try and console distraught relatives and friends.

The hours dragged on but nothing was discovered that day and there was never any explanation of the mysterious Mayday, although subsequently it was to be used to support the theory that the *St Phelim* had been shot down.

Early the following morning the search was resumed. Irish air corps planes and helicopters, four Irish trawlers, two Irish lifeboats and British naval vessels including the frigates *Penelope* and *Hardy*, with British Shackletons, swept the entire sea between Ireland and Wales.

Along the coast a watch was kept on headlands, while people living along the Wicklow and Wexford seashore kept vigil from daybreak, combing the rough seas with binoculars.

Shortly before lunchtime, twenty-four-year-old Lieutenant Commander James Lord, master of the *Hardy*, flashed a signal that a body and some wreckage had been sighted three miles north-northeast of the Tuskar Rock lighthouse.

The *Hardy*, having first sought diplomatic clearance to enter Rosslare Harbour, steamed in at 7.15 p.m. In the gathering dusk, those waiting at the harbour could see that her white ensign was at half mast. She bore the bodies of the first people to be recovered – six women. On the quayside a small group of women wept quietly but in the main relatives and friends of the victims watched mutely.

A portion of the undercarriage and the hydraulic system lay in the bow of the *Hardy*. The searchers also found cabin seats, cushions and a briefcase owned by Gus O'Brien who worked with the Ford Company in Cork. They also found a briefcase stamped with the name of Captain Barney O'Beirne. Later, another British naval vessel, the *Invermoriston*, landed another two bodies and a further two were recovered by one of the searching lifeboats.

It was reported that divers saw the bodies of the crew in their white shirts in the cockpit but were unable to recover them.

The first of the dead to be identified was the Clontarf hostess, Ann Kelly. Later that evening Mrs C. M. O'Halloran was identified. Mrs O'Halloran, whose husband P. J. was also a victim of the crash, had been home on holidays at Gortroe, Youghal for the wedding of Mr O'Halloran's brother, Eamonn.

Led by the Irish naval services ship, L.E. *Macha* the ships searched throughout the night in the eerie glow of lights and parachute flares dropped by circling aircraft.

Hope faded rapidly. The *St Phelim* had sunk in 39 fathoms of water. Over the next few days thirteen bodies were recovered together with cabin furnishings, some baggage, seat cushions and the wheels and inner cylinder from the port main landing gear. One further body was recovered later. Distraught relatives had to cope with the fact that forty-seven people were to remain buried at sea.

The first to be recovered, Ann Kelly, was buried at St Ibar's Cemetery in Wexford. Most Rev. Donal J. Herlihy, bishop of Ferns and Rev. Francis Hegarty of London, whose brother, Fr Edward Hegarty, had also been a victim, were among the concelebrants. Schoolchildren from Ann's old school and Aer Lingus hostesses formed guards of honour.

The other sad funerals followed. A day of mourning was declared in Cork. The list of the tragedies, the heartbreak and the ironies seemed endless.

Forty-six-year-old Desmond Walls, the brother of Aer Lingus deputy general manager, Arthur Walls, and of Dermot Walls, head of quality control at Aer Lingus, was among the victims. His wife, Clare, was the sister of the minister for industry and commerce, George Colley. The minister flew home from a visit to Australia to comfort her.

Mr and Mrs Christy McCarthy had been returning to England with their six-year-old son following a visit to Mrs McCarthy's sister in Skibbereen, when they were killed.

Three members of the staff of the Dairy Research Institute travelling to Reading for a conference perished. Tom Dwane from Castletroy in Limerick was just twenty-four years old. His colleague, Michael Cowhig from Fermoy, was thirty-two, and married with three young children, while John Nyhan, also from Fermoy, was the same age and left a wife and two children.

James Barney O'Rourke of Togher Road, Cork, was on his way to attend a special course arranged by the Norwich Union insurance company. He was due to be married the following Easter Monday.

Rory Delaney was aged twenty-two and had been recently promoted to inspector with the Norwich Union company. He had been home to spend a few days with his mother.

The superintendent of the airport cafeteria, Mrs Sean Bourke, and her mother, Mrs M. O'Callaghan, had been on their way to England on holiday. They had already booked and cancelled two previous flights before electing to fly out on the *St Phelim* that Sunday morning.

Brigadier Maurice Denhan Jephson of Mallow Castle, a member of the board of the Victoria Hospital in Cork, died with his wife.

A former pilot and member of a British management consultancy firm had cancelled his booking on the flight at the last minute when he discovered he had left some relevant papers behind in Dublin. Two years earlier, in 1966, he had cancelled a flight on an Air India plane which crashed at Mont Blanc.

Two German newspapermen owed their lives to a car break-down. Reporter Klaus Haaf aged twenty-seven from Frankfurt and his colleague, photographer Gerd Hoffmeyer, had planned to fly on the *St Phelim*, but missed the flight.

Mr and Mrs E. McCarthy of Leamara, Cork had planned to fly to London for their daughter's religious profession. A few days earlier, Mrs McCarthy's sister refused to go with them by air, so to please her they went by boat.

A young French bride honeymooning in Cahir with her husband mixed up the dates on their air tickets; the mistake saved the lives of Jeanne and Ewald Van Baar.

The position of the wreckage remained obscure in spite of prolonged searches by sonar equipped ships of the British navy and Bord Iascaigh Mhara's *Cu na Mara*.

On 25 March, a considerable amount of debris was found floating northeast of the Tuskar Rock. Eventually, on 5 June, an Irish trawler, *Glendalough*, brought up a quantity of positively identifiable wreckage 1.72 nautical miles from Tuskar Rock, in 39 fathoms of water. In the same area, the *Cu na Mara* also brought up wreckage. The following day the trawlers brought up more wreckage and divers from H.M.S. *Reclaim* confirmed a mass of wreckage 'like a scrapyard' in this position. Subsequently it was found that a major portion of the aircraft was located here.

St Phelim had been totally demolished by its violent impact with the sea. However, about 60–65% of the aircraft was recovered including the major parts of three engines, a few parts of the fourth, all four propellers, almost the complete primary structure of the wings from tip to tip, and the fin and rudder. As part of the wreckage with some bodies inside was being lifted from the seabed the lifting wires cut through it like cheese and it slipped back into the water. Divers again went down to make the recovery.

Within hours of the Tuskar Rock crash, the rumour mill had it that the Viscount had either been brought down by a 'drone' aircraft being fired from the RAF base at Aberporth or because it had to take violent action to avoid some kind of aircraft that strayed into its path.

In 1951, there had been a full public inquiry in the Four Courts after the crash-landing of an Aer Lingus DC-3 in Birmingham which resulted in not a single fatality. But in 1968, with sixty-one people dead in mysterious circumstances, a public inquiry was deemed unnecessary. In his memoirs, *An Irishman's Aviation Sketchbook*, the chief inspector of accidents, R. W. O'Sullivan, claimed that following the crash his telephone had been tapped with the result that covering instructions to inspectors in the field were being reported in a distorted fashion in the newspapers.

As the newly appointed air correspondent of the *Irish Press*, I spent three months in Rosslare during the search for the Viscount. I was so astounded by Mr O'Sullivan's allegations that I requested an interview and went to see him in his home. He was most cordial and friendly, but he wasn't prepared to provide one jot of solid evidence to substantiate his allegation of phone-tapping. Mr O'Sullivan died in June 2000, aged ninety-five.

From the very beginning, all the principal parties – the airline, the civil service and the British authorities combined to obfuscate and impede every legitimate effort at honestly reporting the awful tragedy.

Every legitimate question on behalf of their readers by reporters was suspect and viewed as some form of treachery. Every move by the investigators was sacrosanct under the official secrets act.

Nothing had been learned from the notorious Shannon crash of the KLM Super Constellation *Triton* in 1954 when the bully-boy tactics used to cover up the blatant shortcomings of the rescue services backfired and resulted in grotesque rumours being published in the media all over Europe.

Is it any wonder that the conspiracy theorists lined up like flies swarming towards an open jam jar?

The official report into the crash by the department of transport and power, published in 1970, found the very different descriptions of the sounds heard by witnesses difficult to reconcile, even making due allowance for the subjectivity of interpretations of sounds.

The report of the investigation concluded that the description given by the witnesses inland who heard sounds like thunder agreed closely with that of the sounds caused by a sonic boom. It took the view that those who heard the 'whoosh' sound probably heard the actual impact but that those who heard the noise 'like thunder' heard something else – probably a sound made in the air and carried on the wind. The 'thunder' occurred approximately ten minutes earlier than the probable sound of impact.

It was initially thought that perhaps the people who had seen the plane with the red colour on its wings had actually seen one of the search aeroplanes, a Dove of the air corps, which is coloured silvery grey with bright red/orange 'dayglo' paint on the extremities. However, the only Dove aircraft in the vicinity that day did not arrive there until after 12.45 p.m – well after the crash.

The investigation commission believed that the presence of two small ships in the neighbourhood of Tuskar might have influenced the flight crew to attempt a ditching. However, two factors militate against this, firstly the complete lack of communications and the presence of a very good firm sandy beach between Greenore Point and Carnsore Point of which the crew must have been aware.

The report said the alternative is that after some minutes trying to control the plane it went completely out of control in a stalled condition from a relatively low height and struck the water with a high rate of descent and on a steep flight path. The landing gear was up and the flaps fully retracted and it seems probable that the throttles were deliberately closed shortly before the final impact.

The accident was not survivable. There was evidence that the pilot and co-pilot had fastened their shoulder harnesses and that at least some of the passengers had their seat belts fastened at the time of the crash. There was also an indication that the seat belt sign in the cabin was switched on. While these pointed as possible indications that the crew had some fore knowledge of an emergency the investigators said they were not conclusive.

The recovered wreckage revealed extensive damage to the whole structure, which virtually disintegrated. There were no signs of fire in any of the recovered wreckage. Flight recorders were not carried on the aircraft.

No part of the tail planes or elevators was recovered with the exception of small portions of the spring tab and trim tab. (There are two elevators [hinged flaps] hinged on the tailplane which control an aircraft's ascent and descent. Tabs help the movement of the elevators.) It was later to emerge that the missing elevators might provide the most vital clues.

Six months following the accident it emerged that there had been damage to the tail section of the plane while it was still in flight. Evidence for this was provided by the discovery of a portion of the elevator spring tab on the beach between Rosslare Harbour and Greenore Point, seven miles west of the main wreckage. It was entangled in seaweed and could not be floated. Seaweed was not prevalent at the accident site and tidal currents were not such as to wash the tab ashore the necessary seven miles, so it must have dropped off before the crash.

Owing to the lack of a firm lead to a probable cause, a study was made of every reported accident to Viscount aeroplanes since they were brought into service in 1952 to see if any of these showed any pattern of events which might throw some light on the mysterious events of 24 March 1968. The investigation found no real similarities.

The investigation found it was clear that in the extremely short period (just forty-one seconds) between the last exchange of communications with Shannon and the interception by London Airways of the signal 'Twelve thousand feet descending, spinning rapidly', a catastrophic upset was suffered by the aircraft. This upset brought it from normal cruising at 17,000 feet in relatively good weather conditions, to a situation which could have been either a fully developed spin or a spiral dive, to 12,000, losing height at an average rate of descent of over 120 feet per second. At this rate of descent the aircraft would have hit the sea in another 98.5 seconds.

The report said that although it was very unlikely to have happened, consideration must be given to the possibility that EI-AOM, having descended over the sea in a spin or spiral dive, and having been restored to a degree of controlled flight, then flew westward over Fethard-on-Sea before turning east out to sea near Hook Head, and flying back over the sea to east of the Tuskar Rock where it crashed. However, it stated that it seemed a reasonable assumption that it did fly in a disabled condition for 10–15 minutes over the sea between Strumble and Tuskar.

It accepted that if the aircraft seen over Fethard-on Sea was not the *St Phelim*, then some other aircraft must have been in the vicinity. One witness had described the aircraft as being enveloped in a cloud up to the wings and said that this cloud appeared to be revolving and travelling along with the aeroplane.

This witness also heard a subsequent bang which died away like thunder. Another witness saw the aircraft emerge in a sharp turn from three small black clouds 'as if fired from them'.

The report stated: 'These accounts could be satisfactorily explained by a supersonic aeroplane coming out of a dive, causing a boom and the small clouds then flying past the witness with the wing covered in condensation cloud typical of near sonic speed in humid air.

'The aircraft with part of wing and tail brightly coloured "as if on fire" and seen by other witnesses in Fethard-on-Sea was almost certainly the same one. While enquiries did not elicit any other information abou the possible presence of another aircraft in the vicinity, if the evidence of time of impact is accepted the conclusion that there was such another aircraft in the area is inescapable.'

No aeroplanes were reported missing, but there remains the

possibility of an unmanned aeroplane such as a drone target aircraft or a missile. The UK firing ranges were closed that day however.

The report stated: 'The evidence of those who saw an object in the sea in the vicinity of the Coningmore Half Tide Rock during the afternoon of March 24 would not be inconsistent with the supposition that an unmanned aircraft had fallen in the sea and remained afloat for some hours, but no other evidence of this has come to light and no sighting was made by any of the search aircraft.'

The report said that taking into account all the evidence available at the time and assuming that the observations of sightings, sounds and timing by the few witnesses available were reasonably accurate and reliable, it was possible to evolve a scenario which would account for the otherwise inconsistent elements in the evidence and give a coherent, if improbable story.

This scenario envisaged that while the Viscount was in normal cruising flight at 17,000 feet and within six minutes of reaching Strumble Head, another aircraft, which could have been a manned or unmanned aeroplane, or a missile, passed in close proximity, possibly even colliding with the tail of the Viscount. This caused an upset which led to a manoeuvre which was either a spin or a spiral dive from which the Viscount was recovered in a disabled condition and flew on for about ten minutes over the sea before control was finally lost.

The other aircraft could have been the one seen over Fethard-on-Sea and might have fallen in the sea near the Saltee Islands.

However, in considering what is described as 'this very speculative theory' the report said that there were a number of matters which discounted its credibility: no aircraft, civil or military, manned or unmanned, were reported or known to have been in the area at the relevant times or reported missing; missile and target ranges on the Welsh coast were closed on Sundays and were known to be inoperative on the day of the fatal crash; no aircraft carriers were operating in the area and the altitude of 17,000 feet at which the *St Phelim* was cruising was considered unlikely to be used by military aircraft.

It pointed out that it must also be taken into account that the manoeuvre of recovering a loaded Viscount aeroplane from a spin or a spiral dive would require a very remarkable feat of airmanship on the part of the pilots. In fact there was only one known case in which this was effectively accomplished during a test flight by expert test pilots. Even in that case, the airframe suffered some distortion of the tail unit.

The investigation found that it was difficult to account for the lack of communications during the presumed ten minutes before the final catastrophe. The aircraft may have been too low for VHF communication with ground stations, but if there were transmissions they should have been picked up by other aircraft. However, apart from the other Aer Lingus Viscount and the BOAC Speedbird there were no other aircraft known to have been on that frequency. It is also possible that another aircraft came in on the frequency and could have blocked transmission.

'On account of these matters, the hypothesis must remain in the realm of speculation and on present evidence cannot be given a higher status than a remote possibility,' read the official report.

The report came to the final conclusion: 'For a reason that cannot be determined from the evidence available, the aircraft went into a spin or spiral dive or similar manoeuvre at 17,000 feet, from which a recovery appears to have been effected at some height lower than 12,000 feet. The recovery manoeuvre could not be achieved without inflicting some structural deformation on the airframe, most probably on the tail planes and elevators, causing impairment of controllability in the fore and aft (pitching) plane.

'The aircraft flew in a disabled condition over the sea for at least ten minutes during which no radio signals were received from it, after which fore and aft control was finally lost, and the aircraft descended with a high vertical component of speed in a stalled condition with engines throttled back, until it struck the sea.

'The aircraft was substantially intact when it entered the sea, except for the probable loss of all or part of the elevator spring tab. It was demolished on impact and sank immediately. The impact was unsurvivable.

'There is evidence which could be construed as indicative of the possible presence of another aircraft or airborne object in the vicinity which, by reason of collision or by its proximity causing an evasive manoeuvre to be made, or by its wake turbulence, might have been the initiating cause of an upsetting manoeuvre resulting in the Viscount entering a spin or spiral dive.

'There is no substantiating evidence of such a possibility, but it cannot be excluded for it is compatible with all of the presently available evidence.'

The report found that the accident presented 'a considerable element of mystery not only as to why the accident occurred, but also as to what happened to the aeroplane to account in a rational way for the evidence so far available.'

The report, published on 30 June 1970, stated that while a large amount of wreckage was recovered from the sea, some vital items of evidence were probably still on the sea bed and suggested 'that it would not be impossible for some such item to become washed ashore or otherwise recovered in the future which might provide positive evidence at present lacking'.

As time went by, more and more people took the view that another aircraft – manned or unmanned – had caused the crash.

Conspiracy theories were understandable. But, as time passed, many people also believed it strange that, so many years after the tragedy, not one jot of solid evidence has emerged to prove that the British authorities lied.

That they were capable of doing so is, in the light of massive historical evidence, unquestionable.

But thirty years plus was a long time. Several people would have known.

Someone somewhere must have longed to tell all they knew. Why did no one come forward?

However speculation continued. It ranged from mid-air collision to missiles launched from land and sea, to conspiracy theories of British military involvement and misrepresentation and cover-ups by either the Irish or the UK governments.

In January 1999, it was claimed that documents uncovered by a private investigator alleged that bodies from the air disaster were cremated by the British authorities to cover up evidence that the plane had been hit by a missile fired from a royal navy ship. The documents, allegedly uncovered in America by a private investigator, claimed that the British authorities were anxious that only bodies showing signs of death due to impact with water should be returned to the Irish authorities.

A number of relatives were concerned that much of the crash recovery was effectively handled by the British ministry of defence, which may not have wanted to reveal its military testing arrangements. The ministry of defence consistently denied this, insisting that its only role was to assist in the recovery operations.

The first royal navy ships to reach the scene of the crash were the frigates *Penelope* and *Hardy*. A total of thirteen royal navy vessels participated in the search. This prompted the question as to whether the navy was searching for a manned or unmanned aeroplane or vessel which may have collided with, or just missed, the Viscount.

The royal navy certainly went to extraordinary lengths in its repeated attempts to recover the wreckage of the Viscount. In a report in *Navy News* of October 1968, the salvage operations carried out by HMS *Reclaim* during the summer of 1968 off Tuskar was described as 'the most continuously difficult and dangerous underwater operation ever undertaken by the royal navy'.

Over twenty-six days, ninety-one dives were carried out at depths of around 250 feet. 'Our divers stretched themselves to the limits,' said *Reclaim*'s Commander Peter Messervy. 'To my knowledge no other divers have attempted to sustain this pressure of work at such depths.'

The navy's previous biggest salvage operation, the recovery of a crashed RAF Vulcan in 1959, was estimated at the time to have cost £2 million. Private assessment of the work that must have gone into the Tuskar operation put its value at well over the £2 million mark, yet the Irish government was only charged £136,779.4s.4d.

Nearly two years following the crash, the nose wheel from a Sea Vixen aircraft was found on the beach at Kilpatrick shore, Gorey, Co. Wexford, prompting speculation that it had collided or been involved in a near miss with the *St Phelim*. Since Sea Vixens normally operated from aircraft carriers, this opened up a new avenue of inquiry. It would appear that the only aircraft carrier which might have been in the vicinity of the crash in March 1968 was the *Hermes*. If a Sea Vixen from the *Hermes* had collided with the Viscount its pilot must have ditched and been rescued safely, otherwise it would have been very difficult to cover it up.

It was suggested that the mysterious Mayday calls which were heard by searching ships during the Sunday afternoon of the rescue operations in the Tuskar area, might have come from the ditched pilot who could then have been picked up by one of the British frigates.

It is true that if the testing of sea-launched missiles was being carried out, there would have been very little activity at the RAF base at Aberporth. However, it is unlikely that a light magnesium alloy wheel, which floats easily, would have taken so long to be washed ashore. The ministry of defence's explanation that the wheel was lost from a Sea Vixen which made a bad landing on the carrier *Hermes* two weeks earlier seems most plausible.

Aberporth in Cardiganshire was the royal aircraft establishment's largest and most sophisticated missile testing range stretching out to sea for 200 miles. Missiles are fired either from land at Aberporth or from navy vessels inside the test area. Their targets are drones launched from Llanbedr, away up the coast in Merioneth.

The most popular of all target drones was the Jindivik, a jet powered craft capable of 900 km per hour maximum cruising speed and a range of around 1,000 km. According to *Jane's Weapons System*, the UK had 180 Jindiviks by March 1972 and they had flown over 2,400 sorties at RAE Llanbedr, north Wales.

If the 'fire' reported by some witnesses on the plane seen near Fethard-on-Sea was indeed orange 'dayglo' paint it would tally very closely with that of military target drones like the Jindivik, which are painted with 'dayglo' to make them easier to pick out.

An RTÉ *Prime Time* programme produced on the thirtieth anniversary of the Viscount crash supported the missile theory. The programme suggested that the additional wreckage in the water was taken to the UK – a claim denied by the British ministry of defence. It also reported that although the British government had maintained that there was no missile-testing at the Aberporth testing facility in Wales on the weekend of the crash, there were anomalies in the facility's logbook.

The following year, *Prime Time* said that the British ministry of defence had recently examined its missile capability at the time of the crash and concluded that no land-based British anti-aircraft missile had the range to strike an aircraft off the Irish coast. But significantly, it also reported that the British cabinet papers relating to a missile test site in Wales were extracted from the files in 1982, just as the media renewed its pursuit of the cause of the 1968 crash.

In 1998, following sustained pressure from relatives dissatisfied with the lack of any real explanation, the minister for public enterprise, Mary O'Rourke, in co-operation with the UK government, requested an official review of all relevant files to see if the cause of the accident could be determined.

The review was carried out between 1968 and 2000. The report, published in June 2000, was again inconclusive. It found errors and omissions in the maintenance of the Viscount type aircraft by Aer Lingus and by the airworthiness surveillance office of the department. It discovered that the original investigation found that up to thirty maintenance cards from the penultimate check on the plane carried out three months before it crashed were missing. This was not mentioned in the original report. A certificate of airworthiness was awarded by the department three weeks before the crash in the absence of maintenance records. 'However, there is no evidence that the aircraft's maintenance history was a factor in the accident,' the review emphasised.

It found no evidence of UK involvement in the accident nor any evidence that the UK as a state conspired against the investigating body in an attempt to conceal any facts. Again, it failed to establish the cause of the accident. However, crucially it found that the 1970 reconstruction of the fatal crash ignored some aspects of what had been observed by witnesses in the last minutes of the *St Phelim*'s flight.

In light of this significant new development, Mary O'Rourke promptly commissioned an independent team of aeronautical experts 'to shed further light on the causes of the accident', by making a study of all available documentation, material and/or sources.

The independent specialists selected by the minister were French aeronautical expert, Rear Admiral Yves Lemercier, his associate, Manuel Pech, and Colin Torkington, Australian nominee on the air navigation commission of the international civil aviation organisation (ICAO)

In September 2000, they launched a call for witnesses and, following a large number of interviews as well as a careful examination of the witnesses statements received in 1968, came up with a reconstruction of the last flight of the *St Phelim*. It was fundamentally and dramatically different from that found by the initial 1970 report but again it raised a large number of unanswered questions.

They rejected out of hand any idea of a crash with another aircraft, manned or unmanned. Instead they leaned towards more prosaic ideas such as metal fatigue, corrosion or bird strike.

However, more sensationally, they considered that the original reconstruction was possibly misled by the transcript of the Shannon radio communications. They emphasised that what they were assessing was not the people but the procedures used at Shannon which may have resulted in an irregular transcript.

They went to great pains to emphasise also that if this had occurred it had no actual bearing on what happened to the *St Phelim*, the outcome of the crash or the launch of the search and rescue, which had been adequately handled by London ATC. They were looking at the possibility only in an attempt to shed further light on the accident.

Based on the evidence of witnesses, some of whom were not heard by the original investigating team, the international team built up a new scenario whereby they concluded that the Viscount went into and recovered from not one but two dives.

New witnesses now painted a horrific picture of a terror flight of possibly over half an hour of the *St Phelim* around the southeast coast following its first dive. As passengers crouched forward in their seats the plane plunged, climbed, dived and weaved to avoid obstacles, as its crew fought desperately to control their pitching and disintegrating aircraft.

Based on the evidence of witnesses, the expert report said that what is likely to have occurred is that ten or twelve minutes after the Viscount's take-off from Cork something happened to the horizontal tail – such as metal fatigue, corrosion, flutter or a bird strike – to interrupt the climb of the *St Phelim*, which was then at 9,000 to 10,000 feet. It entered into a spin – possibly a spiral dive – right handed, over land or most likely quite a few nautical miles out at sea between 10.42 a.m. and 10.44 a.m.

Witnesses had come forward to describe in harrowing detail what they had seen over thirty years previously. A farm worker who was in Youghal at the time told how he had seen the plane suddenly turn right in a very steep turn, descend, then spin or spiral almost vertically. This dive was also seen by witnesses in the

Old Parish area of Dungarvan who reported that it spun or spiralled almost vertically. One man said he prayed for the passengers as he thought it would crash at once.

However in a major feat of airmanship, the crew managed to pull out of the spin. The international team believed that with the benefit of Captain O'Beirne's experience on Spitfires, he and First Officer Heffernan succeeded in recovering the plane from its dive and flying it in a disabled condition for probably over half an hour as they tried to land it.

They considered it was a major achievement for the crew to be able to keep this aircraft flying for more than half an hour, with such poor manoeuvrability characteristics. This showed 'remarkable intrinsic and professional level of experience'. They proposed that the pilots should receive a posthumous citation.

They believed that in recovering from the spin there may have been further structural damage, mainly in the tail of the plane.

Initially, they probably tried to return to Cork. The plane was seen making two left turns, above the cliffs at Crobally, then heading northeast, seen or heard from Ballytrissane, Ballymacart, Ballinroad and Ballitlea. During this phase of flight, it flew at low altitude, at a maximum height of not more than 1,000–2,000 feet.

The plane was next seen flying low, over Newtown, South Tramore, crossing Tramore Bay, heading slightly south of Brownstown Head gaining some hundreds of feet.

Then it suddenly turned left descending down to the 'nap' of the earth, heading north.

It then turned right, climbed and headed towards the Saltees, gaining altitude for about 3–4 minutes before going into a second sudden dive in the area of the Kennedy Arboretum, west of Wexford town, at 10.58 a.m.

A young farmer caring for cattle at Tory Hill, who had been watching the Viscount for about fifteen minutes, saw it go into this second dive. Once again the crew recovered at very low altitude, flew around Slievecoitlea Hill and over Ballykelly. Horrified mass goers coming out of Ballykelly Church saw it emerge from behind Slievecoitlea Hill below the horizon line and flying in the exact direction of the Church steeple. As they held their breaths in horror, it turned left to avoid the steeple at the last moment.

It then headed to Fethard at an altitude of around 1,000 feet. The report said it seemed probable that the Viscount arrived from Campile, flew over Dunbrody Abbey and Saltmills, turned right to head to Baginbun Head then carried out a steep turn right towards Slade, after which it headed north and again turned right and flew over Fethard, slightly south of Grange heading to the Keeragh Islands. It is probable that a part snapped off from the aircraft when it was flying 4–5 nautical miles east of Fethard and it is possible that some other part broke off between Black Rock and Carnsore Point before the *St Phelim* made its last plunge into the sea at 11.14 – just thirty-two minutes after the first catastrophic incident.

The investigators concluded that Captain O'Beirne and First Officer Heffernan were so busy trying to stabilise their aircraft following the first spin that they hadn't time to send out a distress call. After the recovery, the radio VHF subsystem could have been damaged and the aircraft was flying too low to be able to communicate with Shannon.

However the investigation acknowledged that this scenario is incompatible with the last communications between *St Phelim* and Shannon air traffic control.

Because over forty independent witnesses recalled sightings supporting the theory that the first dive had occurred much earlier than previously believed, the international team believed the weak side of the inconsistency was that of Shannon ATC's report.

The other possibility, which they discounted as extremely unlikely, was that the crew irregularly reported the aircraft position in its last messages.

The investigators stated that there was no evidence for their opinion that the weak side of the inconsistency was the Shannon

ATC report and they emphasised time and again that in any case it had no direct impact on the accident or rescue processes.

However, they said that their opinion was that the procedures which were applied in ATC Shannon at the time of the accident were either not well adapted (in particular for specific periods of a transition between routine and emergency) or not carefully applied.

They suggested that the distortion between the original recording from the Viscount and the transcripts might result from a misinterpretation of an unreadable message.

At the time of the investigation, the senior officer head of Shannon ATC in 1968, the Shannon supervisor on duty till 11 a.m., and the relief controller taking over at 10.55 a.m., were all deceased.

The Shannon supervisor who took over from 11 a.m. till the end of the afternoon and the controller on duty in the morning up to 10.55 a.m. said that from their recalls, they did not notice anything abnormal in the execution of the procedures on that day, neither by themselves, nor by their fellows on duty. None of them contributed, in accordance with the procedures, to the writing of the transcript of the radio comms; when they reread it, they did not identify anything abnormal.

In a letter to the investigating team, the operational controller on duty at Shannon until 10.55 a.m. on 24 March, writing through his solicitors, rejected their idea of the Shannon inconsistency in so far as it contradicted his own statement and the certified transcripts of the tapes. An attempt to contact him through his solicitors for further elaboration for this book received no reply.

One member of the 1968 investigation commission said that when the commission visited Shannon air traffic control on the Wednesday or Thursday following the accident, he listened by himself to the tape recording.

He said the tape he heard was readable because he had a copy of the transcript made by air traffic control experts. The footnote 'RT transmissions from EI 712 were generally very poor' was put on every transcript. It is the same as 'Errors and omissions excepted'.

The tapes on which the last messages of the *St Phelim* were recorded have now vanished and the London recordings were never made available. The Shannon tapes were reused by air traffic control around 1976 after authorisation had been given to Shannon by Dublin air traffic service. The London transcript had been requested from London air traffic control through the Irish air accident investigation board but the quest was unsuccessful.

One of the main obstacles to the investigation by the 1968 commission was the fact that the plane crashed into the open sea. This delayed the location of the wreckage and explained the non recovery of most of the rear part of the aircraft. Consequently, the tail section could not be considered as a possible causal factor of the accident. This made the investigation report inconclusive.

Dealing with possible causes of the first catastrophic incident the international team's conclusions did not appear to give too much credence to a problem with the door, but saying that on the limited evidence available it must remain 'a possibility'.

Neither did they appear to give too much credence to fuselage failure saying it was difficult to connect a possible bulkhead failure with the loss of the plane, although this part of the aircraft had not been recovered or seen in the field of the wreckage.

The team also considered that the possibility of a birdstrike on one tailplane resulting in partial failure might well be a triggering factor. It discovered that because of the cold winter Irish whooper and bewick swans were still leaving Ireland for Siberia and Russia up to 27 March. The previous year an 'air miss' with Ireland-bound swans had been reported above the Outer Hebrides and an all time record height for these birds of 8,200 metres recorded. In an eerie coincidence these were the same birds which left Ireland in March 1968 and the team concluded that there seems 'little doubt that swan migrations from Kerry, Shannon, Galway and other parts were on collision courses with the track of the *St Phelim*.'

They pointed out that while the 1970 report stated that the

aircraft was substantially intact when it entered the sea, except for the probable loss of all or part of the port elevator spring tab, it appeared that both left and right tailplanes (with the exception of the starboard tab) together with the tailplane centre-section spar were not lying in the sea bed with the main wreckage.

It was therefore not possible to eliminate the possibility of a defect or failure in the elevator and/or tailplanes having contributed to the accident as both elevators, both tailplanes, the tailplane centre-section, the tailcone and the rear pressure bulkhead were not found.

The international experts' view was that the probable cause of this accident was the in-flight fracture of the spigot in the elevator tab circuit. The spigot fitting is a steel quarter-inch spindle mounting which serves as a pivot point in the drive mechanisms. They found that this part had exceeded the 12,000 flight hours retirement life by 21,000 hours resulting in a life of 33,000 hours. If the spigot had fractured, it could have caused the left elevator to fall off in flight. Then the port tail plane and elevator probably fell off which resulted in loss of control of the aircraft.

The team believed that the final chain of events could have started with the metal fatigue failure of the spigot. This would have set up a shuddering in the aircraft which caused the tailplane, complete with its elevator, to fall off.

Subsequently, the retirement life of 12,000 hours for the spigot was made mandatory following a fatigue failure in another aircraft. With respect to EI AOM in 1968 there had been no requirement for an individual track of the spigot.

In summary it appeared that if the spigot was wearing out because it should have been replaced earlier, it would have set up a shuddering in the aircraft and the resultant instability could have caused the tailplane to fall off.

It is not known when the tab free play of the spigot was last checked by Aer Lingus but the Vickers recommended interval was 900 hours. A tab free play inspection was unlikely to have been included in the Aer Lingus 2.04 maintenance inspection, the records of which are missing.

So, it would appear that the Tuskar air disaster was probably caused by structural failure in the plane's tailplane. Possibly the spigot, which is one of the connecting parts of the spring tab and the elevator, fell victim to metal fatigue. The spring tab fell off and separated from the aircraft falling onto the beach at Curracloe seven miles from Tuskar. This theory is supported by the fact that since the spring tab cannot float it must have fallen off before the plane crashed into the sea.

The Viscount was a great aircraft – but it wasn't exactly the world's safest. Up to the end of 1995 there had been 139 reported crashes. There were 1,573 people killed in 66 of these accidents.

The *St Phelim* was by no means the only Viscount to break up in the air. On 12 May 1959, a Capital Airlines Viscount disintegrated in flight near Chase, Maryland, USA, with the loss of all on board.

In 1974, a Viscount of Aerolinas TAO crashed near Cucuta, Colombia, again with the loss of all on board. The official inquiry cited 'fatigue of the tailplane' as the most likely cause.

Some time following the Tuskar crash it is understood that an investigation into another incident involving an Aer Lingus Viscount found that a rod which was part of the plane's elevator control system had failed.

The international team made a number of recommendations and criticisms. It said that the 1968 investigation procedures and report showed some weak points:

- the head of the investigation commission had been responsible for the approval of the certificate of airworthiness for the *St Phelim*;
- the commission accepted that in the investigation the manufacturer took a position higher than that of technical adviser;

- although the investigation was not closed, the aviation department accepted that all material pieces of the recovered wreckage be scrapped;
- most of the very important data was lost after the disclosure of the accident report;
- there were no original tapes of Shannon radio transmission records;
- some pictures given to an inspector by a witness were never returned and were no longer available.

The team recommended that the Irish government promote within Europe an agreement for building up a task force able to search and recover any wreckage lying on the sea bed.

It said that in 1968 the UK test ranges' activities were communicated through a permanent 'Notice to Airmen' (NOTAM) creating a Dangerous Area. Temporary NOTAMs announced those periods when there were no test activities. Accordingly, there were no warnings when test activities took place. This meant that no special warning was issued when the airspace activities had to deal with a real danger. The international experts recommended that the test activities in the UK air space adjacent to the Irish flight information region be clearly announced by the UK to the relevant Irish correspondents.

The team recommended that the files on the *St Phelim* should be closed and that Captain O'Beirne and First Officer Heffernan be given a posthumous citation for their remarkable performance in trying to save their doomed craft.

Again, this latest report produces new questions, new mysteries and no definitive answers. When exactly did the first dive occur? Was there a second fatal dive? In a tragic error, was the *St Phelim* shot out of the sky by a missile from land or sea or struck by an unmanned craft? Did it collide with a high-flying swan en route to the Siberian wastelands? Has the British official secrets act been used to gag army personnel with vital evidence? What did the missing British cabinet papers contain? Was the damage caused by metal fatigue to something as tiny as the spigot connecting the spring tab to the elevator? What did the lost Aer Lingus maintenance records contain? Were the Shannon transmissions misinterpreted? Why were the London tapes never handed over? Why was the assembled wreckage destroyed? And finally, how many aircraft were in the area that fateful Sunday morning?

There are also details given in the latest report of a farm worker in Ballymacart who on the Sunday morning saw 'one plane with four engines ... going towards Cork ... another one ... at the same height was going towards Mine Head ... it was darkish grey colour.' The international team recorded this sighting but made no comment upon it.

Those who lost their loved ones on the *St Phelim* are still seeking the answers which might bring them some sort of closure. Thirty-eight years on it looks as if the only hope of getting any answers may lie in wreckage – possibly a tiny quarter-inch spigot buried 39 fathoms deep in the bed of St George's Channel – or with the very few people who are still privy to lost information and British cabinet papers.

Although the international team has recommended that the file on the crash be closed this seems unlikely to happen given all the queries, question marks, discrepancies and contradictions surrounding the final flight. Surely someone somewhere will yet unearth evidence which will finally reveal why the *St Phelim* disintegrating as it dived, plunged into the sea with the loss of all on board.

ALSO AVAILABLE FROM MERCIER PRESS

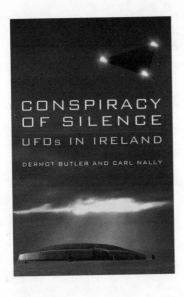

MERCIER PRESS
WHAT YOU NEED TO READ

CONSPIRACY OF SILENCE
UFOs in Ireland

Dermot Butler and Carl Nally

ISBN 1 85635 509 8

UFOs have been sighted in Ireland for over one hundred years. People who have no previous interest in such phenomena have reported bizarre experiences and encounters with the paranormal in almost every county in Ireland, from Derry to Cork, Dublin to Galway.

Here for the first time Nally and Butler present the eye-witness reports, together with their own investigations and interviews with pilots and flight engineers who have, until now, been loathe to talk of their experiences. Certain locations are closely examined, such as Newgrange, where paranormal activity is recorded more often than anywhere else in the country, and the history and official response to UFO activity is explored.

The time is right for the truth about UFOs in Ireland to come out.
This is the story so far ...

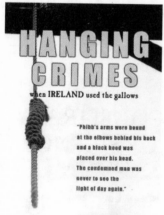

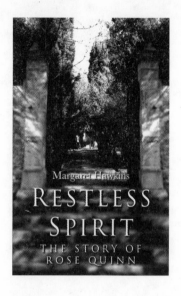

MERCIER PRESS
WHAT YOU NEED TO READ

RESTLESS SPIRIT
The Story of Rose Quinn

Margaret Hawkins

ISBN 1 85635 496 2

Rose Quinn died in an asylum less than a year after being committed by her brother for refusing to live with the man she had been forced to marry. Such was the stigma attached to having had a relative in the asylum that the story remained a family secret until it was revealed three generations later to Rose's great-niece, Patricia.

The news catapulted Patricia into a dedicated search to find out more about the woman she never knew existed. Shocking coincidences were uncovered and an unexpected spiritual connection in the family surfaced. This was to result in finding Rose's burial place – a plot behind the asylum, now known as St Senan's Hospital.

For almost 100 years Rose's fate had been kept secret, but her spirit never died. This is the story of that restless spirit.